TO:

....

FROM:

....

DATE:

....

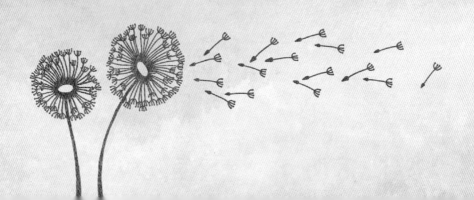

3·MINUTE PRAYERS

FOR

Morning & Evening

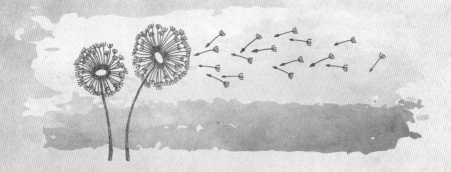

DAILY INSPIRATION
FOR WOMEN

BARBOUR
PUBLISHING

Print ISBN 978-1-63609-592-9

Published by Barbour Publishing, Inc., 1810 Barbour Drive, Uhrichsville, Ohio 44683, www.barbourbooks.com

Our mission is to inspire the world with the life-changing message of the Bible.

Morning and Evening. . .

ENCOURAGEMENT
FOR YOUR SOUL

*Evening, and morning. . .will I pray,
and cry aloud: and he shall hear my voice.*

PSALM 55:17 KJV

This beautiful book will help you experience an intimate connection to the heavenly Father with a brief scripture and prayer—twice a day for every day of the calendar year.

Enhance your spiritual journey with the peaceful time spent in prayer, and come to know just how deeply and tenderly God loves you.

Be blessed!

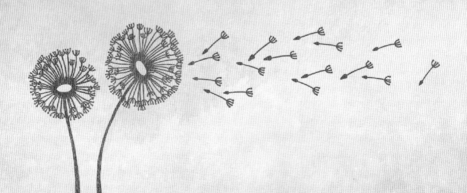

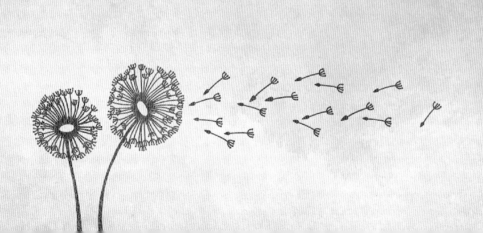

Morning
PRAYER FIRST

And rising very early in the morning, while it was still dark, he departed and went out to a desolate place, and there he prayed.

MARK 1:35 ESV

Some days, before I'm even out of bed, my mind swirls with plans, to-do lists, worries. . .but I forget to come to You, my heavenly Father. I attempt to live life on my own, forgetting that You have promised to walk this earth beside me, sharing my burdens and offering Your wisdom and strength when mine will surely fail. If it is only five minutes on the knees of my heart before rolling out of bed, let my priority be time spent with You. May I follow Jesus' example to put prayer before any other pursuit for the day. Amen.

THINK ABOUT IT:

Do you make time for prayer in the same way you make time for other activities—exercising, fixing hair or makeup, perusing social media—in your morning routine?

Evening
REST FOR SOULS

"Come to me, all who labor and are heavy laden, and I will give you rest. Take my yoke upon you, and learn from me, for I am gentle and lowly in heart, and you will find rest for your souls."

MATTHEW 11:28–29 ESV

My deliverance. My rescue. My salvation. Thank You, Lord, for providing a way back to You. We have all fallen short of righteousness, but through the gift of Your Son's life, we can find rest for our souls. No more striving to live a perfect life—and failing. No more hoping that we're good enough—and realizing we aren't. Through Your incomprehensible love, we become children of the Most High. Christ's righteousness is ours; His yoke is light. As my heart overflows with gratitude, help me share Your love with others. Amen.

THINK ABOUT IT:

How will you find rest in God's gift of grace today?

Morning
WHATEVER IS LOVELY

Finally, brothers and sisters, whatever is true, whatever is noble, whatever is right, whatever is pure, whatever is lovely, whatever is admirable—if anything is excellent or praiseworthy—think about such things.

PHILIPPIANS 4:8 NIV

Oh Lord, our family is bombarded with the world's mess, and it seems to get uglier every week. We're blasted with meanness, violence, lies, bullying, greed, foul language, bigotry, and shocking lewdness everywhere we turn. It comes from TV shows, movies, the news, out on the street, school buses, stores, commercials, magazines, computer games, and social media. We can't always get away from it. Jesus, please protect my family members from these fearsome attacks that keep us from thinking on whatever is good, lovely, and noble. Amen.

THINK ABOUT IT:

What are some practical things God is prompting you to do to limit the world's negative influence on you and your family?

Evening
THAT URGING IN MY SOUL

"Blessed are the peacemakers, for they will be called children of God."

MATTHEW 5:9 NIV

Holy Spirit, I guess You've noticed—painfully so—that I can be a petty person. I sometimes bicker with people needlessly, even with beloved members of my family. I know You want so much more for me than that. In my quiet times, I can feel that divine urging to be more like You. Forgive me for the times I've stirred up trouble instead of goodwill. Please let Your supernatural peace seep into the depths of my soul, and then let the warmth and light of that peacemaking radiance stream like a ray of sunlight on a stormy day onto my family and to the world! Amen.

THINK ABOUT IT:

Is there someone in your life with whom the Holy Spirit might be encouraging you to make peace?

Morning
CASTING PRACTICE

Cast your cares on the LORD and he will sustain you; he will never let the righteous be shaken.

PSALM 55:22 NIV

Dear Father, it's interesting that You tell us to cast our cares on You. Casting something requires effort on my part. The greater the effort, the stronger the cast will be. The more I practice, the better my aim. You want to see that I'm willing to grab all my cares, all my worries and anxieties, put some muscle behind them, and throw them Your way. When I'm worried about something, I tend to freeze up. I stand there, holding my problems, hoping You'll come and take them from me. No more, Father. Today, I cast it all on You. Each time a worrisome thought enters my mind, I'll throw it with all my might in Your direction, for I know You care about every detail of my life.

THINK ABOUT IT:

What things will you cast on the Father today?

Evening
GOD OF DETAILS

In the beginning, God created the heavens and the earth. The earth was without form and void, and darkness was over the face of the deep. And the Spirit of God was hovering over the face of the waters.

GENESIS 1:1–2 ESV

Dear Father, I've read this scripture many times, but it's comforting to come back to this starting point. Before time began, You were there. Why do I worry about my problems when I know the infinite God of the universe is in control? You created every good thing. Without You, nothing would exist. You placed the sun in the sky, scattered the stars like glitter, and positioned the moon just so. You saw to every facet of creation, and You still oversee it all today. I know You can—and will—take care of every detail of my life.

THINK ABOUT IT:

What details will you entrust to the Creator today?

Morning
GOD'S SMILE

So God created the great sea creatures and every living creature that moves, with which the waters swarm, according to their kinds, and every winged bird according to its kind. And God saw that it was good.

GENESIS 1:21 ESV

Dear Father, You must have had so much fun creating all the sea creatures! I can just imagine You laughing, showing Jesus and the Holy Spirit, saying, "Look! This one has eight legs." Then You moved on to the birds, painting their feathers in the most glorious colors, positioning each one just so, to make flight possible. If You took that much time and detail with sea creatures and birds, You must have been even more excited to create me—a person in Your image. When I doubt myself, when I feel anxious about my place in the world, remind me that You created each living thing for Your pleasure, and that includes me. May my words, thoughts, and actions bring You pleasure today, Lord.

THINK ABOUT IT:
How will you make God smile today?

Evening
IN YOUR IMAGE

So God created mankind in his own image, in the image of God he created them; male and female he created them.

GENESIS 1:27 NIV

Dear Father, thank You for this reminder that I was made in Your image. So often, I hear voices in my head that tell me I'm not good enough, not attractive enough, not smart enough, that I'll never measure up. The lies are loud, and they just keep coming. But according to Your Word, I'm made in the image of the perfect, holy, almighty, eternal God. When I doubt myself, remind me of who I am, Lord. Help me to become more and more like You as I develop traits of compassion, kindness, gentleness, and love. When those voices speak, help me silence them. After all, I am a daughter of the Most High God.

THINK ABOUT IT:
What traits do you have that resemble God's character?

Morning
STOP AND KNOW

"Be still, and know that I am God. I will be exalted among the nations, I will be exalted in the earth!"

PSALM 46:10 ESV

Be still. A call to quiet my restless mind—to pause in my endless pursuits. *Know that You are God.* You are almighty. You are Lord. Regardless of what goes on in the world today, Father, I can be still and relish the knowledge that the God who created and controls the universe also resides in my heart. And Your plans will not be shaken—even when my fears shake me to the very core. Deepen my trust, Father; take my head knowledge to my heart so I can feel Your presence in my life, to be still and know that You are God. Amen.

THINK ABOUT IT:

Does stopping to reflect on God's omnipotence bring a sense of peace despite rocky circumstances in the world or your life?

Evening
DEEP BREATH

Then the LORD God formed a man from the dust of the ground and breathed into his nostrils the breath of life, and the man became a living being.

GENESIS 2:7 NIV

Dear Father, You took such special care in making us. You breathed Your own breath into us! Why do I ever doubt Your love for me? Whenever I feel anxious, remind me to breathe. With each breath I take, remind me that it's Your breath giving me life, filling my lungs, spreading to every part of me. Let me feel Your beautiful, serene peace as I relax in Your care. Each time I inhale, bring my thoughts to Your great love, and each time I exhale, help me picture all the worries and cares leaving my body, scattering in the wind. Thank You for Your breath that gives me life.

THINK ABOUT IT:

How will you remind yourself to take deep breaths?

Morning
MAKING FRIENDS

The LORD God said, "It is not good for the man to be alone. I will make a helper suitable for him."
GENESIS 2:18 NIV

Dear Father, You said in Your Word that it's not good for us to be alone. Yet I often feel lonely, Father. Even though I know there are people in my life who care about me, it's hard for me to connect with them. Sometimes I worry about what they'll think or if they're judging me. This fear forces a wall around me and keeps me from deepening my friendships. Whether it's with my spouse, my children, or others in my life, help me to love without fear, Father. Help me focus on others instead of myself. Send people I can connect with and help me develop the friendships I need to stay healthy and accountable.

THINK ABOUT IT:

What can you do today to connect with others and deepen your friendships?

Evening
TO HAVE A FRIEND. . .

Laugh with your happy friends when they're happy; share tears when they're down. Get along with each other; don't be stuck-up. Make friends with nobodies; don't be the great somebody.
ROMANS 12:15–16 MSG

Why does friendship sometimes seem so complicated, Lord? Friendships should be sources of support and joy, but so often conflict and hurt lace them. Instead of resting in their blessing, we labor under their weight. Lord, I read the words in Romans and begin to think that the problem starts in me—in each of us as individuals. Am I approaching friendship with the wrong focus? If my wish is first to *be* a friend and not just *receive* friendship, then my relationships have a chance to blossom. As I spend time with friends this week, refocus me on them, Lord. Amen.

THINK ABOUT IT:

How would your friendships change if you spent more time just being present for your friends?

Morning
INNOCENT

Then the Lord God said to the woman, "What is this you have done?" The woman said, "The serpent deceived me, and I ate."
GENESIS 3:13 NIV

Before sin entered our lives, we were innocent. You perfectly provided for all our needs. After sin, our innocence was lost, and our lives became hard. Something inside me longs for that innocence, Lord. You created me in Your image, but sin has marred that image. You formed me, but sin has *de*-formed me. Before sin, we didn't have to worry about anything, did we? Fear wasn't in the human vocabulary. Help me remember, today and every day, that fear is not from You. Fear is from Satan, and it's not a part of Your plan for my life. Help me trust in You with the innocence of a child.

THINK ABOUT IT:
Can you recall a time of innocence in your life when you didn't worry about anything?

Evening
WHEN WE MESS UP

The Lord God made garments of skin for Adam and his wife and clothed them.
GENESIS 3:21 NIV

Dear Father, this verse so perfectly illustrates who You are. Even though Adam and Eve disobeyed You, You still loved them. You still cared for them and provided for their needs. Instead of responding in anger, You gave them clothes to wear. So many times, I recognize my faults and my mistakes, and I worry that I'm not good enough. I worry that I'll be punished, rejected for my shortcomings. Father, even though others on this earth may judge me harshly, even though they may reject me, I know You never will. All Your actions toward me are born of love, not anger. For that reason, I want to obey You. I want to serve You not out of fear but from a grateful heart.

THINK ABOUT IT:
In what way have you messed up and worried you'd be rejected for it?

Morning
WALK WITH GOD

*Enoch walked with God after he
fathered Methuselah 300 years
and had other sons and daughters.
Thus all the days of Enoch were 365
years. Enoch walked with God, and
he was not, for God took him.*

GENESIS 5:22–24 ESV

Dear Father, what a testimony is contained in these three short verses! Enoch walked with *You*. He lived a long, faithful life, and You spared him from death and took him straight home. I want to live like that, Lord. I want to walk with You. I know from experience that when I stay close to You, when I think about Your promises and talk to You in my heart all day long, worry fades. When worry crowds in today, take my hand, Lord. Remind me of Your presence and help me focus on You. I want each breath, each step to be in time with You.

THINK ABOUT IT:

*What do you think it means to
walk with God like Enoch did?*

Evening
ABRAM'S EXAMPLE

*The LORD had said to Abram, "Go
from your country, your people
and your father's household to the
land I will show you. I will make
you into a great nation, and I will
bless you; I will make your name
great, and you will be a blessing."*

GENESIS 12:1–2 NIV

Abram provides such a great example for me today. You told him to go, but You didn't tell him the destination. You just said, "I'll let you know when you get there." So Abram obeyed, without knowing the future. This is what faith looks like. When it comes to the future, I tend to worry and fret. I want to know what will happen and that it will go the way I want it to. Help me to have Abram's faith. Help me to trust You so much that I'll blindly say, "I don't know what will happen, but I know God will eventually bring me to a good place."

THINK ABOUT IT:

*With what situation do you
need to trust God?*

Morning
FAITHFUL PROMISES

The Lord is trustworthy in all he promises and faithful in all he does.

PSALM 145:13 NIV

The chubby cheeks fill up and blow on the fuzzy dandelion head, and the seeds fly, floating on the breeze, settling on the lawn, tumbling on a wave of air into the distance. And as the seeds drift away, I think of every promise You have given us. Promises to love and take care of us. Promises to watch over us. Promises never to leave us. And each promise of Yours is like a seed in our lives, planting us into Your foundation and giving us hope to grow on. Lord, may I always know Your promises. May I teach others every day through the way I live for You. Amen.

THINK ABOUT IT:

What is one of God's promises that you are counting on?

Evening
A HANDLE FOR LIFE

The fundamental fact of existence is that this trust in God, this faith, is the firm foundation under everything that makes life worth living. It's our handle on what we can't see.

HEBREWS 11:1 MSG

I get so caught up in anxiety, Lord, and when I do, I become blind to the world around me, not to mention the spiritual world. All I see are my imaginary fears (but they seem so real!). Strengthen my faith now, God, I pray. Make it a firm foundation under my unsteady feet. Remind me that You alone are the reason life is worth living, and nothing can ever shake or diminish Your reality. Help me to grab hold of the handle of faith so I can relax and enjoy the life You have given me.

THINK ABOUT IT:

Do you think of faith as the "fundamental fact of existence"? How might your priorities need to change for your faith to become the "handle" that allows you to live with greater confidence in God's love?

Morning
YOUR LOVING EYE ON ME!

I will instruct you and teach you in the way you should go; I will counsel you with my loving eye on you.

PSALM 32:8 NIV

Okay, I admit it, Lord. Some days I like to think of myself as a superwoman. I can almost imagine my back bolt straight, my hands on my hips, and my cape unfurling in the breeze. And at that moment, I'm certain people are whispering, "It's a bird. It's a plane. It's Superwoman!" Then on other days I realize no one would dare think I deserved a recycled thank-you card! I don't know what I'm doing. I need Your help and guidance. Not just on days when I'm panic-ridden and clueless, but every day, Lord. I need Your loving eye on me, Your teachable moments directed at me, and Your divine road map spread before me! Amen.

THINK ABOUT IT:

Why do you pull away from God and His guidance—sometimes even when you need Him most?

Evening
THE FINE ART OF NOISE

Instruct the wise and they will be wiser still; teach the righteous and they will add to their learning.

PROVERBS 9:9 NIV

Okay, so noise really isn't a fine art. . .is it, Lord? But I'd like to do something artsy and useful with noise, since my family produces so much of it! Actually, in all honesty, I want to hide in a deep, dark—and quiet—closet. Maybe I even need a vacation from my daily problems. But since that may not come right away, I turn to You, Lord, for refreshment and calm. And for wisdom. Instruct me so I may become a wiser woman. Show me how to lovingly set boundaries with others and how to balance my life so that, rather than stress over my days, I might savor them! Amen.

THINK ABOUT IT:

What are some of the ways that God's wisdom looks different from human wisdom?

Morning
THE POTHOLE OF PRIDE

The LORD Almighty has a day in store for all the proud and lofty, for all that is exalted (and they will be humbled).
ISAIAH 2:12 NIV

I know we are born with cute little toes and cute little noses; but in this fallen world, we are also born with not-so-cute little egos. And, Lord, I know that like everything else that grows, egos do too! Help me to know how to humble myself before You so You don't have to humble me. And help me train up my family to have confidence in You without falling into a pothole of pride, to be courageous without being arrogant, to be humble without being weak. Such a pursuit seems impossible in this self-absorbed world. But with You, all things are possible! Amen.

THINK ABOUT IT:

What can you do to show your family that humility is a beautiful trait? What Bible verses might help your family— and you—become more humble?

Evening
THIS LIFE JOURNEY

This is the account of Noah and his family. Noah was a righteous man, blameless among the people of his time, and he walked faithfully with God.
GENESIS 6:9 NIV

Lord, I acknowledge that this life journey is not merely in the physical realm. It is a spiritual walk too, and at times it is full of perilous twists and turns, fraught with dangers from my own willful choices, from living in a fallen world, and from the attacks of Satan. I confess that this spiritual trek is hard for me to understand and even harder for me to navigate. Please show me how to walk with You just as Noah did—with faithfulness. Amen.

THINK ABOUT IT:

In his walk with God, Noah showed his faithfulness by building an ark. What is one way you can show your faithfulness to God?

Morning
MERCY

*"Blessed are the merciful,
for they will receive mercy."*
MATTHEW 5:7 NASB

There are some things, Lord, I just can't forgive. People who do hateful things don't deserve to be forgiven! And yet, Spirit, I hear You reminding me that You forgave me for some hateful things I did. I didn't deserve to be forgiven, and yet You did anyway. In Your mercy, You didn't hold my sins against me. Make me more like You, Lord. Give me mercy for others, even those who have done terrible things. Help me to see past their sins to the beautiful souls You created them to be. Show me how to love as You love.

THINK ABOUT IT:

Why do you think you have such a hard time forgiving some people more than others? Can you ask God to make your own heart clear to you?

Evening
FORGIVENESS

*Forgive us our debts,
as we forgive our debtors.*
MATTHEW 6:12 KJV

A debt is something owed; thank You, Jesus, that because of You, I owe no debt for all the ways I've turned away from You and Your plan for my life. You crossed out all my debts, allowing me to walk away free. Help me now, Lord, to extend the same grace to those who have hurt me or harmed me. May I hold nothing against them, but instead, help me to set them free the way You set me free. Give me the strength to forgive, even when it's hard. Remind me that forgiveness doesn't mean I can't protect myself from future hurts, and forgiveness doesn't mean that all consequences of wrongdoing are erased. Make me secure enough in You that I realize I can afford to forgive others. May I love the people who have hurt me, just as You love me.

THINK ABOUT IT:

Why do you think Jesus connected God's forgiveness with ours? How might these two actions (God's and our own) flow together?

DAY 13

Morning
DAILY BREAD

Give us this day our daily bread.
MATTHEW 6:11 KJV

I know You know what I need, Lord God—and I know You'll make sure I have it. But there are a lot of things I *want*, even though I may not *need* them. When those things evade my grasp, I feel so disappointed. There's so much I want in life that I don't have. Help me, Lord, to trust You enough that I can accept that each day You will provide me with what I need, even if I don't always get what I want. Remind me to stop thinking about what I can't have and instead focus on the many blessings You *have* given me. Today, keep my eyes open so that I can see the "daily bread" You give to me. Help me to stop wanting life's cake and candy when I have the Bread of Life.

THINK ABOUT IT:

When Jesus spoke of "daily bread," do you think He meant literal bread? What else might be included in this term? What nourishment does God give to you each day?

Evening
AN APPETITE FOR GOD

"You're blessed when you've worked up a good appetite for God. He's food and drink in the best meal you'll ever eat."
MATTHEW 5:6 MSG

Seems like, Lord, I'm always wanting *more*. I want more clothes in my closet when there are plenty there already. I want second helpings (and thirds) when, really, my stomach was full after the first helping. I want more household items, even though my home is already over-flowing. I want so many things that are newer, bigger, better. It's like I have a hole inside me, and I'm trying to stuff it full of more and more things—when, all along, the only thing that will really fill that hole is You, Holy Spirit. So, I pray, give me an appetite for You. Teach me to desire You more than anything this world can offer. I know that You alone can truly satisfy me.

THINK ABOUT IT:

When you find yourself wanting more, can you take a moment to look inside your heart to see if it might be God you're really wanting?

Morning
MIND AND HEART

"You're blessed when you get your inside world—your mind and heart—put right. Then you can see God in the outside world."

MATTHEW 5:8 MSG

Doubts have been multiplying inside my head, Lord. They started out small, but they keep growing, proliferating. Now they take up so much space that every time I try to talk to You, they get in the way. When I want to feel close to You, I can't anymore. I keep asking myself if maybe I just made You up, if You're nothing more than the adult version of an imaginary friend. God, something inside me has gotten out of alignment. I can't even tell what it is exactly, but I know something feels wrong. I don't know how to fix it. So I'm asking You—in spite of all my doubts—to heal my heart and mind. I want to see Your hand at work in my life. I want to feel close to You again.

THINK ABOUT IT:

What causes the doubts you're feeling? Can you remember when they began? Remember, God loves you, even through your doubts!

Evening
STRENGTH IN THE LORD

David was now in great danger because all his men were very bitter about losing their sons and daughters, and they began to talk of stoning him. But David found strength in the LORD his God.

1 SAMUEL 30:6 NLT

I'm glad, Lord, that the Bible is so full of stories to encourage us. David's enemies kidnapped all the women and children while the soldiers were away—and then his own men turned on him too. I can relate to that story, for I too have made enemies because people thought I had failed to do what I should have. Rather than accept the situation, they blamed me. Lord, when I find myself facing enemies, remind me of this story. Teach me to go to You for strength just as David did. David sought direction from You, and You guided him and went with him, allowing him to rescue all who had been kidnapped. He stood up to his enemies and clung to You. May I do the same.

THINK ABOUT IT:

How can you find strength in the Lord? What do you need to do to be able to face your enemies with the same confidence and wisdom that David did?

DAY 15

Morning
WORDS OF LIFE

The words of the godly are a life-giving fountain; the words of the wicked conceal violent intentions.

PROVERBS 10:11 NLT

I know I'm guilty of telling lies sometimes, Lord, but honestly, I don't have violent intentions! I only tell the sort of lies that smooth over an awkward social situation. Sometimes I lie to avoid upsetting someone or I say what I know the other person wants to hear even if it's not true. Can You really call that "violent"? Or am I concealing my true intentions even from myself? When I deny someone the truth, who am I caring about, really—myself or the other person? Do I really care what's best for the other person, or do I care more about making myself look good? God, help me not to make excuses for myself. May each of my words be spoken in love, with the intention of giving life.

THINK ABOUT IT:

The word the Bible uses for "violent" has to do with doing damage and causing harm. How might even little "polite" lies do damage and cause harm?

Evening
VIOLENT DECEIT

He shall redeem their soul from deceit and violence.

PSALM 72:14 KJV

It's interesting, Lord, that Your Word often pairs lies with violence. Our society is quick to excuse lies as being a "necessary evil," and yet scripture indicates that dishonesty is actually a form of violence. When I look at what has wounded me most over the years, I can see that the lies people told me were truly a form of violence, for they hurt my soul. They smashed my trust. Those who lied to me never hit me or harmed me physically—and yet they harmed my heart. Thank You, God, that You have the power to heal me. You can bring me back and restore clarity and faith to my soul.

THINK ABOUT IT:

The Hebrew word translated as "redeem" in this verse also implies a relationship of kinship. Can you trust in a God who loves you more than family to protect you from the violence of deceit?

Morning
HUMILITY

*Submit to one another out
of reverence for Christ.*
EPHESIANS 5:21 NIV

Lord, I realize that when I get caught up in arguments, it's almost always my selfish nature taking control. No matter how much I believe in my own "cause" (whatever it is), when it comes right down to it, I just want my own way. I want people to see that *I'm right.* I don't have the humility to give in or to compromise; I just dig in my heels and keep arguing. Jesus, teach me Your way instead. I want to model my life on Yours. Take away my selfishness and pride. Open my eyes to other perspectives and viewpoints. Make me willing to learn. Show me others' dignity and wisdom. May I honor You in all my interactions.

THINK ABOUT IT:

*What roles do pride and selfishness
play in your arguments? How
might things look different if you
regarded others with respect and
openness? How might humility
be an antidote for arguments?*

Evening
BRIDGES OF GENTLENESS

*A gentle answer deflects anger,
but harsh words make tempers flare.*
PROVERBS 15:1 NLT

I can hardly remember how this family fight began, Lord. It was probably something little, but over the years, more arguments have piled on top of it. People took sides, each side claiming to be the innocent party. Now there's so much resentment between us that I don't know how to reach past it. These are people I love, God, and yet I've allowed anger to drive us apart. Show me how to begin to heal this terrible division within our family. May I not respond to anger with more anger, adding fuel to the flame; instead, teach me gentleness. Remind me to keep a close hold on my own reactions so that I don't speak harsh words that will cause hurt and more anger. Allow me to build bridges of reconciliation.

THINK ABOUT IT:

*It's never too late to bring an end
to a family feud. What can you do
this week to begin building a bridge
between your family factions?*

DAY 17

Morning
SETTING HEALTHY BOUNDARIES

Don't be naive. There are difficult times ahead. As the end approaches, people are going to be self-absorbed, money-hungry, self-promoting, stuck-up, profane, contemptuous of parents, crude, coarse, dog-eat-dog, unbending, slanderers, impulsively wild, savage, cynical, treacherous, ruthless, bloated windbags, addicted to lust, and allergic to God. They'll make a show of religion, but behind the scenes they're animals. Stay clear of these people.
2 TIMOTHY 3:1–5 MSG

I know You want me to love everyone, Lord, but I also know You want me to steer clear of destructive relationships that can pull me down. Remind me that the qualities described in these verses may be common, but that doesn't make them *healthy*. When I encounter these behaviors and attitudes in other people, may I never dismiss them as "just the way things are." Don't let me absorb them into myself. Show me how to love people like this while still setting healthy boundaries that will protect my relationship with You.

THINK ABOUT IT:
What boundaries do you need to set in your life to protect yourself from destructive and unhealthy influences?

Evening
WHEN I NEED MY FRIENDS

A friend loves at all times, and a brother is born for a time of adversity.
PROVERBS 17:17 NIV

God, I know they are around here somewhere. They used to be here all the time. They were such a huge part of my life once. There was a time when I didn't go a day, or sometimes even an hour, without them. But now, Lord? Where are they now? It seems like my old friends have disappeared. They have lives of their own. I totally understand that. And, yes, there were many times I had to turn them down—times when I just couldn't go out. So why do I feel so neglected and left out? Lord, help me to reconnect with the people I care about. Help me to make the time and find the energy to cultivate good, healthy relationships, Lord. I need some friends. Amen.

THINK ABOUT IT:
What can you do to stay in touch with your friends? What do you do to stay in touch with your friend Jesus?

Morning
A WONDERFUL GOD

Peter and the other apostles replied: "We must obey God rather than human beings!"
ACTS 5:29 NIV

Lord, I confess that the word *obey* makes me squirm sometimes. To obey or submit to You, I'll have to *really* listen to You and Your Word. I may even have to give up my personal agenda. Why does that seem scary? Because I must secretly think that obeying You means I'll no longer be able to enjoy life. What a lie from the enemy—since You are the one who created joy in the first place! Without You, there is no wonder. No gifts. No miracles. None of the good things our spirits long for. Remind me daily, Lord, that the more I get to know You, the more the word *obey* will seem like the perfect and wonderful response to a perfect and wonderful God. Amen.

THINK ABOUT IT:

When you know you're in God's will, how do you feel, and what is the result?

Evening
DOES MY SPIRIT GOOD

Endure hardship as discipline; God is treating you as his children. For what children are not disciplined by their father?
HEBREWS 12:7 NIV

Yes, Lord, I confess I did a bad thing. I disobeyed You, and I'm sorry. To be honest, some part of me doesn't want to face the consequences or take any correction from You. But just as I hope that my children will submit to my loving discipline, I come before You now, surrendering to You. I've learned over the years that even though Your reprimands might be painful for a short time, they do my spirit good in the end. For a good father disciplines his child. And I know that it would always be better to be chastised by You—the one who made me and loves me best—than to be praised mightily by the enemy of my soul. Amen.

THINK ABOUT IT:

Has God disciplined you recently? What did you learn from it?

Morning
RESENTMENT IS BUILDING

*Bear with each other and forgive
one another if any of you has
a grievance against someone.
Forgive as the Lord forgave you.*

COLOSSIANS 3:13 NIV

I am wounded, and I can feel the resentment building. I feel shuffled off, neglected. Lord, I know Your Word says I am to forgive others as You have forgiven me, and that is a good policy—but there is a strange comfort in my anger and in feeling sorry for myself. It's hard to give them up. But I want to do what is right and good in Your sight, Lord, so help me to move beyond my pettiness, to forgive her, and to find a time for some honest but loving dialogue. Amen.

THINK ABOUT IT:

*Do you harbor any unforgiveness
toward someone? How can you
become as ready to forgive him or
her as God has forgiven you?*

Evening
AN ALL-YOU-CAN-FORGIVE MENTALITY

*Then Peter came up and said to him,
"Lord, how often will my brother
sin against me, and I forgive him?
As many as seven times?" Jesus said
to him, "I do not say to you seven
times, but seventy-seven times."*

MATTHEW 18:21–22 ESV

God, at times I struggle to forgive. When others hurt me—sometimes again and again—I am tempted to remain bitter and angry. I feel like they don't deserve forgiveness and often don't care if I offer it. It's easy to want to hold on to wrongs rather than release the burden. But then I think of Your forgiveness toward me. How many times have You granted forgiveness? More times than I care to count. Help me forgive as You forgive—lavishly. Generously. Lovingly. Through my forgiving heart, I reveal Your forgiving nature. Amen.

THINK ABOUT IT:

*God's forgiveness is a gift to us—
how is choosing to forgive a
gift to yourself as well as to the
one who wronged you?*

Morning
GIVE ME COURAGE

"Have I not commanded you? Be strong and courageous. Do not be afraid; do not be discouraged, for the LORD your God will be with you wherever you go."

JOSHUA 1:9 NIV

Lord, some days I feel more cowardly than courageous. In fact, I'm frightened by this world because it seems to be coming apart at the seams. I'm scared of the darkness that seems to get more ominous by the week. And most of all, Lord, I'm scared for the young people in my life. What kind of a world will they grow up in? Will it be a decent place? Or a place so fraught with sin's sickness that they will only be able to live an unfulfilled life—not the beautiful life You intended? Lord Jesus, still my racing heart, and give me courage. Remind me that wherever we go, You go with us as a family—and that is more than enough. Amen.

THINK ABOUT IT:
What does courage look like in today's world? During fearful times, how can you remind yourself of the power of God's presence with you?

Evening
BUT IF NOT. . .

"O Nebuchadnezzar, we have no need to answer you in this matter. If this be so, our God whom we serve is able to deliver us from the burning fiery furnace, and he will deliver us out of your hand, O king. But if not, be it known to you, O king, that we will not serve your gods or worship the golden image that you have set up."

DANIEL 3:16–18 ESV

Father, may I have the courage of Shadrach, Meshach, and Abednego to face the fiery trials, courage to follow Your ways and not bend to the world's, and confidence to know that You will rescue me. And even if You choose not to, Father, may I be committed to remain faithful as You are faithful. Only You are holy and deserve my all. Amen.

THINK ABOUT IT:
How can being resolved to stand firm in faith before trials help you endure them?

Morning
HOW SHALL WE BEGIN?

Her children arise and call her blessed; her husband also, and he praises her: "Many women do noble things, but you surpass them all."

PROVERBS 31:28–29 NIV

When I read about the Proverbs 31 woman, I admit, Lord, I am intimidated. To the max. I'm thinking, *Could that ever be me?* Could I do such noble deeds that my husband would rise up—even before his coffee—and shout my praises? And my kids too? I just can't imagine that. But the thing is, I really would like my life to be that way. I want to be a woman of noble deeds. Of substance and goodness. Yes, I want that. Please. What can I do to make that happen? Lord, how shall I begin? Amen.

THINK ABOUT IT:

What is one good and noble deed God might be nudging you to do today?

Evening
WORTHY WOMEN

"Many women have done excellently, but you surpass them all." Charm is deceitful, and beauty is vain, but a woman who fears the LORD is to be praised. Give her of the fruit of her hands, and let her works praise her in the gates.

PROVERBS 31:29–31 ESV

Lord, how can we as women not be intimidated by the unnamed woman of Proverbs 31? We read of her and begin the mental checklist of all the ways we don't measure up. I have to believe that making women the world over feel inadequate is not Your purpose for these verses, Lord. If I focus less on what she does specifically and more on what she values, I can learn from her; I can grow as a woman of God. Her actions speak of resourcefulness, initiative, generosity, self-respect, faith, and more. . .all qualities I can embody in my own way. Show me how, Lord. May I be worthy of praise. Amen.

THINK ABOUT IT:

In what ways are you a Proverbs 31 woman?

Morning
LOVE ETERNAL

For I am persuaded, that neither death, nor life, nor angels, nor principalities, nor powers, nor things present, nor things to come, nor height, nor depth, nor any other creature, shall be able to separate us from the love of God, which is in Christ Jesus our Lord.

ROMANS 8:38–39 KJV

Lord, that You love me is amazing. You are almighty God. You reign over earth and the heavens; You created the universe! And yet You desire relationship with me—one human among countless others. Your love is immense. . .and it is everlasting. Nothing in this world or out of this world, now or ever, will keep Your love from me. When all else in life seems to disintegrate, I know the love of God will hold me unwaveringly. Words are never enough, Lord, but let me thank You for Your love. Amen.

THINK ABOUT IT:

If love is the greatest power on earth, how much greater is God's love for us?

Evening
LOVE IN SERVICE

Above all, keep loving one another earnestly, since love covers a multitude of sins. . . . As each has received a gift, use it to serve one another, as good stewards of God's varied grace: whoever speaks, as one who speaks oracles of God; whoever serves, as one who serves by the strength that God supplies—in order that in everything God may be glorified.

1 PETER 4:8, 10–11 ESV

God, love puts another before self. It's seeking someone else's good—even when I've been treated poorly. After all, in the greatest display of love, You did not turn Your back on me when sin separated me from You; You reached out and poured Your love over me. Your love encourages me to love others with the same measure. You've equipped me for that purpose. May I use my gifts for Your glory. Amen.

THINK ABOUT IT:

What is it about God's love and grace that prompts us to extend love and grace to others?

Morning
NO EYE HAS SEEN. . .

But, as it is written, "What no eye has seen, nor ear heard, nor the heart of man imagined, what God has prepared for those who love him"—these things God has revealed to us through the Spirit. For the Spirit searches everything, even the depths of God.

1 CORINTHIANS 2:9–10 ESV

God, Your truth is deep, Your wisdom immense. We cannot obtain it like ordinary truth and wisdom—by eyes and ears and mind. The Holy Spirit must reveal it. Open me to Your truth in Your Word and as Your Spirit whispers to my heart. I need Your wisdom guiding me through this life, step by step, moment by moment. Where my understanding is so limited, Yours is unimaginable. But You reveal Your wisdom to the ones You love. Reveal it to me, I pray. Amen.

THINK ABOUT IT:

Is it easy to wait for the revealed wisdom of the Holy Spirit, or do you find yourself relying on the "wisdom of this age" (v. 6)?

Evening
LIKE HONEY TO THE SOUL

My son, eat honey, for it is good, and the drippings of the honeycomb are sweet to your taste. Know that wisdom is such to your soul; if you find it, there will be a future, and your hope will not be cut off.

PROVERBS 24:13–14 ESV

Father, it is easy to think of "wisdom" as dry—something acquired with age. But the scriptures declare wisdom to be sweet—something to be sought even in youth. Wisdom goes deep into our lives and enriches our souls. Wisdom is the nectar we need to thrive. Help me find wisdom, Father. May I daily go to the source of wisdom, Your Word, in search of the insights that bring a future and hope. Whisper to my heart so that I may know You and Your will more fully, so that I may grow in understanding. Amen.

THINK ABOUT IT:

What rewards does wisdom bring to the believer's life?

Morning
HERE FOR NOW

So [Isaac] built an altar there and called upon the name of the LORD and pitched his tent there.

GENESIS 26:25 ESV

Father, if there is one word to describe this life, it might be *impermanent*. People come and go. We move from here to there. Even our emotions shift from day to day. But You, Lord, will never change. Isaac built an altar—an enduring reminder of You—and pitched his tent—a mark of a transitory life. As I go through my life, help me build my faith. Help my worship of You become the one steady point in an often-shifting world. The apostle Paul's words echo in my mind: "The present form of this world is passing away" (1 Corinthians 7:31). May I not cling to earthly things but be ready to follow Your command. Amen.

THINK ABOUT IT:
Do your security and purpose come from eyes fixed on God or in creating an earthly nest?

Evening
"SOMEDAY MY PRINCE WILL COME"

For to us a child is born, to us a son is given; and the government shall be upon his shoulder, and his name shall be called Wonderful Counselor, Mighty God, Everlasting Father, Prince of Peace.

ISAIAH 9:6 ESV

Lord Jesus, how many stories center on a young prince rescuing a fair maiden? The good news is we don't have to wait for Prince Charming to sweep us away from evil. An even greater prince has already come! As our rescuer, our Redeemer, You arrived on earth as a baby to save us from death. You are wise beyond anything humans can comprehend. You are powerful to accomplish Your will. You pour out Your love to us as our heavenly Father. You bring peace. *Someday* is now as we choose to follow You. Amen.

THINK ABOUT IT:
What do each of Christ's titles mean to you in your life?

DAY 25

Morning
THE GOOD PORTION

But the Lord answered her, "Martha, Martha, you are anxious and troubled about many things, but one thing is necessary. Mary has chosen the good portion, which will not be taken away from her."
LUKE 10:41–42 ESV

Father, how many times You must call to me as You did with Martha! When my anxious thoughts run circles in my head . . . When I am worried about all the day holds. . . May I hear You calling my name not as a rebuke but tenderly. You long for me to choose the one necessary thing—relationship with You. May I daily sit at Your feet and soak up Your words. May my focus be on You first, while all else takes second place. Remind me, Father, that what I invest in You will not be taken from me. Amen.

THINK ABOUT IT:
Do you identify more with Martha or Mary—fretting or faith focused?

Evening
AT HAND

The Lord is at hand; do not be anxious about anything, but in everything by prayer and supplication with thanksgiving let your requests be made known to God.
PHILIPPIANS 4:5–6 ESV

Father, when I am worried, I often read the words of Philippians 4:6. But as I follow Your instructions—to pray about my anxious thoughts—remind me of the words that come just before this verse. "The Lord is at hand." You are near, Father. You dwell as high as heaven, yet You are as close as my heart. As I turn my troubles over to You, may my trust grow ever stronger, rooted in Your perfect will. I will not be anxious about anything because You are here with me. Thank You for Your presence. Thank You for caring enough to listen to my prayers. Amen.

THINK ABOUT IT:
What keeps you from surrendering your anxiety fully to God?

Morning
EVEN WHEN I CAN'T SEE IT

Now faith is confidence in what we hope for and assurance about what we do not see.

HEBREWS 11:1 NIV

I'm one of those "see it to believe it" types, Lord. Then again, You already know this about me. Many times I've needed a faith boost, especially when my physical eyes couldn't see what You were up to.

You're teaching me that I can trust You even when I don't see what's coming around the bend. You've never let me down, and You're not going to start now. So I will choose to let You lead the way, no matter how blurry the picture looks. I love You and I trust You, Lord. Amen.

THINK ABOUT IT:

When was the last time you had to lean on your faith in a major way?

Evening
I CAN WALK ON WATER!

"Lord, if it's you," Peter replied, "tell me to come to you on the water." "Come," he said. Then Peter got down out of the boat, walked on the water and came toward Jesus. But when he saw the wind, he was afraid and, beginning to sink, cried out, "Lord, save me!" Immediately Jesus reached out his hand and caught him. "You of little faith," he said, "why did you doubt?"

MATTHEW 14:28–31 NIV

I love this story, Lord! You called out to Peter, and he walked on the water. When he took his eyes off You, he started to sink. Then, just as quickly, he looked Your way and was saved.

I've been there more times than I can count. I was at the near-sinking point; then I shifted my gaze to You and bounced back up again. Thank You for meeting me even on tumultuous seas, Lord. Amen.

THINK ABOUT IT:

Can you think of a time when God proved Himself in spite of your doubt?

Morning
NO MATTER WHAT
. . .HE'S THERE

*"When you pass through the waters,
I will be with you; and through the
rivers, they shall not overwhelm
you; when you walk through fire
you shall not be burned, and the
flame shall not consume you."*

ISAIAH 43:2 ESV

I've been through seasons, Lord, when I felt like I was going to drown. I was up to my eyeballs in chaos and confusion—at work, at home, even with the kids or other loved ones. Yet somehow I managed to stay afloat. I haven't drowned yet, and I know and believe You'll be there to pull me out of the depths of the water again and again.

Thank You for saving me, and thank You for the way You intervene. You're always there, right when I need rescuing. (You're the best lifeguard out there, Lord!)

I won't be overwhelmed. I won't be overtaken. I will trust You even when I pass through deep waters. Amen.

THINK ABOUT IT:

*How did God prove Himself strong
during your last flood or fire season?*

Evening
A PARTING GIFT

*"Peace I leave with you; my peace I
give to you. Not as the world gives do
I give to you. Let not your hearts be
troubled, neither let them be afraid."*

JOHN 14:27 ESV

Lord, I love this verse! Your parting gift to Your followers was peace. Peace to have faith for the things we cannot see. Peace to overcome obstacles. Peace to take the place of turmoil.

It's Your peace, Jesus. As I pause to think it through, I realize this peace passed through Your hands before landing in mine. You don't give me the world's version, filtered through modern-day culture. No, You breathe on it and then pass it directly to me so that my heart and life can be permanently changed.

"Let not your hearts be troubled." Oh, how I love those words! The Savior of the world loves me so much that He left me this amazing parting gift. I'll take it. Apply it. Live it. Thank You, Lord! Amen.

THINK ABOUT IT:

*What do you suppose Jesus meant
when He added, "Not as the
world gives do I give to you"?*

Morning
GET BACK UP AGAIN

The godly may trip seven times,
but they will get up again.
But one disaster is enough to
overthrow the wicked.

PROVERBS 24:16 NLT

I fall down, I get up. I fall down again, I get up again. Over and over this cycle goes.

Oh, I'm not complaining, Lord! Not at all. I'm so grateful You're there to pick me up again. If not for You, I'd still be down after my first tumble. But You won't let that happen. Whenever I trip, You catch me in Your arms and set my feet on solid ground again. How grateful I am for Your strong arms!

Your people are blessed for You provide a supernatural safety net, one the ungodly don't possess. I'm glad I'm one of Your own, Father! Amen.

THINK ABOUT IT:
How do you pick yourself
up after you've fallen?

Evening
I'M AN OVERCOMER!

For everyone who has been born of God
overcomes the world. And this is the
victory that has overcome the world—
our faith. Who is it that overcomes
the world except the one who believes
that Jesus is the Son of God?

1 JOHN 5:4–5 ESV

I'm so grateful for the reminder that I'm an overcomer, Lord! I'm not ruled by my circumstances or feelings. I don't have to give in to fear. I can—and will—have victory in You, even when it feels impossible.

You've overcome sin, death, and the grave. You rose again to new life, and You've given me the power to rise as well— from my past, from my present, and from the problems that seem to plague me.

Have I mentioned I'm grateful for the power You've given me, Father? I am! I lift up praise to You, the one who brings the victory. Amen.

THINK ABOUT IT:
How can you remind yourself daily
that you are an overcomer and
that stress doesn't rule you?

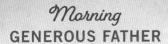

Morning
GENEROUS FATHER

And God said, "Let the earth sprout vegetation, plants yielding seed, and fruit trees bearing fruit in which is their seed, each according to its kind, on the earth." And it was so.
GENESIS 1:11 ESV

Dear Father, You are so generous with us! When I think of fruits and vegetables I grow in my garden or buy at the store, I realize within that single fruit is the potential for dozens, even hundreds more plants. Each seed can produce countless more of its kind, and each of those can produce countless more, and on and on. Your design provides perfectly for all our needs. Why do I worry about what my family will eat, what we'll wear, or how I'll pay the bills? I trust You to provide everything I need. Your generosity over-whelms me.

THINK ABOUT IT:
What kinds of things do you need God to provide for you?

Evening
TIME FOR REST

Then God blessed the seventh day and made it holy, because on it he rested from all the work of creating that he had done.
GENESIS 2:3 NIV

Thank You for this reminder that You rested. I feel like I'm running all the time, Lord. There's always something to do, someone to take care of, some meal to cook or mess to clean or responsibility to tend to. Even when I try to rest, my mind races. I know I feel more anxious about things when I'm tired. I know hard work pleases You, but frantic, nonstop busyness doesn't. Do I even know how to relax, Lord? I want to follow Your example of resting after my work. Will You show me how? Today, help me remember to take time to just rest in Your love, in Your joy, in Your peace.

THINK ABOUT IT:
What will you do differently today so you can rest in Him?

Morning
A REAL PLACE

A river watering the garden flowed from Eden; from there it was separated into four headwaters.
GENESIS 2:10 NIV

It's hard to imagine that Eden was a real place. It's so far removed from my reality that, as much as I try, I can't picture it. But You created the garden perfectly. Before You created man and woman in Your image, You had everything ready for them so they'd lack for nothing. Sin destroyed Your perfect plan, but it didn't destroy Your love for us. When I feel worried, anxious, and stressed, bring to mind this beautiful place called Eden. Remind me that, even now, You're preparing a place for me in heaven, and it will be more glorious than anything I can imagine. Thank You for Jesus and for Your abundant provision for my life both now and for eternity.

THINK ABOUT IT:
When you picture heaven, what do you see?

Evening
SATAN'S SCHEMES

Now the serpent was more crafty than any other beast of the field that the LORD God had made. He said to the woman, "Did God actually say, 'You shall not eat of any tree in the garden'?"
GENESIS 3:1 ESV

Father, Satan hasn't changed his tactics at all. Just as he spoke to Eve in the garden and made her doubt herself and her convictions, he speaks to me in my head all the time. He causes me to doubt what I know is right. He makes me question Your love, Your power, Your faithfulness. When I question who You are and who I am in You, worry is born. Anxiety flourishes in this setting. When Satan plants seeds of doubt in my mind, help me recognize his craftiness and his lies. Make me strong in You. Make me confident in Your promises. Give me the assertiveness to put Satan in his place and call him a liar.

THINK ABOUT IT:
How has Satan caused you to doubt God?

Morning
IN HIS PRESENCE

Then Cain went away from the presence of the LORD and settled in the land of Nod, east of Eden.

GENESIS 4:16 ESV

I don't ever want to leave Your presence. In Your presence, there is joy. There is peace. There is the quiet confidence that I'm wanted, I'm loved, and I belong. But outside Your presence, I find fear and anxiety and every bad thing. When I'm far from You, that's when worry takes over my mind. Forgive me for wandering away from You, Lord. Help me rest in You and delight in Your company. Next time I start to drift away, pull me back. Don't let me go, Father. Even when I'm stubborn and try to fight You, hold on to me. I want to live in Your presence every day, every hour, every minute of my life.

THINK ABOUT IT:

Are you living in God's presence, or have you wandered away from Him?

Evening
I NEED YOU

At that time people began to call upon the name of the LORD.

GENESIS 4:26 ESV

Why did it take people so long to recognize their need for You? If they had called on You sooner, they could have avoided so much heartache. Sin wouldn't have entered the world. Cain wouldn't have killed his brother, breaking his parents' hearts. So many hard things happened, all because they didn't call on You. The same thing is true in my life, Father. When I fail to recognize my need for You, bad things happen. When I don't call on You, life is harder than it needs to be. Help me learn the lesson early and never forget it. I need You. I will call on You every day. I find peace in knowing You will always hear me and You will always answer.

THINK ABOUT IT:

Have you called upon God today and shared your need with Him?

Morning
PROMISE KEEPER

And God said, "This is the sign of the covenant that I make between me and you and every living creature that is with you, for all future generations: I have set my bow in the cloud, and it shall be a sign of the covenant between me and the earth."

GENESIS 9:12–13 ESV

Thank You for this reminder that You always keep Your promises. Every time I see a rainbow, I know You are faithful and true. The promise to never again destroy the earth by flood is just one of Your many promises to mankind and to me, personally. You've promised never to leave me or forsake me. You've promised to take care of me. You've promised to give me peace. The more time I spend in Your Word, the more promises I find. Your faithfulness in every area of my life serves as a gentle reminder that I don't need to worry about anything.

THINK ABOUT IT:
Which of God's promises do you need to remember today?

Evening
REJOICING IN TRIBULATIONS

Hannah prayed and said, "My heart exults in the LORD; my horn is exalted in the LORD. My mouth derides my enemies, because I rejoice in your salvation."

1 SAMUEL 2:1 ESV

I love the story of Hannah, Lord. Even in her tribulations, as she waited and prayed for a child, she never gave up. And when You finally answered her prayer and gave her a son, Samuel, she was quick to praise You.

I want to live my life that way! Even in times of tribulation, may I lift my voice to You. Even when things look bleak, may I place my trust in You. You have always come through for me, Lord. I know You won't fail me now. I want to be a Hannah—faithful until I see the promise fulfilled. Help me, I pray. Amen.

THINK ABOUT IT:
Did you stop to praise God the last time He came through for you?

Morning
ANXIOUS FOR NOTHING

*Do not be anxious about anything,
but in everything by prayer and
supplication with thanksgiving let
your requests be made known to God.
And the peace of God, which surpasses
all understanding, will guard your
hearts and your minds in Christ Jesus.*

PHILIPPIANS 4:6–7 ESV

Lord, sometimes I get so wound up!
I'm like a ticking bomb, about to go off.
Stresses add up, one on top of the other,
and I don't always handle them the way I
should. Then I'm reminded of Your Word:
"Do not be anxious about anything."

You have a great plan to turn things
around, but it requires action on my part.
You want to involve me in the process. So
here I am, Father, pouring out my sup-
plications with thanksgiving in my heart
because I know You'll answer my prayers
when and how You choose. My choice,
Lord, is to trust You in the process. Thanks
for loving me enough to care about my
anxieties! I'm so grateful, Father. Amen.

THINK ABOUT IT:
How do you turn your anxiety around?

Evening
HE WILL DELIVER ME

*Moses answered the people, "Do not
be afraid. Stand firm and you will see
the deliverance the Lord will bring you
today. The Egyptians you see today
you will never see again. The Lord will
fight for you; you need only to be still."*

EXODUS 14:13–14 NIV

Lord, I'll be honest—there are days when
I'm so stressed out, I can't think straight.
On those days, it's like I forget who You
are and what You're capable of. I'm overwhelmed by my circumstances, unable to
see past them.

Then I'm reminded of this story
from Your Word. If You could deliver the
Israelites from the hands of their enemies,
surely You have me covered as well. So,
I won't stress out. I'll stand firm just as
You asked them to do. And I know that I
will see deliverance just as they did. How
I praise You for Your supernatural intervention, Lord! Amen.

THINK ABOUT IT:
*Can you remember a
specific time when God
intervened in your situation?*

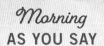

Morning
AS YOU SAY

Mary said, "I am the servant of the Lord. Let this happen to me as you say!" Then the angel went away.

LUKE 1:38 NCV

Lord, I love the story of how Mary submitted herself to Your authority. She spoke the words "As you say." They serve as a reminder that Your way is higher. Your way is wiser.

I'm facing a lot of chaos in my life. I want things the way I want them. But Mary's story also reminds me that I'm not really in charge of my own life. You are. And if she could trust You, I can too. So I'll say the words that she spoke: "As you say, Lord."

As You say in my relationships. As You say in my work. As You say in my provision. As You say in my hopes and dreams. Your way is better. As You say. Amen.

THINK ABOUT IT:

Can you think of a time when you preferred to do things your way and not God's? Did your way lead to peace or stress?

Evening
FIERY TRIALS

Shadrach, Meshach, and Abednego answered and said to the king, "O Nebuchadnezzar, we have no need to answer you in this matter. If this be so, our God whom we serve is able to deliver us from the burning fiery furnace, and he will deliver us out of your hand, O king. But if not, be it known to you, O king, that we will not serve your gods or worship the golden image that you have set up."

DANIEL 3:16–18 ESV

I know You never promised me a fire-free journey, Lord. But this story of Shadrach, Meshach, and Abednego is a great reminder that even in the most fiery trials, You're right there in the midst of the flames.

Sometimes I feel like I'll be consumed, if I'm being honest. But You saved these three Hebrew men who put their trust in You, and You'll save me too. No stress, no problem, no heartache is so big that You can't pull me out of it. Thank You for delivering me, Lord! Amen.

THINK ABOUT IT:

Do you believe God is able to deliver you from impossible situations?

Morning
THAT KIND OF LOVE

For I am convinced that neither death nor life, neither angels nor demons, neither the present nor the future, nor any powers, neither height nor depth, nor anything else in all creation, will be able to separate us from the love of God that is in Christ Jesus our Lord.

ROMANS 8:38–39 NIV

Lord, I appreciate Your love for me. The profound love You talk about in Romans 8 is just what I long for—all the way to my innermost being. It makes me want to rise up early and put a smile on the day. It helps me know I can call on You for whatever I need as a person. It reminds me that no matter what kind of horrors the world is embroiled in today, You are there, holding my hand, my heart, my life. I love You too! Amen.

THINK ABOUT IT:

What are some ways you can show others how much God loves them?

Evening
A SERIOUS CASE OF THE GRINS

A merry heart doeth good like a medicine: but a broken spirit drieth the bones.

PROVERBS 17:22 KJV

Oh, how I love it when the sun comes out bright and warm after a season of rain. It's so welcome, and it always does my heart good. For too long, Lord, I've been in a dreary mood—like those old dry bones the Bible talks about—and it's reflecting on my whole life. Please help me learn how to have a merry heart and to teach others how to enjoy a good belly laugh. The whole world needs a lot less scowls and a lot more smiles. And please let that serious case of the grins begin with me! Amen.

THINK ABOUT IT:

How does it change your attitude knowing God would rather see a grin than a grimace?

DAY 36

Morning
IN GOOD COMPANY

*He is despised and rejected by men,
a Man of sorrows and acquainted
with grief. And we hid, as it were, our
faces from Him; He was despised,
and we did not esteem Him.*

ISAIAH 53:3 NKJV

Lord, I've heard You referred to in Your Word as a "man of sorrows." I can't imagine the unthinkable horrors You endured while You were here on this earth. Sometimes when I watch the news, as a witness of the world's ills, I feel a soulful sorrow too. The horrors of the world are all too numerous to mention and too dark to fathom. But I know that even in Your sorrow, You gave the ultimate gift—Your perfect body for our sin-stained ones. You offer us new life, real love, and the bridge to heaven! Show me how to share this glorious news with others. And may my life become a daily celebration of Your gift—Your glory. Amen.

THINK ABOUT IT:
*How have you celebrated
the gift of Jesus today?*

Evening
IT'S A ME-FIRST WORLD

*"In everything I did, I showed you that
by this kind of hard work we must help
the weak, remembering the words
the Lord Jesus himself said: 'It is more
blessed to give than to receive.'"*

ACTS 20:35 NIV

Lord, I admit to sometimes succumbing to that selfish notion of wanting what I want when I want it. And having the mentality that I'd better "get while the getting is good." I know in my heart these life slogans are not Your ways. Unfortunately, my kids have been watching me too closely, so they're starting to act and sound like me! That isn't always good. I think I need an overhaul, and I give You permission right now to do it. And please, Lord, help me to remember Your teachings—that it is better to give than it is to receive. Amen.

THINK ABOUT IT:
*In the past, how did it feel to share
God's blessings with others?*

DAY 37

Morning
BRUISES THAT DON'T GO AWAY

But the wisdom that comes from heaven is first of all pure; then peace-loving, considerate, submissive, full of mercy and good fruit, impartial and sincere.

JAMES 3:17 NIV

I saw a little one tumble off his bike. He shed a few tears, and so did I. Maybe You did too, Lord. He'll probably get a bruise, but I'm glad it will heal quickly. That moment made me think of all the bruises we all get growing up—ones that we might not see. The verbal barbs that affect us within. Perhaps the hurt on someone will come from me—some harsh criticism that might wound her spirit—which she might carry with her always. Lord, please don't let it be so! Guard my tongue, and always let my words be pure and full of mercy and good fruit! Amen.

THINK ABOUT IT:

When anger rises and you feel some stinging words coming on, what are some things you can do instead of releasing a critical remark? What Bible verse might God want you to take to heart to help you in this endeavor?

Evening
THE GARDENER

"I am the true vine, and my Father is the gardener. He cuts off every branch in me that bears no fruit, while every branch that does bear fruit he prunes so that it will be even more fruitful."

JOHN 15:1-2 NIV

I love being happy, Lord, but it's like a butterfly landing for a moment, and then it's gone. This is a fallen world, so I understand that perfect, unspoiled happiness will only be in heaven. But I do find myself wishing for more of it on earth too. I see in John 15 that You prune even the branches that bear fruit. *Ouch!* That sounds a bit painful. Please help me to realize that when I become holier from pruning, I also find a more joyful way of life. Let me accept that truth—to embrace it—and to willingly change into whomever You created me to be as Your child. Amen.

THINK ABOUT IT:

What are some ways that God has pruned you recently, and what were the results?

DAY 38

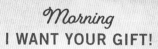

Morning
I WANT YOUR GIFT!

If the whole body were an eye,
where would be the sense of hearing?
If the whole body were an ear, where
would be the sense of smell? But as it
is, God arranged the members in the
body, each one of them, as he chose.

1 CORINTHIANS 12:17–18 ESV

Father, Christians are the hands and feet, the eyes and ears—the members of the body of Christ, each designed perfectly to spread Your glory. In Your wisdom, You have gifted me in specific and intentional ways. Sometimes I struggle with contentment, wishing I had a different gift. Forgive my jealousy, Father. Help me recognize my place. Help me rejoice in the *me* You created. Only I can fill the role You have appointed to me. And I can only blossom in my role through You. Amen.

THINK ABOUT IT:

In what ways can you appreciate and
use the spiritual gifts that God has
graciously and purposely given you?

Evening
SUPERNATURAL STRENGTH

He gives strength to the weary and
increases the power of the weak.

ISAIAH 40:29 NIV

I love the word *supernatural*, Lord. Anything You offer me is above and beyond this natural world. Your imagination? I can't even begin to fathom the things that go on in Your mind. Your love for me? It amazes me too! Your grace? Wow! So far beyond what I could imagine!

Your best gifts are *all* supernatural. So why would I doubt that You can empower me with supernatural strength? If You can give me hope, if You can give me peace, if You can supernaturally infuse me with joy, then I can count on You to give me strength for the journey, the kind that comes straight from Your throne to my weary body. It's supernatural! Amen.

THINK ABOUT IT:

Are you having to rely on
God's supernatural strength?

Morning
TRYING TO IMPRESS

"And when you pray, do not heap up empty phrases as the Gentiles do, for they think that they will be heard for their many words. Do not be like them, for your Father knows what you need before you ask him."

MATTHEW 6:7–8 ESV

Dear Father,

Sometimes I want to impress others so they'll think well of me. I want them to think I'm good and kind and righteous and holy. I do good things, hoping for their approval. Forgive me for doing the right things with the wrong motives. Change my heart. Make me humble, because I know humility pleases You. Help me stop worrying about what others think and focus on honoring You with my thoughts, words, and actions. I want to be just like Jesus.

THINK ABOUT IT:

Do you care more about what others think or what God thinks? Do you need to shift your motives at all?

Evening
BLESSED WITH PEACE (NOT STRESS!)

The LORD gives strength to his people; the LORD blesses his people with peace.

PSALM 29:11 NIV

When I think of all the gifts my parents have passed down, I'm so grateful. And when I think of all the gifts that You, my heavenly Father, have passed down. . . I get even more excited!

You give me things like hope, joy, and peace. Every gift is life-giving. So when I'm feeling stressed? When I'm feeling overwhelmed? Those feelings aren't from You. They're definitely not gifts! Usually, they've come because I'm in over my head.

But You, Lord, offer the gift of peace even in situations that feel overwhelming! And with that peace comes great strength. Oh, how I appreciate that strength on the rough days! Amen.

THINK ABOUT IT:

When was the last time God gave you strength and peace in place of your anxiety?

Morning
ESCAPE ROUTE

No temptation has overtaken you that is not common to man. God is faithful, and he will not let you be tempted beyond your ability, but with the temptation he will also provide the way of escape, that you may be able to endure it.

1 Corinthians 10:13 esv

Sometimes I seem to struggle with the same temptations. But there is hope! I read in Your Word that You will provide a way out. Open my eyes to see the escape route. Reach out to me as I grasp for Your hand. Lift my focus from the temptation to You. I want to live a life of victory over sin. I know this is only possible through Your power. Alone, I will fail; together with You, I will overcome. Thank You for Your faithfulness. Amen.

THINK ABOUT IT:

How do the words of 1 Corinthians 10:13 encourage you when you face temptation?

Evening
LASER FOCUSED

He said, "Come." So Peter got out of the boat and walked on the water and came to Jesus. But when he saw the wind, he was afraid.

Matthew 14:29–30 esv

Lord, I see myself in Peter. On good days, I am confident, stepping into life with my eyes trained on You. But then the storm rolls in. The wind begins to blow, and my focus falters. I look away from You, and suddenly I am afraid. What joy there is in the rest of Matthew's account! Peter cries out—and You take hold of him. Be my rescue in the storms. But more than that, increase my faith so I will not doubt Your presence or Your power to calm the wind. May my eyes be ever focused on You, Father. Amen.

THINK ABOUT IT:

Like a pirouetting dancer always orienting her head to a single focal point, how important is it for Christians to remain focused on God?

Morning
GETTING CREDIT

"Thus, when you give to the needy, sound no trumpet before you, as the hypocrites do in the synagogues and in the streets, that they may be praised by others. Truly, I say to you, they have received their reward. But when you give to the needy, do not let your left hand know what your right hand is doing, so that your giving may be in secret. And your Father who sees in secret will reward you."
MATTHEW 6:2–4 ESV

Dear Father, too often, I worry about what others think of me. I want them to be impressed, so I do things in order to get credit. But my only concern should be what You think of me. Forgive me for wanting the spotlight. True humility does good things in private, without needing credit. Give me a humble nature. Help me honor You without worrying about what others think.

THINK ABOUT IT:

When was the last time you did something good without getting credit? How did it make you feel?

Evening
ALL OF MY ANXIETIES

Casting all your anxieties on him, because he cares for you.
1 PETER 5:7 ESV

You ask me to cast all of my anxieties on You, Lord. To release them from my tight grip and toss them all the way to Your loving hands. No one else I know would make an offer like that. Who in the world would want to carry all of my burdens, especially with the stress I've been under lately? No one!

But You? You're not only willing but *able* to carry them all. And You desire to lift these burdens from me because You care so deeply for me. Your love means everything to me, Father. Thank You for reminding me I don't have to bear my problems alone. Amen.

THINK ABOUT IT:

Casting is a fishing term. When was the last time you "cast" your cares on the Lord?

Morning
PROFITLESS

"And which of you by being anxious can add a single hour to his span of life?"
MATTHEW 6:27 ESV

Father, so many times I am reminded of this verse in my life. I worry—a lot—about something, and the "problem" I anticipate resolves itself easily or never surfaces at all. Or something else, something I never would have known to anticipate, ends up being a problem! My response is not to be a bundle of nerves perpetually, fearing life and what might catch me unawares. I need a daily reminder of the futility of worry, Father. You call me to a life of peace. Even if my world crumbles, my soul is safe with You. And You promise to walk with me through debris and clear paths alike. Thank You for Your presence. Amen.

THINK ABOUT IT:

Has worry ever had a positive or constructive influence on a difficult situation in your life?

Evening
HEAVEN IS WORTH A FORTUNE

"The kingdom of heaven is like treasure hidden in a field, which a man found and covered up. Then in his joy he goes and sells all that he has and buys that field."
MATTHEW 13:44 ESV

It's so easy to lose sight of heaven, Lord. I'm bombarded by all that this world offers, and I begin to build my "kingdom" on earth. I forget that my life does not end here, but it continues forever with You. Am I willing to let go of all I have—materially and emotionally—to gain spiritual rewards that are beyond comprehension? Is the promise of heaven worth my all? Yes! Fix my heart on You, Father. Fill it with the joy of the man who sold everything in commitment to the treasure that awaits. Amen.

THINK ABOUT IT:

How can you develop a heart attitude of being all in for Christ and His kingdom?

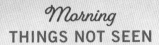

Morning
THINGS NOT SEEN

*Now faith is the assurance of
things hoped for, the conviction
of things not seen.*
HEBREWS 11:1 ESV

When I'm going through a stressful season, Lord, it's almost as if I'm staggering around in a dark room. I keep waiting for someone to turn on the lights, but it doesn't happen. Darkness surrounds me. In my imagination, the stresses will disappear when I'm able to see things more clearly.

You have a different way of seeing things. You're asking for my faith right now, right here, even in the middle of these stressful circumstances. Even when I can't see what's coming and don't know how to find my way out of this situation. Give me that kind of faith, I pray! I want the assurance of things I haven't yet seen, things I'm hoping for. Amen.

THINK ABOUT IT:
*What things are you hoping
for but haven't seen yet?*

Evening
NO REASON TO FEAR

*Fear not, for I am with you;
be not dismayed, for I am your
God; I will strengthen you, I will
help you, I will uphold you with
my righteous right hand.*
ISAIAH 41:10 ESV

I'll admit it, Lord. Most of my stresses come from taking my eyes off You. When I begin to look in other directions, I get overwhelmed. I forget where my help comes from. Fear creeps in. It wriggles its way up my spine and hijacks my thoughts.

You are calling me to take anxious thoughts captive and to give my fears to You. Today I choose to lay my burdens at Your feet, heavenly Father. I'm counting on Your help to overcome my worry and angst. Amen.

THINK ABOUT IT:
Is your stress triggered by fear?

Morning
A TREE PLANTED
BY THE WATER

*"Blessed is the man who trusts in
the Lord, whose trust is the Lord. He
is like a tree planted by water, that
sends out its roots by the stream,
and does not fear when heat comes,
for its leaves remain green, and is
not anxious in the year of drought,
for it does not cease to bear fruit."*

JEREMIAH 17:7–8 ESV

I want to be like that tree standing by the water, Lord. I want my roots to go down so deep that strong winds can't possibly blow me over. I don't want to be wobbly when stresses come. I want my leaves to remain green because I'm being fed and watered by You. I can only flourish when my roots run deep.

Thank You for removing my worry and anxiety, Lord. May this tree never cease to bear good fruit. Amen.

THINK ABOUT IT:

Are your leaves currently green?

Evening
NO TRAPS FOR ME!

*The fear of man lays a snare,
but whoever trusts in the Lord is safe.*

PROVERBS 29:25 ESV

My emotions go up and down a lot, Lord! I go in and out of stressful seasons like some people go through a revolving door. I'm fickle at times, like a mouse chasing after elusive bits of cheese, not realizing he's about to be caught in a trap.

I know You're not the one who lays these traps, hoping to catch me off guard. The enemy of my soul places snares in my path. But I'm on to him! I will be more cautious. I know things can go poorly when I feel trapped and unsafe, so I will avoid his snares at every cost and put my trust in You! Amen.

THINK ABOUT IT:

*How do you tend to respond
when you feel trapped?*

Morning
BACK TO THE BEGINNING

From the Negev he went from place to place until he came to Bethel, to the place between Bethel and Ai where his tent had been earlier and where he had first built an altar. There Abram called on the name of the Lord.

GENESIS 13:3–4 NIV

It's interesting that Abram went back to where You showed him in the beginning. Why did he leave there in the first place? Why do I walk away from the places and things You show me? Do I think the world can offer anything better than my loving heavenly Father? Forgive me for seeking security outside of Your love, outside of Your promises. Help me rest in Your goodness and stay in Your presence. When I feel anxious and worried, ground me, Father, and pull me back to my safe place—right in Your arms.

THINK ABOUT IT:

Do you need to return to God's presence and rest in His promises today?

Evening
MY SHIELD

After these things the word of the Lord came to Abram in a vision, saying, "Do not fear, Abram, I am a shield to you; your reward shall be very great."

GENESIS 15:1 NASB

When I read this verse, I know I can substitute my name for Abram's. When I feel worried and afraid, I can hear You saying, "Do not fear, _____. I'm your shield." You truly are my protector, Lord. I know You surround me, and You'll guard me from Satan's arrows. Even when bad things happen, I know You're right there with me, fighting for me. I don't have to do anything except trust You and stay close to You. When Satan tries to draw me away from Your presence by pulling me into worry and fear, remind me that he is a liar, and pull me back to You. Thank You for being my shield, Father.

THINK ABOUT IT:

Against what circumstance do you need God to be your shield?

Morning
WHEN WE BEGIN TO JAW

Set a guard over my mouth, LORD;
keep watch over the door of my lips.

PSALM 141:3 NIV

I know the routine, Lord. Moms gather. They joke around. They laugh. They share their hearts in sweet fellowship. Good stuff. But sometimes, Lord, I know all too well what else can happen in those little circles of friendship—gossip. First, a few juicy words pop out, but with a bit of encouragement, what started out as a beneficial and amiable dialogue can turn into a rumormongering free-for-all! And I know, Lord, that gossip can have serious and permanent consequences. Hurt feelings. Destroyed relationships. Ruined reputations. On and on it goes. So please keep me from spewing gossip or even encouraging it. May I every day pray that You, Lord, "keep watch over the door of my lips"! Amen.

THINK ABOUT IT:

The last time you released a few morsels of gossip, what were the consequences? What did God teach you in that moment?

Evening
THE FACE OF COMPASSION

Therefore, as God's chosen people,
holy and dearly loved, clothe
yourselves with compassion, kindness,
humility, gentleness and patience.

COLOSSIANS 3:12 NIV

Lord, what does compassion look like? Hmm. Do I remember to hold the door for an elderly person? Do I bake something yummy for the family that just moved into the neighborhood? Do I watch out for widows and orphans and feed the homeless? Do I really listen to friends? Really grieve with those who grieve? Am I truly being compassionate and kindhearted? I know it would be better for others to see these lovely attributes in me rather than preach sermons on the verse above. Lord, show me the way. I really would love to have people see *Your* compassion adorning me! In Jesus' name I pray. Amen.

THINK ABOUT IT:

What was your last act of compassion that reflected Christ's?

Morning
TRUST VS. REVENGE

*Dear friends, never take revenge.
Leave that to the righteous
anger of God.*
ROMANS 12:19 NLT

Some people, Lord, *deserve* to suffer a little. I have an especially hard time forgiving those who have hurt people I love. Maybe I won't plot ways to get even with them (though sometimes I do!), but at the very least, I'm going to make it clear to these people that I dislike them because of what they did. I'm going to turn away when they say hello, and I'll answer their smiles with scowls. Can You really expect anything else from me, Lord, after what they did? But then I come across a verse like this one, and I know You don't approve of my desire for revenge. That's not Your way. So okay, God, I'll let my anger go. I'll surrender it into Your hands. I'll let You sort out the damage these people have done, and I'll mind my own business. I'll trust Your Spirit to work in their hearts.

THINK ABOUT IT:

*Does revenge ever
accomplish anything?*

Evening
FORGIVEN AND FORGOTTEN

*"Their sins and lawless acts I will
remember no more." And where
these have been forgiven, sacrifice
for sin is no longer necessary.*
HEBREWS 10:17–18 NIV

I keep going over my failures, Lord. At night they haunt me. They interrupt my thoughts when I'm driving. They even distract me from my work. I'm so sorry I let You down. I wish I could go back and undo the past. I'm ashamed of myself. But Jesus, Your Word tells me I can let go of the past. You don't hold my failures against me. You don't even remember them! I don't have to keep saying I'm sorry, and I don't have to find ways to punish myself. I am truly freed from everything I did. I can serve You with a clean heart for You have restored my innocence and made me whole. Empower me now to live for You.

THINK ABOUT IT:

*As human beings, we can forgive,
but we can't usually forget. But God
is not like us. What does it mean to
you to have your failures not only
forgiven by God but also forgotten?
How does it make you feel?*

Morning
THE FIXER

So Sarai said to Abram, "See now, the Lord has prevented me from bearing children. Please have relations with my slave woman; perhaps I will obtain children through her." And Abram listened to the voice of Sarai.

GENESIS 16:2 NASB

Dear Father, Sarai tried to fix things. Instead of trusting You to keep Your promise to her, she took things into her own hands. How often do I do the same thing? I trust You for a little while, but when answers don't come and problems aren't solved as quickly as I hoped, I jump in and try to control the situation. I think I can fix things, instead of trusting You. Forgive me for that, Lord. Help me to be patient and trust Your timing instead of worrying and fretting and trying to manipulate things to go the way I think they should go.

THINK ABOUT IT:
What situation have you tried to fix recently?

Evening
THINKING TOO SMALL

So Sarah laughed to herself, saying, "After I have become old, am I to have pleasure, my lord being old also?"

GENESIS 18:12 NASB

It's easy to judge Sarah for laughing, because I know the end of the story. I know that despite her age, she did have a son, and that was the beginning of the nation of Israel. But if I'd been in her place, I might have laughed too. How often do I think something is too big or too hard for You? How often do I look at a problem and think it's an impossible situation? Instead of trusting Your sovereignty, I worry and fret. Teach me to have Abraham's faith, Father. Help me to believe Your promises for yesterday, today, and all future days. Forgive me for thinking too small for You, Lord. Forgive me for laughing instead of having faith.

THINK ABOUT IT:
What problem seems impossible to you today?

Morning
RUN TO HIM

*When he raised his eyes and looked,
behold, three men were standing
opposite him; and when he saw
them, he ran from the tent door to
meet them and bowed down to the
ground, and said, "My Lord, if now
I have found favor in Your sight,
please do not pass Your servant by."*

GENESIS 18:2–3 NASB

I love this picture of Abraham running to meet You. Scholars say these three men were Your Holy Trinity: Father, Son, and Holy Spirit. Abraham was so excited by Your presence that he ran to meet You. He begged You to stay with him. Am I that excited to spend time with You, Lord? I want to be. I want to see You. I want to be in Your presence, for I know that's where I'll find the peace I long for. My request is the same: if I've found favor in Your sight, please don't pass me by.

THINK ABOUT IT:

*Are you excited by God's presence?
Do you run to Him each day?*

Evening
IS ANYTHING TOO HARD?

*But the LORD said to Abraham,
"Why did Sarah laugh, saying, 'Shall
I actually give birth to a child, when
I am so old?' Is anything too difficult
for the LORD? At the appointed time I
will return to you, at this time next
year, and Sarah will have a son."*

GENESIS 18:13–14 NASB

Father, is anything too difficult for You? The answer is no. Nothing is too hard for You, Father. Yet I find myself worrying, overcome with anxiety, afraid things won't work out the way I want them to. Help me take my hands off the situation, Lord. I worry because I want to be in control, but I'm not the right person to control any situation. I'd rather have You in the driver's seat, Lord. Teach me to relax in You, to trust Your goodness, and to say, "Nothing is too hard for my Father."

THINK ABOUT IT:

*What situation are you
trying to control?*

DAY 50

Morning
GLORY IS COMING!

*For I consider that the sufferings
of this present time are not
worth comparing with the glory
that is to be revealed to us.*

ROMANS 8:18 ESV

"In the light of eternity." How I love these words! The things I'm fretting over today—the very things I've lost sleep over—won't matter at all when I get to heaven. I won't even remember them.

Until then, please help me keep things in perspective, Lord. Your perspective. When it comes to the non-eternal things, help me to push them aside in my mind so that I'm not fixated on them. Only when I do so will I really rise above my circumstances to walk a faith-filled life with You. I can't wait to spend eternity with You, Lord! Amen.

THINK ABOUT IT:
Have you ever pondered eternity?

Evening
YOUR DIVINE POWER

*His divine power has given us
everything we need for a godly
life through our knowledge
of him who called us by his
own glory and goodness.*

2 PETER 1:3 NIV

Sometimes I watch those superhero movies and wish I could have the kind of power they seem to possess. Watching all of the miraculous feats they perform is mind-blowing!

Then I remember that Your power is greater still. And You've shared that power with me! Your Word says that You've given me everything I need to get through this life. Everything, Lord? Wow! I might not be able to scale buildings in a single bound, but I can leap over problems and soar above challenges. I can speak to mountains and watch them fall in the name of Jesus!

You really have given me all I need, and I praise You today for calling me to a life of power! Amen.

THINK ABOUT IT:
*What has God's divine
power given you?*

Morning
I'LL BUILD THEM UP

Therefore encourage one another and build each other up, just as in fact you are doing.

1 Thessalonians 5:11 niv

The world is filled with people who love to cut each other down. They can't wait to find flaws—in their loved ones, coworkers, even their closest friends.

Your Word tells us to have the opposite spirit—to encourage others and build them up. No limitation is placed on that command. Your Word doesn't say, "Only when they're behaving right," or "Only when they do what you want them to do." No, we're to offer encouragement and to build up others no matter how a situation is unpacking itself.

Building others up isn't always easy for me, Lord. I'll admit it. But with Your help, I'll become one of the best encouragers around. You've been that for me, after all! It's the least I can do in return. Amen.

THINK ABOUT IT:

What can you do today to build up those you love?

Evening
LIVING WISELY

Be very careful, then, how you live— not as unwise but as wise, making the most of every opportunity, because the days are evil.

Ephesians 5:15–16 niv

I'll admit it, Lord! Sometimes (okay, *many* times) I don't think before I leap. I make quick, impulsive decisions or choices and then live to regret them.

You want me to make wisdom my BFF, to give it a permanent room in my home. I won't have anything to regret after the fact if I allow Your wisdom to lead me. Best of all, I can live stress-free if I choose wisdom every time. I won't give way to the enemy (that roaring lion). I won't let him bring me down. No, not anymore! I'm on to him. I'm done falling into his trap. Wisdom lives in my house! Thank You for giving it to me as a gift. Amen.

THINK ABOUT IT:

How do you keep your spiritual antennae up during these precarious days?

Morning
I TRUST YOU, LORD

*But those who trust in the LORD will
find new strength. They will soar
high on wings like eagles. They
will run and not grow weary.
They will walk and not faint.*

ISAIAH 40:31 NLT

I wonder why I'm zapped. I wonder why I feel like I'm running on empty. Then I realize I've shifted my trust—from You to me. I didn't do it on purpose, Lord, but it happened.

It's time to turn this situation around, but I'm going to need Your help. I'm tired of relying on myself! I want to rise up from my weariness to soar high on wings like eagles, as Your Word says. So I place my trust in You. In You, I find energy to keep running the race without growing exhausted. I can walk—no matter how long it takes—and not faint.

Thank You for the joy You bring when I trust in You! Amen.

THINK ABOUT IT:

*What does it mean to soar
high on eagles' wings?*

Evening
STRATEGIES FOR RELATIONAL HEALING

*Be kind and compassionate to
one another, forgiving each other,
just as in Christ God forgave you.*

EPHESIANS 4:32 NIV

I love when the pieces of a broken relationship come back together quickly, Lord! You can certainly mend broken hearts and put the pieces back together in a hurry. Other times, the healing seems to take forever. I start to wonder if things will ever be right again.

In the gap in between—before true relational healing comes—You've asked for my participation: to be kind, compassionate, and forgiving. I know that exhibiting this kind of attitude will help mend the broken places, so I'll do my best, Father. I'll go on loving even if the other person makes it difficult. I'll offer forgiveness even if they don't ask, because You forgave me. After all, I've experienced firsthand the power of forgiveness. How could I help but offer it to others?

Thank You for mending broken relationships, Lord! Amen.

THINK ABOUT IT:

*What does it mean to forgive
as Christ forgave you?*

Morning
GOD OF THE IMPOSSIBLE

"What do you mean, 'If I can'?"
Jesus asked. "Anything is
possible if a person believes."
MARK 9:23 NLT

If it feels completely impossible to me, Lord, I know You're not feeling that way. In fact, the more impossible it seems, the more I'm forced to depend on You.

There's no need to ask if You can, Lord. I know You can. You're capable of parting the seas, toppling walls, and putting broken lives back together. And You tell me that anything is possible if I will just believe.

So I'm tossing my "impossibles," Lord! With You, nothing is impossible. I'll wait with fervent faith to see how You turn this situation around. And until then, I'll keep on hoping, keep on believing, and keep on speaking in faith. Amen.

THINK ABOUT IT:
What feels impossible to you right now?

Evening
HAPPY IN YOU

Be happy in the Lord. And He will
give you the desires of your heart.
PSALM 37:4 NLV

I'm learning that happiness is a choice, Lord. I can choose to be happy in You even when circumstances cry out, "Give up! Give in to despair!"

I won't give in. I'll make the right choice. And when I do, You will give me the desires of my heart. Honestly? This verse makes me wonder how many times I had to wait for the desires of my heart because I chose despair instead of faith.

I'll be happy. I'll choose joy. And I'll anticipate Your miraculous intervention followed by a marvelous outpouring of Your compassion and love. Amen.

THINK ABOUT IT:
What are the desires of your heart?

Morning
HE'S NEVER FAR AWAY

*When the righteous cry for help,
the Lord hears and delivers them
out of all their troubles. The Lord
is near to the brokenhearted and
saves the crushed in spirit.*

PSALM 34:17–18 ESV

You're not going anywhere, Lord. You've never left me, and You never will. When I cry out for help, You are right there, already at my side. You hear me. Even if I whisper a prayer, You don't miss a word. Best of all, You intervene! You deliver me from all my troubles.

Your nearness brings me hope, reminding me I don't have to walk alone during stressful seasons. I'll keep my eyes on You and remember that You're ready, willing, and able to deliver me, if only I call. Amen.

THINK ABOUT IT:

*Do you sense God's nearness
when you're in the middle of a
stressful situation, or do you tend
to push thoughts of Him aside?*

Evening
EVEN WHEN I FEEL LIKE I CAN'T

*I can do all things through
him who strengthens me.*

PHILIPPIANS 4:13 ESV

Here's the thing, Lord: I know I can't. By myself, I really can't. I know because I've tried in my own strength so many times and failed. But when I go to You, when I count on You to strengthen me from the inside out and give me the wisdom only You can give. . .then I can.

It's not me; it's You. I recognize that. From now on, please help me to recognize it before I waste precious time trying to be a superhero on my own. I won't attempt to go it alone anymore, Father. When I do, I always end up exhausted, afraid, and stressed out. I'm so glad You're ready to do the heavy lifting, Lord. Amen.

THINK ABOUT IT:

How often do you use the word can't?

Morning
PRAYERS FROM HEAVEN

*"Simon, Simon, behold, Satan
demanded to have you, that he might
sift you like wheat, but I have prayed
for you that your faith may not fail."*
LUKE 22:31–32 ESV

Lord, this world is full of trials. Refining trials. Trials that test me but ultimately make me purer. Though Peter failed by denying You, his faith survived. I wonder if, looking back, he was encouraged or comforted by Your prayer—to know that the God who sees all—who knew Peter's weaknesses beforehand—prayed for his faith victory. As I go through my own life's trials, pray for me, Lord. I need all the support I can get! Too often I'm like Peter, failing again and again and again. But my faith endures. Praise God, I have an advocate in You! Amen.

THINK ABOUT IT:

*Does the idea of Jesus coming
alongside us as an advocate
(1 John 2:1) encourage you to
conquer sin and to remain faithful?*

Evening
AN ALL-IMPORTANT QUESTION

*And he asked them, "But who do
you say that I am?" Peter answered
him, "You are the Christ."*
MARK 8:29 ESV

Heavenly Father, of all the questions in the Bible, this is one of the most important. Who is Jesus? Everyone must respond, and the answer will mean either eternal life or death. Who do I say that Jesus is? Jesus is the Son of God—Your Son. He lived a perfect life on earth to die for humanity's sin. Without Him, I will be eternally separated from You. But by repenting of my sin and accepting Your loving gift of grace and Christ's righteousness, I am Your child, destined for heaven. May my answer to this all-important question be more than facts, Father; may it be alive in my heart, just as Your Holy Spirit is alive in my heart. Thank You for Christ. Amen.

THINK ABOUT IT:
Who do you say that Jesus is?

Morning
ABIDING

"By this my Father is glorified, that you bear much fruit and so prove to be my disciples. As the Father has loved me, so have I loved you. Abide in my love."

JOHN 15:8–9 ESV

Heavenly Father, as Your Son, Jesus was the model of perfect obedience to You. Although I cannot expect to be perfect, I can follow in Jesus' path of obedience. I can make Your commandments the framework of my life. By living under Your commands in obedience, I place myself in the shelter of Your love, abiding there, remaining there. I can't do it alone, Father. I pray for an obedient heart. I pray for the power of the Holy Spirit to resist the temptation to follow my own path. I bow to Your wisdom in knowing what is best for me. Amen.

THINK ABOUT IT:

How can you improve your obedience to God—and abide in His love more fully?

Evening
DIVINE PURPOSE

"But rise and stand upon your feet, for I have appeared to you for this purpose, to appoint you as a servant and witness. . .delivering you from your people and from the Gentiles—to whom I am sending you to open their eyes, so that they may turn from darkness to light."

ACTS 26:16–18 ESV

Father, when I read about Paul's conversion and calling to a life of faith, I can't help but think that this becomes the purpose of all believers. I can't help but frame these words in the context of my life. How can I be a servant to those around me, showering Your love and displaying the others-centered focus of Jesus as He walked this earth? How can I better witness to the countless lost souls, opening their eyes so they turn from darkness to the light of Your saving grace? Show me how, Father. Amen.

THINK ABOUT IT:

Have you felt called to be a servant and witness to the faith?

Morning
A TREE OF LIFE

The soothing tongue is a tree of life, but a perverse tongue crushes the spirit.

PROVERBS 15:4 NIV

I remember, Lord, the scraped knees I had growing up. I was sad to see it but glad that the wound healed quickly. Then I thought of all the tiny injuries we have on our hearts—those hidden from everyone but You, Lord. The ones that come from hurtful words. Proverbs says that a vicious tongue can crush a person's spirit; but on the other hand, soothing words are like a tree of life. What a difference! May my friends always know I'm there for them when they have a hidden hurt, but more importantly, may we know we can run to You with every care—knowing Your healing touch will meet us there. Amen.

THINK ABOUT IT:

What injuries of the heart did you receive growing up? Have you let God heal them all?

Evening
LIVING FOREVER

But our citizenship is in heaven. And we eagerly await a Savior from there, the Lord Jesus Christ, who, by the power that enables him to bring everything under his control, will transform our lowly bodies so that they will be like his glorious body.

PHILIPPIANS 3:20–21 NIV

Lord, I know our society is always looking for the perfect supplement to live way beyond our years. Yes, long life is a gift, but if we truly had the choice, would we choose to live forever in this broken state? What would seem like a miracle would eventually become a curse, since we would long to shed these lowly bodies for glorious ones. Lord, may I live this life to the fullest with You by my side and be joyful, knowing as a Christian that this fallen earth is not the last stop. My citizenship is in heaven! Amen.

THINK ABOUT IT:

Have you told someone about the saving grace of Jesus Christ and the wonders of heaven?

Morning
MY REFUGE IN TIMES OF TROUBLE

The LORD also will be a refuge for the oppressed, a refuge in times of trouble. And they that know thy name will put their trust in thee: for thou, LORD, hast not forsaken them that seek thee.

PSALM 9:9–10 KJV

I feel oppressed in so many ways, Lord. I'm weighted down with such a heavy load of responsibilities that I get tired just thinking about it. On top of that, every day seems to bring some new and unexpected challenge for me to deal with. And then there's the bigger world out there, a world that is overflowing with problems, problems that are so big I can't even begin to know the solutions. But, Lord, You know the answers. And Your presence is my hiding place whenever life seems too much to handle. Teach me to truly know Your name. I'm putting my trust in You today. Show me Your presence in my life and in the world around me. I know You will never forsake me.

THINK ABOUT IT:

Sometimes, when we feel particularly challenged by life, we forget to seek God. How can you intentionally make time to seek His presence today?

Evening
GOD IS WITH YOU

At that time Abimelek and Phicol the commander of his forces said to Abraham, "God is with you in everything you do."

GENESIS 21:22 NIV

Thank You for this reminder that when we live in Your will, when Your favor is on us, people notice. These men had watched Abraham, and they saw clearly that You were with him. I know people watch me because they know I'm a Christian, and they want to see if You make a difference in my life. When I show worry and fear, I subconsciously tell others that I don't trust You. Mark me as Yours, Lord. Help me to live each day with such faith, such total trust, that others will know You are with me in all that I do.

THINK ABOUT IT:

When others watch your actions and listen to your words, is there evidence that you belong to God?

Morning
GOD'S GOODNESS

*Before he had finished praying,
Rebekah came out with her jar on
her shoulder. She was the daughter
of Bethuel son of Milkah, who was
the wife of Abraham's brother Nahor.
The woman was very beautiful, a
virgin; no man had ever slept with
her. She went down to the spring,
filled her jar and came up again.*

GENESIS 24:15–16 NIV

Why am I surprised at Your goodness?
You didn't just provide Isaac with any
girl. You brought him a beautiful young
woman of appropriate age, with a simi-
lar background, to be his wife. She was
generous and kind and pleasing in every
way. Sometimes I make up my mind about
what I want before consulting You. That's
so silly because I know what You have for
me is far superior to what I might choose
for myself. Forgive me for doubting Your
goodness, Lord. Help me trust You with
everything.

THINK ABOUT IT:

*What do you need to
trust God with today?*

Evening
THE RICHES OF
GOD'S GLORY

*My God will meet all your
needs according to the riches
of his glory in Christ Jesus.*

PHILIPPIANS 4:19 NIV

I feel such a terrifying mixture of emotions, Lord: embarrassment, guilt, anger,
shame, fear. All those feelings keep swirling around in my head. They keep me
awake at night, and they're there waiting for me as soon as I wake up in the
morning. I never imagined that I would
find myself in such dire financial straits.
I keep looking for someone to blame—
but then I turn around and feel ashamed
of the mistakes I made. I'm scared of what
the future holds. The only place I can find
rest for my thoughts is in You, God. I am
so grateful that You are taking care of me
even now. My financial mess is not too big
for You to handle.

THINK ABOUT IT:

*Have you given your finances to
God? Or are you still trying to handle
them yourself? What might change
in your life and in your heart if you
relied completely on God's "riches"?*

Morning
NO FEAR

There is no fear in love. But perfect love drives out fear, because fear has to do with punishment. The one who fears is not made perfect in love.

1 JOHN 4:18 NIV

Father, You are love. Time and again in Your Word, You reveal this truth. Time and again in my life, You've shown Your goodness. When I worry about things, when I let fear control my thoughts, I'm choosing to live outside of Your great love. It doesn't make any sense, yet I do it anyway. Forgive me for focusing on fear instead of sinking deep into Your perfect love. With You in control of my life, I have nothing to fear. Even when things don't go as I want them to, I can have confidence that Your plans for me are good. Help me to stay in Your perfect love.

THINK ABOUT IT:

What is your biggest fear right now? How does that fear contrast to God's love for you?

Evening
GIVE YOUR WORRY TO GOD

Cast all your anxiety on him because he cares for you.

1 PETER 5:7 NIV

Sometimes, Lord, my mind becomes obsessed with worries. My worries are both big and small, both selfless and selfish: I worry about the health of my loved ones. I worry about my children's safety. I worry about our finances. I worry about the state of the world. I worry about my weight. I worry what people will think of me. I worry about my job. Especially at night, when I'm trying to sleep, all these worries just tumble around in my head like heavy, wet towels in a dryer. But those "towels" never get dry; they just tumble and tumble and tumble, going nowhere, spinning endlessly. So, dear Lord, I'm giving them to You. Take the whole heavy, lumpy load of worry out of my mind. Thank You for loving me so much that You're right there beside me, ready to help as soon as I let You.

THINK ABOUT IT:

It's hard to control our thoughts, but with practice, we can learn to quickly turn over our worries to the God who loves us. How can you remind yourself today to stop worrying and start trusting?

Morning
PREPARING THE WAY

*And it came to pass, when he saw
the earring and bracelets upon his
sister's hands, and when he heard the
words of Rebekah his sister, saying,
Thus spake the man unto me; that
he came unto the man; and, behold,
he stood by the camels at the well.
And he said, Come in, thou blessed
of the LORD; wherefore standest thou
without? for I have prepared the
house, and room for the camels.*

GENESIS 24:30–31 KJV

Abraham sent his servant to find a wife for
his son Isaac. He wanted a young woman
from his own people, who shared his
faith. It must have seemed like a random,
impossible task to the servant, to travel
into this unknown-to-him land looking for
an appropriate bride for his master's son.
What if Isaac wasn't pleased? But when
You send us on a journey, You always
prepare the way, don't You, Father? Thank
You for preparing the way for me.

THINK ABOUT IT:
*What impossible task
do you face today?*

Evening
GOD'S BEST

*And Isaac brought her into his
mother Sarah's tent, and took
Rebekah, and she became his wife;
and he loved her: and Isaac was
comforted after his mother's death.*

GENESIS 24:67 KJV

This is better than any Hallmark romance
because it's not fiction. It really happened.
You didn't just provide any woman for
Isaac. You sent him a love match! In
Rebekah, You gave Isaac more than he
could hope for. I know You have wonderful things in store for my life as well.
Why do I worry that You'd give me the
bare minimum when You're always so
generous? Sometimes I lower my standards because I don't trust that You have
something better for me. Forgive me for
ever settling for less than Your best for my
life. Forgive me for forgetting how lavish
Your love is. Teach me to trust in Your
goodness, Your kindness, and Your love.

THINK ABOUT IT:
*In what ways have you settled
for less than God's best for you?*

Morning
ANTIDOTE FOR ANXIETY

"Be strong and courageous! Do not be afraid or discouraged. For the LORD your God is with you wherever you go."

JOSHUA 1:9 NLT

I'm feeling spiritually weak, Lord, but also emotionally and physically weak. Anxiety is eating me up inside. It feels like an animal gnawing on my stomach, making me sick. It's hard to breathe, hard to swallow. I can't seem to get my thoughts together. My heart is constantly racing. God, I need Your help! I'm desperate. Please give me Your strength and courage. Take away my fear. Send Your Spirit to encourage me. Reveal to me Your presence at my side. I'm too weak to deal with this anxiety on my own. I need Your help.

THINK ABOUT IT:

Try something different today. Whenever anxiety starts to consume you, repeat to yourself, "The Lord my God is with me wherever I go." See what happens.

Evening
POSSIBILITIES

"All things are possible for the one who believes."

MARK 9:23 NASB

I seem to have run out of hope, God. I look at my life, and I just can't imagine anything changing. Maybe I've hit rock bottom, and now there's no place to go but up—but that's not how I feel. I feel trapped, like there's no escape from the situation. I don't see a way out. I'm so discouraged that just getting up in the morning is a real effort. Lord, now, when I have nothing left to cling to, I'm turning to You. Maybe You needed to get me to this place where I had no hope left, where I've been forced to realize that I've used up all my own ideas and skills. Here, God, at the bottom of this pit of hopelessness, I choose to put my hand in Yours. I believe in You. I don't know the way out of this situation, but I believe You do. Do the impossible, the way You always do. Show me the way to go from here. Reveal to me Your possibilities.

THINK ABOUT IT:

How can God use your hopelessnes to get you to depend on Him in a new and fuller way?

Morning
THE WISDOM OF THE PRESENT MOMENT

Do not say, "Why were the old days better than these?" For it is not wise to ask such questions.

ECCLESIASTES 7:10 NIV

I'm so tired of hurting, Lord. This pain of mine never goes away. It interrupts my sleep, and it cuts into my productivity during the day. It robs me of joy and peace. It even interferes with my relationships with my friends and family. I just want things to go back to the way they used to be, before this pain was eating me alive, day after day. I want my life to be the way it was when I was younger and stronger and pain-free. I know, though, that it doesn't do me any good to keep looking backward at the past. The answers to my life don't lie behind me. Instead, I'm going to look for You to reveal Yourself to me in a different way today. I give You this pain of mine—and I ask You to do something new in my life. Show me that You are here with me right now, in this very moment. Don't let this pain come between my heart and Yours.

THINK ABOUT IT:

How does dwelling on the past hold you back? How can you find ways to seek God in the present moment today?

Evening
DIG ANOTHER WELL

And he removed from thence, and digged another well; and for that they strove not: and he called the name of it Rehoboth; and he said, For now the Lord hath made room for us, and we shall be fruitful in the land.

GENESIS 26:22 KJV

Sometimes, for reasons that are out of our control, we have to start over. This has happened many times in my life, Lord. When that happens, I want to be like Isaac. He didn't waste time or breath lamenting how unfair life was. Instead, he just dug another well. He simply moved on, again and again, as many times as it took. Father, help me to move on from my past. Help me to dig another well like Isaac did, again and again, until I arrive at the place where You want me to stop. You blessed Isaac's perseverance, Lord. Give me strength to persevere too.

THINK ABOUT IT:

From what circumstance do you need to move forward? What new well do you need to dig?

Morning
A PUDDLE IN
THE CORNER

*How long, Lord? Will you forget
me forever? How long will you
hide your face from me?*

PSALM 13:1 NIV

It's been one of those days, Lord. Is the whole world disgusted with me? Are You? I'm worried that You too will hide Your holy face from me. That You will forget me or run from me. I know if I were You, God, *I* would run from me! I'm discouraged. And disheartened. No more than a puddle of tears in the corner. Help me, Lord. I don't even know exactly what to ask for. But in Your infinite knowledge and mercy, You know what I need. I will rest in that assurance always, just as David did all those many years ago. Amen.

THINK ABOUT IT:

*What are some of the scriptures
in Psalms that refer to David
being rescued by God?*

Evening
I CAN'T DO THIS
THING ALONE

*I keep my eyes always on the
Lord. With him at my right
hand, I will not be shaken.*

PSALM 16:8 NIV

I didn't see it coming. I thought I knew best. I got the idea that if I could memorize a handful of scriptures, breathe a prayer from time to time, and attend church services—well, that would take care of the spiritual part of my life. But that's when I found out the hard way that I can't do this thing alone. I need You, Lord, to help me every day. Every hour. I have to keep my eyes on You, Jesus, all the time. I need to hold Your hand not only through the hard years but all of my life. Amen.

THINK ABOUT IT:

*What are some ways you
can teach your kids to rely
on the Lord all the time?*

Morning
RAIN DOWN ON ME

*But the wisdom that comes
from heaven is first of all pure;
then peace-loving, considerate,
submissive, full of mercy and good
fruit, impartial and sincere.*

JAMES 3:17 NIV

Lord, I confess, there are days when I am anything but wise. I can be a royal goof. And not just the guileless, funny kind of goof. I mean the kind You refer to in Proverbs as a fool—someone who has made decisions without knowledge, common sense, and biblical understanding. Lord, forgive me for my foolishness. Rain down on me with Your refreshing wisdom. I need a daily shower of it on my spirit. I know You love it when we ask for wisdom, so I humbly come before You now, seeking Your knowledge and understanding. Thank You, Lord! Amen.

THINK ABOUT IT:

*How can you teach yourself to be wise?
What scriptures might help you?*

Evening
CLOSE TO HIS HEART

*He tends his flock like a shepherd:
he gathers the lambs in his arms
and carries them close to his heart;
he gently leads those that have young.*

ISAIAH 40:11 NIV

Your words in Isaiah 40:11, Lord, are some of the most beautiful, tender, and heart-stirring in the Bible. What insight into Your love for me! What peace and joy I receive from this short passage! I can see that flock of bleating sheep, all of them plump and fluffy, bumping into each other as You ever-so-gently lead them safely along a stony path. I can see You, Lord, picking up one of the wanderers and bringing that little one up to Your heart, keeping her close, because that is what is needed. That is what is yearned for by the lamb and by the Shepherd. To be close. To be loved. To be always. Amen.

THINK ABOUT IT:

*Think about a time when you felt
that sweet, intimate closeness
with the Great Shepherd.*

DAY 66

Morning
TOO DEEP FOR WORDS

*Likewise the Spirit helps us in our
weakness. For we do not know what
to pray for as we ought, but the
Spirit himself intercedes for us with
groanings too deep for words.*
ROMANS 8:26 ESV

Father, this earthly life can be overwhelming. Suffering abounds. It's hard to maintain hope of a bright future when the present seems so dismal. At times it's even difficult to put the weight of what I feel into words. But Your Holy Spirit intercedes for us. From heaven, You listen and You're faithful. Your plans will come to pass. You keep Your promises. You are good, and You desire ultimate good for Your children. Remind me of Your love, Father. When my words fail, let the groanings of the Spirit be my voice. You'll hear them loud and clear! Amen.

THINK ABOUT IT:

*When prayer is a struggle, how
often do you sit in silence and
let the Holy Spirit take over?*

Evening
LIE DOWN AND SLEEP

*In peace I will both lie down and
sleep; for you alone, O LORD,
make me dwell in safety.*
PSALM 4:8 ESV

When I can't fall asleep, night becomes endless. My mind fills the silence with unspoken thoughts about troubles. It fills the darkness with images of an uncertain future. But it doesn't have to be like this. King David knew more chaos and danger, yet he trusted in Your care and found sleep. Nothing can happen to me that You have not foreseen; I can close my eyes and rest in Your will. When I can't fall asleep, let Your promises of love fall over me like the words of a lullaby. Let Your peace surround me like a warm blanket. You are God. You are good. I trust in Your care and find sleep. Amen.

THINK ABOUT IT:

*What verses create a sense of calm
when you have trouble sleeping?*

Morning
UNTO HIM

Now unto him that is able to keep you from falling, and to present you faultless before the presence of his glory with exceeding joy, to the only wise God our Saviour, be glory and majesty, dominion and power, both now and ever. Amen.

JUDE 24–25 KJV

Lord God, I kneel today with Jude's words in my mind as a beautiful reflection of the prayer in my own soul, because more and more I realize that You are *all* to me. Without You, I'd stumble, but You uphold me. Without You, I'd have no hope of heaven, but You offer grace; You'll present me in eternity with Your righteousness as mine and not with reluctance but with *exceeding joy.* Such an amazing thought! God, You alone are worthy—worthy of all glory, all majesty, all dominion, all power—for all time. Amen.

THINK ABOUT IT:

How can you honor God for all He means to you?

Evening
CELEBRATE!

Then Miriam the prophetess, the sister of Aaron, took a tambourine in her hand, and all the women went out after her with tambourines and dancing. And Miriam sang to them: "Sing to the LORD, for he has triumphed gloriously; the horse and his rider he has thrown into the sea."

EXODUS 15:20–21 ESV

Lord, these verses lift my spirit. I can almost feel the celebration in the words. You brought victory, and Miriam and the other women were ready to rejoice. Out of tune or not, it's time for me to sing to You, Lord. Today and every day is a chance to offer praise for all You've done—and are yet to do. I'll lift my voice in song; I'll move with joy in dance. Because You are glorious, Lord. You are glorious! Amen.

THINK ABOUT IT:

When was the last time you let go and celebrated God through music or dancing?

Morning
BY EXAMPLE

Therefore, since we are surrounded by so great a cloud of witnesses, let us also lay aside every weight, and sin which clings so closely, and let us run with endurance the race that is set before us.

HEBREWS 12:1 ESV

Father, thank You for so many people who show what it means to follow You each day. Thank You for giving me examples in Your Word of faith lived out. It's no secret that the faith path gets bumpy. When I wear down, I look to You; I look to Your presence in those who have gone before and shined! I'm in the race, Father. Show me what entangles me, trips me. I'm determined to run my best for You. And I know You cheer me on as I take each step in faith. Amen.

THINK ABOUT IT:

Who is in your own "cloud of witnesses"? How do their lives motivate you?

Evening
ELEPHANTINE MEMORY

The LORD answers, "Can a woman forget the baby she nurses? Can she feel no kindness for the child to which she gave birth? Even if she could forget her children, I will not forget you. See, I have written your name on my hand."

ISAIAH 49:15–16 NCV

Lord, You have designed a loving bond between mother and child. After nine months of pregnancy and then years of tender care as the child grows, a mother isn't likely to forget. It *seems* unthinkable. Your promise to remember Your children goes even further. It *is* unthinkable; You will never forget, Lord. When I feel insignificant, just one of many billions lost in a crowd, You remember me still. I am precious to You so much so that You died on the cross to bring me life. May I never forget Your love. Amen.

THINK ABOUT IT:

Do the words of Isaiah change how you see yourself?

Morning
LOOK AHEAD

*The sun had risen on the earth when Lot came to Zoar. Then the L*ORD *rained on Sodom and Gomorrah sulfur and fire from the L*ORD *out of heaven. . . . But Lot's wife, behind him, looked back, and she became a pillar of salt.*

GENESIS 19:23–24, 26 ESV

God, when You call me to new life in You, You call me to leave behind my old life of sin—for my good! While on the surface sin is attractive, it is also deadly. I will thrive through obedience. If Satan tempts me to look back longingly, keep my eyes riveted on You, God. Looking forward to eternity with You is worth much more than any backward glance. In "giving up" the past, I have only to gain. Amen.

THINK ABOUT IT:

How do prayer and spending time in God's Word help diminish the pull to disobey?

Evening
SUCH A TIME

Then Mordecai told them to reply to Esther, . . . "If you keep silent at this time, relief and deliverance will rise for the Jews from another place, but you and your father's house will perish. And who knows whether you have not come to the kingdom for such a time as this?"

ESTHER 4:13–14 ESV

God, You have every last detail mapped out. No matter how confusing this world becomes, I can rest knowing Your plan will unfold—perfectly. And rather than working alone from heaven, You include Your children in what moves Your plan forward here on earth. Even in my weakness, You can use me! You have me right where I need to be to fit into Your plan—perfectly. When I am hesitant to act—when I'm on the verge of keeping silent like Esther—remind me of the honor and blessing of risking all for You. Amen.

THINK ABOUT IT:

How have you seen God's perfect timing in your life? In others' lives?

Morning
GIVING UP CONTROL

Jacob said to his father, "I am Esau your firstborn. I have done as you told me; now sit up and eat of my game, that your soul may bless me."
GENESIS 27:19 ESV

Jacob lied to his father. But it goes much deeper than a lie. Rebekah, Jacob's mother, set up the farce. She was worried that things wouldn't go the way she thought they should, so she decided to help things along. You had promised her that Jacob would be blessed, but she didn't trust You.

How often have I done the same thing, Lord? Maybe I haven't encouraged my children to lie, but I've certainly tried to manipulate things to my advantage instead of trusting You with the outcome. If I'll just step back, have patience, and let You work, I know I'll save myself a lot of grief and heartache. Help me act in faith, Father.

THINK ABOUT IT:
What situation do you need to give to God today?

Evening
HE WILL SHOW
ME COMPASSION

Yet the LORD longs to be gracious to you; therefore he will rise up to show you compassion. For the LORD is a God of justice. Blessed are all who wait for him!
ISAIAH 30:18 NIV

I blew it again, Lord. You were a first-hand witness to my catastrophe. Now I'm paying the price. Now the stresses of what I've caused are adding up and spilling over. What a fiasco.

But You? You're not mad at me. You're not pointing the finger and saying, "Good grief! What have you done?" No, You're right here, forgiving, loving, and encouraging me. . .as always. Give me that same compassionate heart toward others, I pray. May I learn to be gracious with others just as You have been with me. Amen.

THINK ABOUT IT:
Does the idea of "waiting" on God cause more stress for you or does it bring peace?

Morning
HE PROMISED

"Behold, I am with you and will keep you wherever you go, and will bring you back to this land; for I will not leave you until I have done that of which I have spoken to you."

GENESIS 28:15 RSV

You made this promise to Jacob despite all the low-down, manipulative things he did to his father and his brother. I know You make the same promise to me in spite of all my failures. When I'm tempted to worry about my future, bring these words to mind. I don't have to fear being alone because You will stay with me and keep me wherever I go. I don't have to be afraid that Your plans won't come to fruition. As long as I trust You and stay close to You, You will fulfill Your purpose in my life. Because You are good and loving and kind, I know my future is safe with You.

THINK ABOUT IT:

What about your future causes you the most anxiety? Can you trust God with it?

Evening
HIS BURDEN IS LIGHT

"Come to me, all who labor and are heavy laden, and I will give you rest. Take my yoke upon you, and learn from me, for I am gentle and lowly in heart, and you will find rest for your souls. For my yoke is easy, and my burden is light."

MATTHEW 11:28–30 ESV

I love Your swap plan, Lord. I give You chaos, You give me peace. I give You turmoil, You give me comfort. I give You heaviness, You give me featherlight freedom.

You ask me to take Your yoke upon me. That sounds heavy at first, but I've learned that Your yoke isn't weighty at all! It's freedom. It's joy. It's abundance. It's peace. It's the very opposite of what the world can give.

Today I celebrate the "burden" You ask me to carry. In You, I find answers to every problem I could ever face. How grateful I am to be free, Lord. I'll rest easy in You. Amen!

THINK ABOUT IT:

When was the last time you truly rested in the Lord?

Morning
WHY? BECAUSE YOU CARE FOR ME!

Humble yourselves, therefore, under the mighty hand of God so that at the proper time he may exalt you, casting all your anxieties on him, because he cares for you.
1 PETER 5:6–7 ESV

Sometimes I feel like no one notices me. In fact, sometimes I wonder if anyone cares at all. I go through deep valleys, and no one seems to notice or respond to the pain I'm in. I realize that You do, of course! You notice. You care. You're right beside me, ready to lift me up when I'm down.

During those low seasons, You ask me to humble myself so that You can lift me up. I'll confess, I often don't feel like doing that. Things are tough enough already, and humility just doesn't come naturally. But today I choose to humble myself in obedience, knowing You will bless me as I lay my whole life before You. Thank You for loving me! Amen.

THINK ABOUT IT:
Does humility come naturally to you?

Evening
I'M NOT GETTING ANY YOUNGER

"And which of you by being anxious can add a single hour to his span of life?"
MATTHEW 6:27 ESV

Worry, worry, worry. Anxiety, anxiety, anxiety. Stress, stress, stress. It's a vicious cycle, Lord! I get worried, and then I panic. With panic comes fear. With fear comes doubt. With doubt comes a lack of faith. Finally, a lack of faith leads to hopelessness.

You have a better way, one meant to add years to my life. Give up the worry! Hand it over to You. I like this plan, Lord. I'm not getting any younger, after all. I need all the days (and hours) I can get, so I'll pass my troubles to You and age well. May my life span be free of anxiety as I put my hope in You! Amen.

THINK ABOUT IT:
When you consider the notion that stress can shorten your life, do you want to do a better job dealing with it?

Morning
HARDSHIPS AND BLESSINGS

Before the year of famine came, Joseph had two sons, whom As'enath, the daughter of Poti'phera priest of On, bore to him. Joseph called the name of the first-born Manas'seh, "For," he said, "God has made me forget all my hardship and all my father's house." The name of the second he called E'phraim, "For God has made me fruitful in the land of my affliction."
GENESIS 41:50–52 RSV

Dear Father, Joseph spent thirteen years from the time his brothers put him in the pit until his rise to greatness. He had many ups and downs. Help me remember to trust You when hard times come. Help me to hang in there and be faithful. I know You are good and that Your blessings are coming.

THINK ABOUT IT:

*Are you in a season of blessing?
Thank God for your blessings.
Are you in a season of hardship?
Trust Him for tomorrow.*

Evening
LETTING GO

"So it was not you who sent me here, but God; and he has made me a father to Pharaoh, and lord of all his house and ruler over all the land of Egypt."
GENESIS 45:8 RSV

Joseph was able to forgive his brothers because he saw Your hand in all that had happened to him. I know much of my worry and anxiety often stems from not being able to let go of the past. Help me learn from Joseph's example. I know You don't cause bad things to happen to me, but sometimes You allow them so that they will propel me forward into a better future. Help me forgive others and let go of my past, knowing You are leading me into a future filled with Your promises and blessings.

THINK ABOUT IT:

*Is there anyone you need to forgive?
Is there something from your past you need to let go of?*

Morning
I CAN'T RUN AWAY

But Jonah ran away from the Lord and headed for Tarshish. He went down to Joppa, where he found a ship bound for that port. After paying the fare, he went aboard and sailed for Tarshish to flee from the Lord.

JONAH 1:3 NIV

How many times have I tried to run, Lord? A hundred? Two? I'm a flight risk for sure! Troubles come, and I'm out the door, headed for safety.

Only safety can never be found out there. I'm only safe when I turn to You. Lesson learned. (The hard way, at times!) I don't want to be a Jonah. When You call, I want to respond with "Yes, Lord," even when it's hard. Really, really hard.

Stresses come when I say no to You. So today I say yes to Your call, Your plan, Your way. Thank You for holding tight to me, especially when I'm tempted to run. Amen.

THINK ABOUT IT:
When was the last time you tried to run away from a problem? How did that story end?

Evening
AN UNTROUBLED HEART

"Let not your hearts be troubled. Believe in God; believe also in me."

JOHN 14:1 ESV

There are days, Lord, when things just feel off. I can't quite put my finger on what's wrong, but I feel troubled deep down in my soul. I'm unsettled. Fretful. Worried without any logical reason. This verse reminds me that I can have an untroubled heart. That nagging sensation has to leave when I invite You into the picture.

I invite You into my emotions. Into my pain. Into my stress. Into my troubles. You're right there, standing at my heart's door, knocking. I swing wide the gate and say, "Yes, Lord! Come on in and take control." What a relief to give this troubled heart to You! You handle it with great care, and I'm so grateful. Amen.

THINK ABOUT IT:
When you hear the phrase "troubled heart," what images come to mind?

Morning
A SOGGY OLD DISH TOWEL

*I can do all this through him
who gives me strength.*
PHILIPPIANS 4:13 NIV

I am exhausted today, Lord. I have mounds of laundry to wash, meals to cook, diapers to change, cleaning, driving, shopping, and a dozen other chores. The problem is I don't even feel like getting out of bed! I'm not mighty after all; instead, I feel more like a soggy old dish towel. Limp. Lifeless. And at risk of being tossed in the trash heap. So I come before You and ask for Your assistance—Your supernatural help. I need strength in every way, and I ask that You fulfill Your promise in Philippians 4:13. Ah, thank You, Lord. I accept Your strength. I rise up and thank You. Together, let us make this a joy-filled day to remember! Amen.

THINK ABOUT IT:

*Name a time when you had to rely
completely on the strength of the Lord.*

Evening
MY STRENGTH AND MY SHIELD

*The LORD is my strength and my
shield; my heart trusts in him, and
he helps me. My heart leaps for joy,
and with my song I praise him.*
PSALM 28:7 NIV

I'm feeling pretty weak right now, Lord. I'm overwhelmed, and I just don't know where to find the strength to keep going. But wait a minute, that's not right! I *do* know where to find the strength I need, the same place I've found it over and over down through the years—in *You*! Be my strength, God. Wrap Your loving arms around all that is weak in me. I know I can trust You to help me physically, emotionally, spiritually. I know I don't need to be embarrassed to confess to You how weak I am. You have me covered.

THINK ABOUT IT:

*As you turn your attention
to God and His love for you,
can you also praise Him, even in
the midst of your weakness?*

Morning
EMOTIONAL BAGGAGE

Jesus replied, "No one who puts a hand to the plow and looks back is fit for service in the kingdom of God."
LUKE 9:62 NIV

Lord, I want to have a joyful, creative, and active home, but I can't have that if I'm dragging emotional baggage around with me. It's wearing me out spiritually—and, as it turns out, physically. I'm exhausted. I'm at Your mercy, which I know is the very best place to be. You remind us in Your Word that if we are constantly looking back, we won't be fit for service in Your kingdom. So please remove any emotional baggage in me that is keeping me bound to the past and unable to move forward. I accept Your healing touch. I praise You for Your supernatural freedom. I embrace it fully! Amen.

THINK ABOUT IT:
How is God helping you move forward?

Evening
CONFIDENT HOPE

I pray that God, the source of hope, will fill you completely with joy and peace because you trust in him. Then you will overflow with confident hope through the power of the Holy Spirit.
ROMANS 15:13 NLT

When I feel like giving up hope, God, remind me that the power of Your Spirit has no limits. Even when everything else ends up being a dead end, Your path stretches into eternity. Teach me not to rely on anything but You. Sharpen my focus on Your love and energy so that I stop looking to other sources that sooner or later will let me down. Fill me with Your joy and peace. May I overflow with Your hope so that I bring hope to every situation and person I encounter today. Make me confident in You, I pray.

THINK ABOUT IT:
Is God the source of your hope? Or have you been relying on other things?

Morning
A SUPER-HONEST MOMENT

May these words of my mouth and this meditation of my heart be pleasing in your sight, Lord, my Rock and my Redeemer.

PSALM 19:14 NIV

If we're going to have a super-honest moment, Lord, here it is: I wouldn't want my friends and neighbors to hear me behind closed doors. I can really let fly with some ugly and unkind words. On top of that, my thought life is a mess at times—full of vain imaginings, less than lovely ponderings, and serious doubts about You (just to name a few). But I also know there is no such thing as "behind closed doors" with You. All is laid bare for You to hear and see. Oh Lord, I come to You, knowing these truths, and I ask You to make Psalm 19:14 my life verse. Please write its words on my heart and help me follow them diligently. Amen.

THINK ABOUT IT:

In what ways might you tend to become two very different people: one who puts on a pious face in public and a different one at home? How can knowing that God sees all help you be wholly pleasing to Him?

Evening
EVERY GOOD AND PERFECT GIFT

Every good and perfect gift is from above, coming down from the Father of the heavenly lights, who does not change like shifting shadows.

JAMES 1:17 NIV

Dear Lord, today I have cleaned and cooked and driven and listened and taught and disciplined and tended and mended . . .and then dropped in exhaustion. Sometimes I get so bogged down in the mundane chores of life that I forget how blessed I am. I acknowledge that every good gift comes from You, Father. Even after a very long day, help me to always remember that truth—that life is full of wonder and mystery and laughter and beauty! In Jesus' name I pray. Amen.

THINK ABOUT IT:

Have you seen lately what an amazing gift life is? Do so today!

Morning
THE EVERLASTING GOD!

Do you not know? Have you not heard?
The Lord is the everlasting God, the
Creator of the ends of the earth. He
will not grow tired or weary, and his
understanding no one can fathom.
ISAIAH 40:28 NIV

Oh Lord, my God, when I look at Your handiwork, I am spellbound. Mesmerized by the luminosities of Your night sky. Fascinated by Your world under a microscope. Captivated by Your dragonflies, ghost fish, and wombats. Your majestic mountain spires, shimmering seas, and underwater caves. I cannot fathom the vastness and details of Your creation, Your knowledge, Your power. And I cannot comprehend Your love for us. . . for me. I am such a tiny dot in Your vast universe, and yet I can feel Your tender love for me and my family. I love You, God, and I offer You my profoundly grateful heart. In Jesus' name I pray. Amen.

THINK ABOUT IT:

What part of God's creation do
you love the most and why?

Evening
SHINE YOUR LIGHT

Woe to those who call evil good and
good evil, who put darkness for light
and light for darkness, who put bitter
for sweet and sweet for bitter.
ISAIAH 5:20 NIV

I watch the news, Lord, and I shiver in my soul. I watch my fellow man bickering, fist-fighting, plotting evil schemes, and I shake my head. Sometimes I look in the mirror, Lord, and I don't even know myself; I see, within the shadows of my spirit, sin that needs to be forgiven. Many people have come to a place where they call evil "good" and good "evil." It's a poisonous switch in morality that will destroy our souls if we let it. Please deliver us from evil and shine Your light in all the dark crevices of our hearts. We need You now, Lord Jesus! Come! Amen.

THINK ABOUT IT:

What are some moral choices society
calls good that are really evil in the
eyes of the Lord? How might you
shine some of God's light on them?

Morning
TALKING TO GOD

Pray continually.
1 THESSALONIANS 5:17 NIV

Lord, when You say we should "pray continually," what does that mean exactly? Maybe You mean that when I see an ambulance on the way to work, I should pray for those who've been hurt. Or when I experience tension at church or my child is struggling with homework, I need to ask You to work in our midst. Or when sin comes calling, I should ask for Your help in resisting those temptations throughout the day. Or as I witness a sunset that ignites the evening sky with color, perhaps I should breathe a prayer of thanksgiving. Maybe praying frequently isn't giving up my time, but fellowshipping with the one who has the power to work all things for my good, the one who loves me best, the one who can forgive my sins, and the one who is worthy of my praise. Lord, may I never stop fellowshipping with You! Amen.

THINK ABOUT IT:

What are some ways you "pray continually" throughout the day?

Evening
SWEET FREEDOM

"Therefore, if you are offering your gift at the altar and there remember that your brother or sister has something against you, leave your gift there in front of the altar. First go and be reconciled to them; then come and offer your gift."
MATTHEW 5:23–24 NIV

Lord, why is saying "I'm sorry" so hard? Even the thought of making amends with a coworker, my husband, children, friends, or church members makes me sweat. I guess it's pride. Nobody likes to admit to being the bad guy. It's so much more satisfying to know *I've* been wronged. But the bottom line is that I want to follow Your teachings, Lord; and I can see in Matthew 5 that You'd like people to make amends, whether it is an apology, a reparation, or whatever might make the relationship right again. Please help me learn that I am not ensnared by reconciliation but am, on the contrary, given sweet freedom in it. Amen.

THINK ABOUT IT:

Is there someone with whom you need to make amends? How does it help knowing that you must forgive others to receive God's forgiveness?

Morning
WARDROBE STAPLES

Stand therefore, having fastened on the belt of truth, and having put on the breastplate of righteousness, and, as shoes for your feet, having put on the readiness given by the gospel of peace. In all circumstances take up the shield of faith, with which you can extinguish all the flaming darts of the evil one; and take the helmet of salvation, and the sword of the Spirit, which is the word of God.

EPHESIANS 6:14–17 ESV

God, as I get dressed each morning, don't let me walk out the door before I put on my most important "accessories." More than adornment, Your armor is essential. Without it, I'm left bare to Satan's assault, the evil that tries to hinder my walk with You. But with it, I am ready to face the day—not just with style—but with Your truth, righteousness, peace, faith, salvation, and words. Amen.

THINK ABOUT IT:

How does God's armor equip you for daily spiritual battles against Satan?

Evening
A GOOD NAME

Now there was in Joppa a disciple named Tabitha, which, translated, means Dorcas. She was full of good works and acts of charity.

ACTS 9:36 ESV

Father, I sometimes wonder what others will remember about how I lived. I hope that I am building a reputation like Tabitha. How beautiful that she was known for doing good—and not just a little bit; she was *full* of charity. The widows wept at her death, recalling all she had done. More beautiful than this is the fact that You used her life to lead others to faith. Father, fill me with a desire to reach out in kindness, to let my life tell of Your truth. May it be said of me that I was filled with good works—that through Your work in me, others believed. Amen.

THINK ABOUT IT:

In what ways are you like or can you become like Tabitha?

Morning
SEQUOIA-LIKE

As you received Christ Jesus the Lord, so continue to live in him. Keep your roots deep in him and have your lives built on him. Be strong in the faith, just as you were taught, and always be thankful.

COLOSSIANS 2:6–7 NCV

Lord, when I first turned to You, my new life was like a sapling. With shallow roots, it would have been easy to pull out. But You have grown me through Your Word and through Your tender care. I'll continue to grow with You, Lord. Each day, I want my spiritual roots to go deeper still. Redwoods aren't easily uprooted. . . and neither is a life planted firmly in You! It is able to withstand the harshest winds; it is a beautiful reflection of You. Thank You for all You do to keep me rooted. Amen.

THINK ABOUT IT:
What do you do to remain rooted in Christ?

Evening
ABOVE AND BEYOND

"And if anyone forces you to go one mile, go with him two miles. Give to the one who begs from you, and do not refuse the one who would borrow from you."

MATTHEW 5:41–42 ESV

Lord, You call me to be stingy in grudges and generous in love. You know I struggle with this at times. My default is to protect my own interests, especially when someone treats me badly. Help me model my character after You. You are the greatest example of responding sacrificially. You were condemned and abused, yet You held nothing back, even Your life, to benefit those who nailed You to the cross. Be with me as I go that extra mile, as I give with open hands, just as You did for me. Amen.

THINK ABOUT IT:
Why is it so difficult to turn the other cheek when wronged? How does Christ's example and presence enable you to do just that?

Morning
ON A MISSION

And when his parents saw him, they were astonished. And his mother said to him, "Son, why have you treated us so? Behold, your father and I have been searching for you in great distress." And he said to them, "Why were you looking for me? Did you not know that I must be in my Father's house?"

LUKE 2:48–49 ESV

Lord, I sometimes feel lost in where I should be and what I should be doing for You. I'm more like Mary—frantic, missing the big picture—when You knew precisely what Your purpose was and how You should go about it. I'll never have Your clear vision on my own, Lord. Please reveal Your plan in Your time. Nudge me toward the *where* and *what*. At the end of each day, and at the end of my life, I want to be found doing my Father's will. Amen.

THINK ABOUT IT:

Are you confident in your calling? If not, how can you carve out time to seek God's direction?

Evening
BETTER THAN

For a day in your courts is better than a thousand elsewhere. I would rather be a doorkeeper in the house of my God than dwell in the tents of wickedness. For the LORD God is a sun and shield; the LORD bestows favor and honor. No good thing does he withhold from those who walk uprightly. O LORD of hosts, blessed is the one who trusts in you!

PSALM 84:10–12 ESV

Father, this world is all I really know. I have the promise of heaven, but until then, my reality is the here and now. When I am tempted to make choices based solely on today, speak the truth of this psalm to my heart. One day with You is better than a thousand anywhere else. Your blessings are beyond anything this world could offer. May I never stop short of the promise. Amen.

THINK ABOUT IT:

Does shortsightedness impact how you live for God—that is, living in the moment versus living for eternity?

DAY 83

Morning
MIND CHANGER

But Moses implored the LORD his God and said, "O LORD, why does your wrath burn hot against your people, whom you have brought out of the land of Egypt with great power and with a mighty hand?" . . . And the LORD relented from the disaster that he had spoken of bringing on his people.

EXODUS 32:11, 14 ESV

God, what an amazing thought! You listen to believers. You hear what I whisper in my heart or cry out loud. Like a good father, You won't always do what I say, but You will receive my prayers. And sometimes, as Moses experienced, You will change Your mind. Even in hopeless situations, remind me to never stop *asking*. . .to never stop approaching You with reverence and faith. You will always do what's best. Thank You for being such an amazing God! Amen.

THINK ABOUT IT:
Does Moses' example give you a renewed sense of the power of prayer?

Evening
MIGHTY SMALL FAITH

He said to them, ". . .For truly, I say to you, if you have faith like a grain of mustard seed, you will say to this mountain, 'Move from here to there,' and it will move, and nothing will be impossible for you."

MATTHEW 17:20 ESV

God, no matter what size my faith, You have the power to accomplish great things in and through me. When I am in Your will, nothing is impossible for me because nothing is impossible for You in achieving Your purposes. What appear to be mountains in my life are just molehills in Your sight. That sin I struggle with. . .a friend I'm afraid to witness to. . .the times this world calls my beliefs into question and I feel weak to remain rooted in You. . . With Your power, I can command "mountains." Please never let me forget it! Amen.

THINK ABOUT IT:
What obstacles can you face with new confidence when you internalize Christ's words in Matthew?

Morning
SEIZE THE DAY

*So watch your step. Use your head.
Make the most of every chance you get.
These are desperate times! Don't live
carelessly, unthinkingly. Make sure you
understand what the Master wants.*

EPHESIANS 5:15–17 MSG

Father, it is so easy to get wrapped up in
the day to day, so easy to get caught up
in emotion and decide to go one way or
another, do one thing or another, without seeing You in the process. You offer
me Your wisdom and direction. . .why
do I not come to You more often? I only
have a set number of days to live out Your
will here on earth. Help me as Your Word
says to make the most of them. I don't
want to waste opportunities to be a witness to You. I don't want to stray from
Your purposes. May I pause first and think
on You before moving forward. Amen.

THINK ABOUT IT:

*What distracts you from the goal
of living every moment for God?*

Evening
DON'T FORGET

*When you eat all you want and build
nice houses and live in them, when
your herds and flocks grow large
and your silver and gold increase,
when you have more of everything,
then your heart will become proud.
You will forget the Lord your God.*

DEUTERONOMY 8:12–14 NCV

Father, may I take this warning to heart;
may the truth of its words never become
the pattern of my life. Because it is so
true, so humbling, so frightening. The
more that fills my life, the more likely I
am to ignore You. Forgive me for those
times! Nothing is more valuable than You.
Everything comes from You. I thank You
for the many blessings You have given me.
Use them to point to You and snuff out
my pride in what *I* gain. Amen.

THINK ABOUT IT:

*Why do possessions sometimes crowd
out God and make room for pride?*

Morning
WHEN WE THINK OF HONOR

"You know the commandments: 'You shall not commit adultery, you shall not murder, you shall not steal, you shall not give false testimony, honor your father and mother.'"

LUKE 18:20 NIV

Lord, I have read Your Ten Commandments, and I know You want children to honor their parents; but to be honest, some days I don't feel that "honored." That particular word seems to have lost its popularity in this modern age. When I think of being honored, it makes me think of respect, admiration, and devotion. But too many times my kids holler at me, ignore me, and disobey me. Lord, help me to encourage them to respect me and their father, but also help me to give my children plenty of reasons to look up to, admire, and honor me. Amen.

THINK ABOUT IT:

Which of those commandments might God be wanting you to pray on?

Evening
PLUMB WORN OUT

Let us not become weary in doing good, for at the proper time we will reap a harvest if we do not give up.

GALATIANS 6:9 NIV

Okay, I've baked a casserole for my elderly neighbor. I've sewn costumes for my daughter's school play. I've volunteered at the local food pantry. I've worked my way into goodwill giddy gladness. Except, Lord, to be truly honest, I'm more harried than happy. I'm tired of doing so many nice things for so many people. In fact, no one appreciates all my hard work. I don't want to be a servant anymore. I don't see very many fringe benefits! Okay, I'm done with my pity party now. Lord, heal me of this clunky attitude. Show me how to rest and be refreshed in You. Then bring me back to Your Word that tells me to not let myself get weary of doing good deeds for Your beloved. Amen.

THINK ABOUT IT:

What are some ways you can rest and refresh today so you can once again give with a joyful spirit? What Bible verse might reenergize you?

Morning
MY HIDING PLACE

You are my hiding place; you will protect me from trouble and surround me with songs of deliverance.

PSALM 32:7 NIV

Lord, I sense danger all around my family, and I'm scared. I hear about terrible accidents of all kinds. I see children growing up in rebellion. I even hear about young people taking their own lives. These terrors are just a glimpse of what can go wrong with a family—and it sometimes paralyzes me with fear. I know we are not to live with anxiety and dread, Lord, so I will choose to put my trust in You. Please protect our family from harm and evil. Surround us with Your loving care and Your songs of deliverance. And when You do allow trouble to pass through our lives, stay near us, help us to bear it, and please work it for Your and ultimately our good. Amen.

THINK ABOUT IT:

How did the Lord help you when you or a family member were going through a rough time?

Evening
YOUR PEACE

"All your children will be taught by the LORD, and great will be their peace."

ISAIAH 54:13 NIV

Oh Lord, many days it feels as if our world is spinning out of control. I've tried to shelter my children from the division and hatred around us, but the task is getting harder by the day. They see discord everywhere and are beginning to talk about it. I'm concerned that this abrasive and conflict-ridden society of ours will influence my family. I think it already has. I want my children to be taught by You, Lord, so please allow Your Holy Spirit to give me the right words to say; help me to use those teachable moments wisely and to live a life that exemplifies Your biblical precepts. I pray that peace—Your peace that passes all understanding—will rain down on our family. Amen.

THINK ABOUT IT:

How is the peace of God different from the peace the world promotes?

Morning
YOU ARE THE WAY

*Jesus answered, "I am the way and
the truth and the life. No one comes
to the Father except through me."*
JOHN 14:6 NIV

Lord, throughout history, some people
have tried to run from Your message of
salvation, or they try to poison it. But I
have read Your Word—the Bible—and I
know You make it very clear that You,
Jesus, are the truth. You are the life. And
You are the *only* way to heaven. As a concerned Christian, help me to know how
to keep my family safe from the world's
dangerous dilution of Your message and
how I can pray for a sinful world that
needs Your beautiful truth, Your merciful forgiveness, and Your everlasting
life! Amen.

THINK ABOUT IT:

*When you gather around the table
for family meals, how can you
promote a discussion of current
issues, scriptures, and truth?*

Evening
MUSIC FROM
YOUR HEART

*Speaking to one another with
psalms, hymns, and songs from
the Spirit. Sing and make music
from your heart to the Lord.*
EPHESIANS 5:19 NIV

Lord, if I suddenly burst out into song, my
kids would think I'd lost my mind. *And*
I have a tin ear, which makes my voice
sound more like a wail than a croon.
But maybe You just want a joyful noise
and a willing heart. Well, *that* I can do. I
want to rejoice in the new day, Lord, and I
want to praise You for everything You
do, since You are worthy of my worship.
I suppose if my family can shout cheers
at sporting events with utter abandon,
then we can learn to sing praises to You,
the Almighty! Amen.

THINK ABOUT IT:

*What are some ways you can
make music to the Lord?*

DAY 88

Morning
EMPOWERED BY YOU

But God made the earth by his power; he founded the world by his wisdom and stretched out the heavens by his understanding.

JEREMIAH 10:12 NIV

Lord, society keeps telling me I'm supposed to be empowered. But by whom? *Me?* I'm certainly not powerful enough for such a monstrous mission. Or I'm told I should take control of my life. Yet what human really governs anything in this life? If humans appear to be in full command, it's only an illusion. I know that You, God, are truly in control of all things. You made the whole universe with Your supernatural power—and You made me. I surrender to that truth. I acknowledge You as the maker of all things, and I choose to be empowered by You alone, God! Guide my every step. Amen.

THINK ABOUT IT:

Have you given God full control of all areas of your life?

Evening
THE SUBLIME BEAUTY OF GOD

One thing I ask from the LORD, this only do I seek: that I may dwell in the house of the LORD all the days of my life, to gaze on the beauty of the LORD and to seek him in his temple.

PSALM 27:4 NIV

Psalm 27 tells me You are beautiful, Lord. You are sublime—exalted and transcendent and glorious! And Your creation is exquisite as well. Because I am made in Your image, I want to be more like You in every way. I want to create a life of beauty all around me, whether it emanates from my hands as art or from my heart as an offering. Oh Lord, my God, I want to know the essence of who You are on a deeper level so that I can live a life of beauty! Amen.

THINK ABOUT IT:

What can you create today (whether from your hands or your heart) that will celebrate the beauty of God and His creation?

Morning
THE WONDERFUL DAYS TO COME

"Here I am! I stand at the door and knock. If anyone hears my voice and opens the door, I will come in and eat with that person, and they with me."

REVELATION 3:20 NIV

I imagine it like this, Lord: I iron my finest tablecloth, and I put out my best china. I cook my most beloved dish, and I pull out the chair at the head of the table—for You. I don't need to worry that You'll be late. You come to eat with me, and we talk about our relationship to each other and our Father God. And we toast to all the love and joy and all the wonderful days to come. Thank You, Lord, for coming to be with me, to sup with me, to live a life hand in hand with me. So beautiful is that life, in fact, that I'm looking forward to an eternity of it! Amen.

THINK ABOUT IT:

How can you show others that Christianity is not a religion but a relationship?

Evening
MY BUMBLY WAYS

We all, like sheep, have gone astray, each of us has turned to our own way; and the LORD has laid on him the iniquity of us all.

ISAIAH 53:6 NIV

Sometimes when I look at the reckless and random ways people live their lives, it looks sort of muddled from the outside. Maybe it looks muddled from the inside too. Is that the way I live my life, Lord? Am I guilty of going my own way willy-nilly? Have I become that little sheep full of bumbly ways—too silly and senseless to even know the perils all around me? If so, I am sorry, Lord. Please forgive me. And help me see the benefits of staying near to You and Your loving guidance as the Good Shepherd of my soul. Amen.

THINK ABOUT IT:

How do you know when you've gone astray from the Good Shepherd? And what do you do about it?

Morning
GOOD THINGS TO COME

When Jacob finished charging his sons, he drew up his feet into the bed, and breathed his last, and was gathered to his people. Then Joseph fell on his father's face, and wept over him, and kissed him.

GENESIS 49:33–50:1 RSV

You were so gracious to Joseph to allow him to see his father, Jacob, again before he died. It had been so long, and Joseph could have easily lost hope of that ever happening. But You always have good things in store for those who love You, don't You, Father? When I'm tempted to lose hope, when I think nothing good will ever happen, remind me of this story and Your goodness. Help me to lay down my worry, because worry is simply a belief that bad things will happen. Hope is the belief that good things will come. Help me to hope in You.

THINK ABOUT IT:
How can you turn your worry into hope?

Evening
LETTING GO

"Fear not, for am I in the place of God? As for you, you meant evil against me; but God meant it for good, to bring it about that many people should be kept alive, as they are today. So do not fear; I will provide for you and your little ones." Thus he reassured them and comforted them.

GENESIS 50:19–21 RSV

This passage is as much about forgiveness as it is about Your plan for us. Joseph would have carried so much anguish with him if he'd refused to forgive his brothers. He would have missed out on seeing his father again. He would have forfeited a future relationship with his brothers, including the younger brother he'd never met. I know when I refuse to forgive, it causes anxiety and stress to build up inside me. Help me to truly forgive those who have hurt me.

THINK ABOUT IT:
Whom do you need to forgive? Ask God to help you.

DAY 91

Morning
MILK AND HONEY

"And I have come down to deliver them out of the hand of the Egyptians and to bring them up out of that land to a good and broad land, a land flowing with milk and honey."
EXODUS 3:8 ESV

You promised Your people a land flowing with milk and honey. This promise was fulfilled in spite of their ongoing rebellion and disobedience. Why do I worry about things when I know You always have good things in store for those who love You? I know that worry really means I don't have faith in Your goodness. It means that, deep down, I struggle to believe Your promises. Forgive me for my lack of faith, Father. When I'm tempted to worry about the future, remind me of this land of milk and honey and of the good things You always have in store for Your children.

THINK ABOUT IT:
What are some things on your "milk and honey" list? Trust God for the good things He wants to give you.

Evening
FROM FEAR TO CONFIDENCE

But Moses said to the Lord, "Oh, my Lord, I am not eloquent, either in the past or since you have spoken to your servant, but I am slow of speech and of tongue." Then the Lord said to him, "Who has made man's mouth?... Is it not I, the Lord?"
EXODUS 4:10–11 ESV

I can so relate to Moses in this passage. There are things I want to do, things I feel You calling me to do, but I hesitate because I don't feel qualified. Thank You for this reminder to Moses that You created us, and You will qualify us to do the things You need us to do. Next time I feel anxious and unqualified, bring this passage to mind. Replace worry with confidence and fear with hope.

THINK ABOUT IT:
In what areas do you feel unqualified? How can you reframe your fears to reflect confidence in God?

Morning
GOD RESTORES

"I will restore to you the years that the swarming locust has eaten, the hopper, the destroyer, and the cutter, my great army, which I sent among you. You shall eat in plenty and be satisfied, and praise the name of the LORD your God, who has dealt wondrously with you."

JOEL 2:25–26 ESV

Long before Joel penned these words, Moses led Your people out of bondage. You sent plagues of swarming locusts, among other things, to demonstrate Your power. Here, You promise Your people that even when we're devastated, even when all seems lost, You have the power to restore. Sometimes I look at the bad things that have happened in my past, and I project those events onto the future. Change my heart and my way of thinking, Lord. I know that no matter what's happened in the past, I can hope in Your goodness.

THINK ABOUT IT:
What would you like God to restore for you?

Evening
EVEN YOUR ENEMIES

The people of Israel had also done as Moses told them, for they had asked the Egyptians for silver and gold jewelry and for clothing. And the LORD had given the people favor in the sight of the Egyptians, so that they let them have what they asked. Thus they plundered the Egyptians.

EXODUS 12:35–36 ESV

Thank You for this reminder that You can cause even our enemies to do nice things for us. Sometimes I worry about people who don't like me, and I lose sleep over those relationships. But I know when I walk with You, when I find favor with You, I also find favor in relationships. You can change people's hearts. Help me find favor even with those people who don't like me, Father. Help me to show them love and kindness in every situation. May my behavior reflect Your goodness and point them to You.

THINK ABOUT IT:
What relationships cause you concern? Talk to God about them.

Morning
TALK ABOUT IT

*Then Moses said to the people,
"Remember this day in which you
came out from Egypt, out of the house
of slavery, for by a strong hand the
Lord brought you out from this place."*

EXODUS 13:3 ESV

Just as the Israelites were commanded to
remember and talk about the good things
You did for them, I know You want me
to do the same. When I remember Your
goodness and Your faithfulness to me in
the past, I'm less likely to worry. When
I tell others about all the great things
You've done for me, it builds my faith.
When I'm tempted to give in to fear and
anxiety, bring to mind all the amazing
ways You've shown Your love to me. Open
doors for me to tell others about Your
greatness. Keep my focus on You, Lord,
instead of on my circumstances.

THINK ABOUT IT:
*What are three of the most amazing
things God has done for you?*

Evening
WHEN IT DOESN'T
MAKE SENSE

*When Pharaoh let the people go, God
did not lead them by way of the land
of the Philistines, although that was
near. For God said, "Lest the people
change their minds when they see
war and return to Egypt." But God
led the people around by way of the
wilderness toward the Red Sea. And
the people of Israel went up out of the
land of Egypt equipped for battle.*

EXODUS 13:17–18 ESV

Sometimes You do things that don't make
sense to me at the time. But I know You
always have a good reason for everything
You take me through. In this passage,
You wanted Your people to escape. You
knew they'd become disheartened and
return to bondage if they had to fight the
Philistines, so You took them the long
way around. Forgive me for doubting You
when things don't make sense to me. I
know Your ways are higher than my ways.

THINK ABOUT IT:
*What in your life doesn't
make sense right now?*

Morning
STILL AND SILENT

"The LORD will fight for you,
and you have only to be silent."
EXODUS 14:14 ESV

I don't know why I fight so hard for things to go my way. I try to maintain control when You only want me to be still. You are already fighting my battles for me, and You do a much better job than I can ever hope to do on my own. Help me to stop worrying and complaining. Teach me to sit back and watch You work, popcorn in hand, waiting to see what great things You will do. I trust You, Father. Forgive me for working and fighting and stressing out when all I need to do is step aside, get out of Your way, and witness Your greatness and glory in action.

THINK ABOUT IT:

Have you been fighting your own
battles? Practice being still and silent
today, and see what God does.

Evening
NOT ALONE

Moses' father-in-law said to him,
"What you are doing is not good.
You and the people with you will
certainly wear yourselves out,
for the thing is too heavy for you.
You are not able to do it alone."
EXODUS 18:17–18 ESV

I must be a lot like Moses, trying to do everything alone. I don't know why I worry about things so much. Worry is my way of trying to maintain control, I guess. Thank You for the wisdom of Moses' father-in-law and for the reminder that we weren't meant to do life alone. You are always with me, fighting my battles, caring for me. When needed, You send others into my life to help. Forgive me for trying to work things out for myself. Help me to trust You with all my cares and concerns.

THINK ABOUT IT:

What things are you trying to do
alone? Give them to God today.

Morning
I WON'T WORRY ABOUT TOMORROW

"But seek first the kingdom of God and his righteousness, and all these things will be added to you. Therefore do not be anxious about tomorrow, for tomorrow will be anxious for itself. Sufficient for the day is its own trouble."
MATTHEW 6:33–34 ESV

Why do I worry about tomorrow, Lord? It's not even here yet! I have enough to deal with today without fretting over tomorrow and the days after that.

And yet I still struggle with fear regarding the unknown. I know—deep in the recesses of my heart—that the only way out of this fear is to give my tomorrows to You. I've trusted You with my yesterdays, and You've always come through. I trust You with today and sense Your presence. Why, then, would I give up on tomorrow before it even arrives?

I won't. I look forward with anticipation and hope, not fear. Thank You for joining me in my tomorrows, Father! Amen.

THINK ABOUT IT:
What actions can you take to avoid worrying about things that haven't happened yet?

Evening
YOU BIND MY WOUNDS

He heals the brokenhearted and binds up their wounds.
PSALM 147:3 ESV

Sometimes I feel like my heart has a gaping wound, Lord. If You didn't reach down and bind it, I might bleed out. The cruel words spoken over me, the ugly actions of others, even my own self-loathing. . .they've done a number on me.

I'm so grateful for Your TLC in moments like these. You're like a paramedic, reaching down to put pressure on the wound to keep it from depleting me. Then You supernaturally infuse me with Your blood, Your power, Your joy. And somehow—in spite of the pain and trials—I keep going. The wound doesn't take me down. You cure me and set me aright, healthy and whole. Thank You for such great care, heavenly Father. How tenderly You treat this heart of mine! I'm so grateful. Amen.

THINK ABOUT IT:
What specific wounds from your past has God healed?

DAY 96

Morning
A QUIET, PEACEFUL PLACE

The LORD is my shepherd;
I shall not want. He makes
me lie down in green pastures.
He leads me beside still waters.

PSALM 23:1–2 ESV

You make me lie down in green pastures. I'll admit, there are times when I don't want to. I want to keep going, going, going. . .until my body and my will give out. But You? You know better. So You lead me to quiet streams with shade trees nearby. You woo me with Your gentle words, encouraging me to rest. To relax. To be with You.

When I take the time to enjoy the stillness with You, the stresses of life have no choice but to flee! So today I choose still waters over chaos. I choose shade trees over the beating sun. I choose peace over turmoil. And I choose You over me. Thank You for leading me beside still waters, Lord. Amen.

THINK ABOUT IT:

How has God "made you" lie down
in green pastures in the past?

Evening
ALL THINGS ARE POSSIBLE

"For nothing will be
impossible with God."

LUKE 1:37 ESV

If I'm being honest, Lord, I have to confess that I haven't always believed You to be capable of "all" things. There were certain things—people, relationships, situations—that I gave up on. I just couldn't see it happening, so I didn't bother asking You to intervene. Or maybe I asked but then quickly gave up.

Now I see the futility of my approach. You wanted to be free to move on my behalf, but I limited You. I said, "Never mind that person, Lord. She's never going to change." Today I ask for Your intervention in the situations that seem impossible to me. May I watch the impossible change to possible once You take the reins! Amen.

THINK ABOUT IT:

Do you have faith to believe
that "all" things are possible?

Morning
HE FIGHTS MY ENEMIES

David said to the Philistine, "You come against me with sword and spear and javelin, but I come against you in the name of the Lord Almighty, the God of the armies of Israel, whom you have defied."

1 SAMUEL 17:45 NIV

Oh, how I love David's bold words in today's scripture, Lord! How dare that evil giant think he stood a chance against a man of God! How dare he lift his sword and spear to take down one of God's anointed!

You've got our backs, Lord—even when we face strong (giant!) opposition. Even then we come out swinging not with weapons of warfare like the world uses but in Your name. We come against the forces of darkness in the name of the Lord Almighty, the God of the armies of Israel. When those who speak against God rear their heads, we take them down with smooth stones, not earthly weapons. And we do it with Your power, Your strength, and Your confidence. Thank You for making us battle-ready, Lord. Amen.

THINK ABOUT IT:
How can you hand the reins over to the Lord today so that your stresses can be relieved?

Evening
GETTING OUT OF MY HEAD

Trust in the Lord with all your heart, and do not lean on your own understanding. In all your ways acknowledge him, and he will make straight your paths.

PROVERBS 3:5–6 ESV

Most of the time, it's so hard to get out of my head, Lord. I get wrapped up in my thoughts, my plans, my worries, my vain imaginings, and I forget to put my trust in You. I wonder why I end up with my stomach in knots and my hands trembling. It's because I tried to take Your place.

Today I give my thoughts, my worries, my anxieties to You. I won't lean on my own understanding. (This is going to be hard for me, but You already know that!) I'll stop, take a breath, and acknowledge Your rightful place as the solver of all my problems. And when I do, I know You'll straighten my path and show me which way to go.

Whew! I'm so glad I can trust You, Father! Amen.

THINK ABOUT IT:
What are some techniques you can use to get out of your head and trust God more?

Morning
WHEN MY KNEES ARE KNOCKING

"Be strong and courageous. Do not fear or be in dread of them, for it is the Lord your God who goes with you. He will not leave you or forsake you."

DEUTERONOMY 31:6 ESV

"Do not fear or be in dread." I read those words in today's verse and want to ask, "How do I *do* that, Lord? When I'm totally stressed out—when things are going the very opposite of how I hoped they would go—how do I keep from becoming fearful? How can I push away dread, especially when the enemy is taunting or intimidating me?"

Then I read the rest of this verse and get my answer. You're going with me. Whew! You're right beside me. You won't leave, no matter how heated the battle gets. In fact, the tougher the battle, the tighter You stick to me. I'll trust You, Lord. Even in the battle. *Especially* in the battle. Amen.

THINK ABOUT IT:

Are you easily intimidated?

Evening
EVERY NEED. . .MET!

And my God will supply every need of yours according to his riches in glory in Christ Jesus.

PHILIPPIANS 4:19 ESV

Okay, I'll admit it—sometimes I get worried and worked up over things that haven't even happened yet. A bill comes in the mail, and I panic without even considering how You will make provision. I get totally stressed out and ignore Your gentle reminder: "Hey, haven't I taken care of every single need in the past? Do you really think I'm going to start letting you down now?"

I know You won't, Lord. You're a way-maker. You're a need-meeter. You supply every good thing for those who love You and are called according to Your purpose. I trust You, Father, even when the need seems great. Amen.

THINK ABOUT IT:

What (particular) needs are you praying God will supply today?

DAY 99

Morning
EVEN THEN. . .

Even though I walk through the valley of the shadow of death, I will fear no evil, for you are with me; your rod and your staff, they comfort me.

PSALM 23:4 ESV

We've been through some hard seasons, You and me. I've trudged through valleys so deep, so dark, that I questioned Your existence. I've been on seas so turbulent that I felt sure I wouldn't pull through.

But You. . . Even then, in the midst of the despair, You always showed up and showed off! I don't have to be afraid because I've seen You intervene in the past and I know You'll do it again. And again. And again. Even when things are at their worst, I can trust You. Today I choose to do just that. Amen.

THINK ABOUT IT:

How are you comforted by God's rod and staff?

Evening
YOU'VE BEEN THERE, LORD

And Jesus, full of the Holy Spirit, returned from the Jordan and was led by the Spirit in the wilderness for forty days, being tempted by the devil. And he ate nothing during those days. And when they were ended, he was hungry.

LUKE 4:1–2 ESV

Knowing You've walked a mile in my shoes brings me so much hope, Lord. You understand what it's like to be tempted. You know how it feels to be in pain. You've experienced betrayal, anger, and frustration too. You've been hungry. And thirsty. And weary. And yet—through the power of Your Spirit—You overcame it all.

You're teaching me to overcome too. Help me to lean into You on days when I'm feeling weak. Even when I'm feeling strong, I want to fully rely on You. Thank You for leading the way. Amen.

THINK ABOUT IT:

How do you feel knowing that Jesus has walked a mile in your shoes?

Morning
A CHANGE OF ATTITUDE

For I consider that the sufferings of this present time are not worthy to be compared with the glory that is to be revealed to us.

ROMANS 8:18 NASB

When I'm worried about money, Lord, it's so easy to lose my sense of perspective. The size of my bank account starts to seem like the most important thing in the world. I forget that I'm living in eternity right now, even while I'm living in this world; I forget that You are in control of my life, and You are working even in the midst of this financial strain I'm experiencing. Remind me, God, that in the big scheme of things—Your scheme—my finances are a very small concern. The financial limitations I'm experiencing now are nothing—truly nothing!—compared to all You have in store for me. So, Lord, I'm asking You to shift my perspective. Help me to see my life with Your eyes. Reveal Your glory in me, I pray.

THINK ABOUT IT:

Imagine the worst thing that might happen because of your financial problems. Now imagine yourself putting that imaginary situation in God's hands. As you do so, open yourself to the glory of the Holy Spirit. Can you feel the change in your attitude?

Evening
BROKENHEARTED JOY

So be truly glad. There is wonderful joy ahead, even though you must endure many trials for a little while.

1 PETER 1:6 NLT

God, I've always struggled with this verse, and now I'm *really* struggling. How can I be "truly glad" when so much has fallen apart? That just doesn't make sense to me. I feel such hurt and betrayal, such shame and failure, such sorrow and heartache. Your joy seems far, far away from my heart. Even so, Lord, I'm going to cling to this verse. I'm going to keep believing that You are working in this situation. I do not know the future, but You do, and I know that one day, one way or another, You will heal my broken heart. You will help me to be glad again. I'm trusting You.

THINK ABOUT IT:

Have you confided all your deepest feelings about your brokenness to the Lord? Set aside some time to do that as soon as you can. And then open yourself to God's joy, a joy that doesn't depend on circumstances.

Morning
AVOID THE TRAFFIC JAMS!

"Step out of the traffic! Take a long, loving look at me, your High God, above politics, above everything."
PSALM 46:10 MSG

The injustice in the world is weighing heavy on my heart, Lord. It seems like every day there's a new story about people who are suffering and oppressed. Sometimes I just don't want to hear anymore. I want to plug my ears and shut my eyes so I don't have to know the terrible realities that others are experiencing. I feel so helpless to do anything, and so I'd rather just not know. I'm tired of all the fighting and polarization, all the protests and politics. I'd like to hide from them and think about something else. But I know, God, that many people don't have the luxury of hiding; they have to face injustice in their daily lives. And so, God, today I'm stepping out of all the noise and arguing, the anger and the accusations. Instead, I'm going to fix my eyes on You. Show me Your way of justice. Reveal to me what I am called to do to build Your kingdom.

THINK ABOUT IT:

What is the "traffic" in your life that you may need to step away from in order to hear God's call to justice more clearly?

Evening
BUILDING INSTEAD OF ARGUING

Encourage one another and build one another up.
1 THESSALONIANS 5:11 NASB

It seems like the world is full of arguments lately, God. One side sees things one way, and they're absolutely certain they're right—meanwhile, the other side sees things just as clearly in the exact opposite way, and they're equally positive that they're holding the correct position. It's hard not to get sucked into the arguments when they're everywhere: in social media, between friends and family, between neighbors, even within the church. We just can't seem to agree on so many important issues. Lord, we need Your help. We need to stop looking at all the ways we disagree and instead begin focusing on how we can encourage each other and build each other up. God, I ask that You help me do my part. Help me to resist arguing so that Your love can flow through me (even to the people I disagree with).

THINK ABOUT IT:

What do you think is more important— being right or being loving?

DAY 102

Morning
THE FUTURE STARTS NOW

We've been given a brand-new life and have everything to live for, including a future in heaven—and the future starts now! God is keeping careful watch over us and the future. The Day is coming when you'll have it all—life healed and whole.

1 PETER 1:3–5 MSG

My pain defines each day, Lord. I can't get away from it. It's always there with me, no matter what I'm doing. I try to ignore it, but it's like a nagging child, pulling at my sleeve until I pay attention to it. Teach me ways to gently tell my pain to wait so that I can take a few moments to focus on You. Thank You that the life You have planned for me isn't defined by my pain. I believe that one day You will heal me; in the meantime, I will trust You to guard me and bless me. Even on my most painful days, give me hope in You. Remind me that my life with You begins now.

THINK ABOUT IT:

Have you allowed your pain to come between you and God?

Evening
UPHELD!

"Do not fear, for I am with you; do not be afraid, for I am your God. I will strengthen you, I will also help you, I will also uphold you with My righteous right hand."

ISAIAH 41:10 NASB

The thought of losing our home terrifies me, Lord. Our home is the place where our family goes to be together, to enjoy each other's presence, to rest, to be safe. And now our home—the physical symbol of our family—is going to be taken away from us. How are we going to survive? How can we ever feel safe and secure again? Thank You, God, that *You* are our safety. You are our home. Show us the right way to go from here. As we find our security in You, lead us to a new physical home. Uphold us with Your hand and take away my fear.

THINK ABOUT IT:

God wants to help you with every problem that comes your way. Have you hesitated to ask His help with this situation?

Morning
GOD'S PEACE GUARD

Don't worry about anything;
instead, pray about everything.
Tell God what you need, and thank
him for all he has done. Then you
will experience God's peace, which
exceeds anything we can understand.
His peace will guard your hearts and
minds as you live in Christ Jesus.
PHILIPPIANS 4:6–7 NLT

God, when financial worries threaten to overwhelm my mind, remind me of all You have done for me in the past. You have never abandoned me, and I know You won't now. When I look back, I see all the ways You have provided for me and my family. Even the worst situations somehow worked out, and You were with us every step of the way. And so now, Lord, I need to spend some time praying about my finances. I'm going to go through every bill, and I'm going to put each one in Your hands.

THINK ABOUT IT:

How is God's peace different from
the peace that comes from knowing
you have plenty of money in
your bank account? Which peace
would you rather have?

Evening
GOD IS ON YOUR SIDE!

If God be for us, who can be against us?
ROMANS 8:31 KJV

I was counting on these people, Lord. I thought they respected and liked me. I was sure they would help me get ahead in life. I believed these were useful contacts You had brought into my life to help me do Your work. And now it turns out they had their own agenda. They didn't care about helping me; they only wanted to use me to help themselves. I feel embarrassed and betrayed—but even worse, I feel so disappointed. I really thought we could accomplish great things together, and now I feel as though everything I had hoped for has fallen into pieces. But now, Lord, remind me that Your will for my life won't ever be limited by anything people can do or say. You are on my side, and I am on Yours. Together we will do great things in this world, things that will bring love and healing to the people You love. Help me to put this setback behind me and move on, confident that You have everything under control.

THINK ABOUT IT:

How would your attitude change
if you became convinced that
God was truly on your side?

Morning
MOTIVATION

Let us think of ways to motivate one another to acts of love and good works.
HEBREWS 10:24 NLT

I'm afraid I've gotten into a rut with my family, Lord—a negative rut. Everything they do seems to irritate me. When I'm talking to them, almost every word that comes out of my mouth is a criticism. I feel like my complaints are legitimate (if they'd just listen to me, everything in our household would go so much more smoothly!), but I realize that my constant negativity has become a burden for our family. I ask for Your forgiveness, Lord. Today, help me not to notice all the things my family does wrong, but to look for ways to motivate them to do better. Remind me to build them up, not tear them down.

THINK ABOUT IT:

Does angry criticism motivate you to do better? Do you think it motivates your family?

Evening
PRAYER IN THE MIDST OF DISAPPOINTMENT

Be joyful in hope, patient in affliction, faithful in prayer.
ROMANS 12:12 NIV

Once again, Lord, I had my heart set on something—and then it never materialized. This time I was so sure it was actually going to happen. It didn't seem like anything could go wrong. But now here I am again, my heart aching with disappointment. Is this a definite no, Lord? Or are You asking me to wait a little longer for Your perfect timing? Either way, I'm going to need Your help with this. Give me Your joy, Your hope, I pray: a joy and hope that don't depend on circumstances, that are firmly grounded in Your unchanging love. I also ask for patience and endurance. Keep my eyes fixed on You. Remind me not to obsess about my disappointment but instead to keep bringing it to You in prayer. Thank You that You always listen, You always care.

THINK ABOUT IT:

When you are disappointed, are you faithful in prayer?

Morning
TAKE HEART!

"I have told you these things, so that in me you may have peace. In this world you will have trouble. But take heart! I have overcome the world."

JOHN 16:33 NIV

Life seems so full of pain. Whenever I watch the news on television, my chest grows tight with anxiety; it's just one terrible story after another. And then my personal life hasn't exactly been a walk in the park lately. Every morning as I face a new day, I can't help but wonder what will go wrong. Some days it feels as though anxiety is my obligation, a heavy burden I'm duty-bound to constantly carry around with me. Remind me, Lord, that anxiety is optional. As Your child, I have the choice to trust You instead. You never promised that the world wouldn't be full of trouble—but You did promise that You are greater than anything the world can throw at me. Teach me to dwell on Your good news rather than on the nightly news. Give me Your peace, I pray.

THINK ABOUT IT:

What would it take to convince you today that your anxiety is optional? What do you need to do to grab hold of the peace of Jesus?

Evening
WAITING UPON THE LORD

They that wait upon the LORD shall renew their strength; they shall mount up with wings as eagles; they shall run, and not be weary; and they shall walk, and not faint.

ISAIAH 40:31 KJV

God, I'm so exhausted. My body is tired, my mind is tired, my heart is tired. The stress of my life has sapped all my strength away, leaving me weak and vulnerable. I'm on the verge of getting sick or sinking into depression. I'm in desperate need of a dose of divine strength. Show me the practical steps I need to take to renew my energy and stamina. Let me know where I need to cut back on the things I'm doing—and then give me the strength to follow through. Remind me that only You are omnipotent; my strength will always be limited. Help me to be a good steward of the energy and skills You've given me. Most of all, Lord, lift me up on the eagle wings of Your Spirit. Draw me closer to You, the source of all my strength. Let me always wait upon You.

THINK ABOUT IT:

Can you identify two things that are consuming your strength right now? Do you think God might want you to cut back on anything?

Morning
GOD'S CARE FOR YOU

*Give all your worries and cares
to God, for he cares about you.*

1 Peter 5:7 nlt

My stomach is in knots, Lord, as I think about this situation. I'm scared of what might happen. I worry about the wisest course of action. Everyone in my life has their own ideas about what I should do, but I don't know who to trust. I'm so confused. Thank You, God, that I can bring this situation to You. You know all the ins and outs of my case, better even than any others. You understand my feelings better than even my friends and family do. I trust You to guide me. I know I'll keep pulling my worries back out of Your hands, but I'm going to keep on giving them right back to You, no matter how many times it takes. Give me wisdom. Give everyone concerned clear eyes to see what is right. Thank You for loving me and never abandoning me, no matter what the future brings.

THINK ABOUT IT:
Can you trust God?

Evening
OPPORTUNITY FOR JOY

*When troubles of any kind come your
way, consider it an opportunity for
great joy. For you know that when
your faith is tested, your endurance
has a chance to grow. So let it grow,
for when your endurance is fully
developed, you will be perfect and
complete, needing nothing.*

James 1:2–4 nlt

Lord, it seems as though Your Word is always telling me the same, almost impossible thing: find joy even in the hard things. I read the words, but they don't make sense to my heart. How can *this* situation be an opportunity for joy? I feel like I need to be practical. I need to focus on what I have to do to recover from disaster. I don't have time to be spiritual right now. God, I need Your help with my attitude. I need You to shift my perspective so that I see You at the center of this trouble. Use this crisis to make me stronger in You. Teach me that even when my finances are in shambles, I have absolutely everything I need in You.

THINK ABOUT IT:
*How is your faith being tested
by this situation? How might
God be asking you to grow?*

Morning
THE "THORN" OF WEAKNESS

*I was given a thorn in my flesh. . . .
Three different times I begged the
Lord to take it away. Each time he
said, "My grace is all you need. My
power works best in weakness."*

2 Corinthians 12:7–9 nlt

I don't like feeling weak, Lord. I would
much rather be strong and competent. I
want to impress people with how well I
do things. I don't want them to feel sorry
for me because I'm too weak right now
to keep up with my responsibilities. I feel
so frustrated with myself! I just want You
to make me strong, the way I used to
be. But maybe that's not Your will for
me right now. If the apostle Paul had to
live with his weakness, his "thorn in the
flesh" (whatever it was), then help me
also to accept myself the way I am right
now. Clearly, You were able to use Paul
in all sorts of amazing ways, regardless of
his weakness. So if that's what You want,
Lord, then go ahead—use my weakness
to reveal Yourself in the world. Teach me
to rely on Your grace rather than my own
strength.

THINK ABOUT IT:
*How might you allow God's power to
work through your weakness today?*

Evening
SPIRIT WIND

*Those who enter into Christ's
being-here-for-us no longer
have to live under a continuous,
low-lying black cloud. A new power
is in operation. The Spirit of life
in Christ, like a strong wind, has
magnificently cleared the air, freeing
you from a fated lifetime of brutal
tyranny at the hands of sin and death.*

Romans 8:1–2 msg

Our world is so full of violence, Lord.
My heart aches each time I hear about
another shooting, one more act of senseless rage against innocent people. The
world seems to be smothering under a
thick cloud of hatred and death. Thank
You, God, that Your Spirit has the power
to blow away the clouds. Thanks to Your
presence, I can breathe in the cool, clear
air of love and hope, even in the midst of
this world's sin.

THINK ABOUT IT:
*What does the phrase "Christ's
being-here-for-us" mean to you?
Can you look back at the past few
days and find examples when you
knew Christ was with you?*

Morning
DON'T FRET!

*Do not fret because of those
who are evil or be envious
of those who do wrong.*
PSALM 37:1 NIV

I find myself caught up in arguments so easily, Lord. Lately, there are countless things to argue about: politics, health precautions, race, sex, the environment. There are so many issues, and we can't seem to agree on any of them. My own point of view truly does seem like the right one! I really believe it is—and then I get so upset with the people who don't agree with me. I feel that they're not following You the way they should. The harder I try to persuade them, the more bitter our arguments become. I find myself feeling so angry, brooding about them, wishing there was some way to convince them. God, I realize I've been letting these arguments rob me of the peace You want me to have. I've been fretting when I should have been trusting You. And so, Lord, I give You all these issues. You know how strongly I feel about them; You know I truly want what's best. I put them all into Your hands. I'm not going to argue anymore.

THINK ABOUT IT:

*What are the issues you
feel most passionate about?
Can you trust them to God?*

Evening
STAY ALERT!

*Then GOD's Message came
again. . . . "Stay alert! I am GOD,
the God of everything living.
Is there anything I can't do?"*
JEREMIAH 32:26 MSG

My sense of helplessness has turned into apathy, God. There's nothing I can do to change things, so why should I care anymore? I've been drifting through my days in a fog of discouragement. I've given up. I just don't want to keep trying. But, Lord, the Bible reminds me that I'm not the first person to feel this way. Your people have always had times of doubt and discouragement, times when they could see no way out of their situation, when they felt completely helpless. And yet every time, You stepped in and saved them. Down through the centuries, no situation has ever been too hard for You to handle. So, God, I ask You today to wake me up out of my fog. Remind me to look around me and see what You are already doing. Keep me expectant, eager to see what You will do next. Remind me that even when I am helpless, You are strong.

THINK ABOUT IT:

*What can you do today to "stay alert"
to what God is doing in your life?*

Morning
UNCONDITIONAL LOVE

Love never gives up, never loses faith, is always hopeful, and endures through every circumstance.
1 Corinthians 13:7 NLT

I've messed up, God. I made mistakes that have had consequences, and now I feel like such a failure. I've let people down, and I'm disappointed in myself. But, Lord, I'm so glad that You are never disappointed in me. This Bible verse that's so often read at marriage ceremonies applies just as much to Your love for me. You never give up on me, no matter how badly I mess up. You never lose faith in me, no matter how many other people I may have disappointed. You have hope for my future, and You share that hope with me. Your love endures even when I fail. I don't have to do anything to earn Your love, because You will always love me just the way I am.

THINK ABOUT IT:

Do you believe that God's love is unconditional? What would it take to convince you?

Evening
ABSOLUTE TRUST

Though he slay me, yet will I trust in him.
Job 13:15 KJV

I don't like to think about dying, Lord. I don't want to leave the people I love, and there are still so many things I want to accomplish in life. Worst of all, no one *really* knows what lies on the other side of death. When I think about the reality that I too must one day die (just like everyone does sooner or later), I feel scared. I shift my thoughts as quickly as I can to something else. But God, even though I don't know what eternity will be like, I do know *You*. I know You have never treated me unkindly; You have never shown me anything but love. When I look back at my life, I see You were always there with me, right from the beginning. And so I will trust You with my death as well. I will put my confidence in Your unfailing love. No matter what happens, I have faith in You. You will keep me safe in this world—and the next.

THINK ABOUT IT:

Can you trust God with your own death? If not, what holds you back? What makes you afraid to rely on God's love to carry you into eternity?

Morning
RULING IN MY HEART

*And let the peace of Christ rule in your
hearts, to which indeed you were
called in one body. And be thankful.*
COLOSSIANS 3:15 ESV

I have to confess, I've been ruled by many
things over the years, Lord. My temper. My
poor attitude. My jealousy. My frustration.
These and other things have taken control
of my heart at different times, and poor
actions always followed.

But no more! Now I'm ruled by Your
peace. I'm giving it first place in my heart.
I'm so thankful for Your supernatural
peace because I know it will affect my
actions and others will notice. And once
they see the change in me, I'll be able to
share more freely about all You're doing
in my life. Being ruled by peace is a beautiful cycle! I'm so grateful I can live this
way. Amen.

THINK ABOUT IT:
*What does it mean
to be ruled by peace?*

Evening
NO FEAR IN LOVE

*There is no fear in love, but perfect
love casts out fear. For fear has to
do with punishment, and whoever
fears has not been perfected in love.*
1 JOHN 4:18 ESV

I read this verse, Lord, and I'm mesmerized. I'm trying to figure out how to get
rid of the fear and anxiety in my life, and
the answer is right in front of me—love.
When I'm fully convinced of Your great
love for me, when I'm overwhelmed by
Your grace, no room is left for fear or
stress.

Consume me with Your love and
grace today, I pray. Take hold of those
things that trouble me most deeply. Wash
away my fears with Your peace. Remove
angst. Leave behind only joy, flowing from
the wellspring of Your Spirit. I give myself
over to this way of living, Lord. Thank You
for providing a way out of stress. Amen.

THINK ABOUT IT:
*What do fear and love have
to do with each other?*

Morning
GET OVER IT!

Refrain from anger, and forsake wrath!
Fret not yourself; it tends only to evil.
PSALM 37:8 ESV

You ask me to forsake wrath, Lord. But forsaking wrath isn't as easy as it sounds. More often than not, I lose it! Oh, I never mean to. It always seems to hit from out of the blue. Someone gets on my last nerve, and I come out swinging, exhibiting the very opposite of this verse: I'm angry. Filled with wrath. Fretting. And in those moments, I really do have a propensity toward evil.

But You have a different way. What a relief to know there's a way out. Today I swap out anger and wrath for God-breathed peace. I trade in my fretting for trust. And I turn my back on evil, refusing to give the enemy a foothold in my life.

Thank You for giving Your children a better way, Lord. Amen.

THINK ABOUT IT:

Are you one of those people who has a hard time getting over things?

Evening
BECAUSE I TRUST IN YOU

You keep him in perfect peace
whose mind is stayed on you,
because he trusts in you.
ISAIAH 26:3 ESV

Sometimes I wonder what "perfect" peace looks like. Is it mountain streams or ocean waves? Is it a baby's coo or a puppy's cuddles? Is it a cozy blanket and a cup of tea on a cold day?

You show up with feelings of peace in all sorts of ways, Father God, but by far Your best offering came through the sacrifice of Your Son, Jesus, on the cross. Because of Your amazing gift, I can have lasting peace to carry me through not just the situations I'm facing today but all of the stresses of tomorrow.

The world can't give this peace to me, and no circumstances are strong enough to take it away. Perfect peace comes through the blood of Jesus, the one who cleansed me from my sin and set my feet on a rock. How grateful I am for this overcoming peace! Amen.

THINK ABOUT IT:
What do the words
perfect peace *mean to you?*

Morning
KNEES. . .STOP KNOCKING!

"Have I not commanded you?
Be strong and courageous. Do
not be frightened, and do not be
dismayed, for the LORD your God
is with you wherever you go."
JOSHUA 1:9 ESV

I'm noticing a cycle, Lord. My most stressful moments come when I forget to place my trust in You. I panic, and then fear sets in. But You've commanded me to be strong. I think it's a little sad that You have to command this—courage should come naturally to me, but it doesn't.

I take Your commands seriously, Lord. You obviously care a great deal about courage if You commanded it! "Do not be frightened" is easier said than done. "Don't be dismayed"? Only possible through You, Lord!

Here's my favorite part of that verse: "For the LORD your God is with you wherever you go." And that, of course, is the answer to how and why it is possible to rise above fear. Thank You, Lord! Amen.

THINK ABOUT IT:
Why do you suppose God
made courage a command
instead of a suggestion?

Evening
I'M TOSSING IT YOUR WAY, LORD!

Cast your burden on the LORD,
and he will sustain you; he will never
permit the righteous to be moved.
PSALM 55:22 ESV

When I think of how You sustain me, Lord, I imagine a net holding me above my troubles. You lift me out of them in much the same way a mother scoops her child into her arms. It's easy to cast my burden on You when I picture You holding me like that. You care—about my chaos, my confusion, my struggles, my pain. And because You care, You sustain. (That safety net is there anytime I need it.)

The word *sustain* gives me courage to look ahead. If You're willing to sustain me today, I can count on it tomorrow too. Thanks for giving me a way to rise above my problems, Lord. Amen.

THINK ABOUT IT:
In what ways has God
sustained you this week?

DAY 113

Morning
A FIXED MIND

*You keep him in perfect peace
whose mind is stayed on you,
because he trusts in you.*
ISAIAH 26:3 ESV

Today I choose to fix my mind on You, Lord. I'm tempted to look to the right. No, I'm tempted to look to the left. I'm tempted to look every way the wind blows, if I'm being honest. Distractions beckon. Temptations abound. They cry out for my attention, but I'm not falling into their trap! I've done that before, and things didn't end well.

This time things *will* end well because I've made up my mind to keep my heart, my thoughts, and my attitude firmly fixed on You—Your Word, Your plan, Your way. I won't give up if things don't come together instantly. I'll stick with You. You've stuck with me, after all. (Have I mentioned how grateful I am for that, Lord?) Amen.

THINK ABOUT IT:

What does it mean to "fix" your mind?

Evening
YOU STARTED IT, YOU'LL FINISH IT

*And I am sure of this, that he who
began a good work in you will bring it
to completion at the day of Jesus Christ.*
PHILIPPIANS 1:6 ESV

I don't always finish what I start, do I, Lord? It's a real problem. I'll come up with a craft project or redecorating scheme on a whim. Things get off to a great start, but then my ambition fizzles out. I get stuck. I give up. I leave rooms half-finished.

You, though? You don't get stuck. You've renovated my heart and taken the project all the way! If You start something in my life, I can count on You to follow through on Your word to complete what You've started.

Teach me Your ways, Lord! Show me how to be a good finisher, not just a good starter. Amen.

THINK ABOUT IT:

What would you like God to finish?

DAY 114

Morning
YOU CREATED ME, LORD!

*As you do not know the path
of the wind, or how the body is
formed in a mother's womb,
so you cannot understand the work
of God, the Maker of all things.*

ECCLESIASTES 11:5 NIV

The next time I start to fret over this circumstance or that circumstance, remind me of how I was created in my mother's womb, Lord. You didn't leave out one teensy-tiny detail. You formed me long before Mom knew I was coming!

If You took the time to knit me together with such delicacy, surely I can trust You with the running of my life now. You've been running it all along, after all! So I won't fret. (Hey, I didn't fret when I was tucked away in my mother's womb!) I won't worry about how things are going to turn out. (Did I worry then? No way!) I'll trust You now as I trusted You then—wholly and completely. Amen.

THINK ABOUT IT:

*How do you feel knowing that the
same God who created you sees what
you're going through right now?*

Evening
KEEP THE PAST
IN THE PAST

*This is what the LORD says—he who
made a way through the sea, a path
through the mighty waters, who
drew out the chariots and horses,
the army and reinforcements
together, and they lay there, never
to rise again, extinguished, snuffed
out like a wick: "Forget the former
things; do not dwell on the past.
See, I am doing a new thing!"*

ISAIAH 43:16–19 NIV

"Forget the former things." Oh, how easy that sounds, Lord! But how hard it is to do! I have so many regrets, so many unresolved situations. How do I just leave them there? I need Your help to do so.

You've performed so many miracles—rescuing, saving, delivering Your people. And in every situation, You offered the same advice: "Don't look back." There must be something to it. The past haunts me at times, but I can't look back or I won't move forward. Today I'll do my best to keep my eyes on today, not yesterday. Amen.

THINK ABOUT IT:

*What can you do today to
put the past in the past?*

Morning
WHEN I SAY GOODBYE

*Her children arise and call her
blessed; her husband also, and he
praises her: "Many women do noble
things, but you surpass them all."*

PROVERBS 31:28–29 NIV

Lord, when I say a final goodbye to this
old world—and I know that day will come
for all of us—I wonder what people will
say about me. When they gather to say
a handful of words that summarize my
years here, what will those words be?
How will friends and relatives remember
me? For my wisdom and acts of kindness
and faith? Or will their memory recall a
woman of less virtue? Lord, help me in
this. I really do want to live a life that
reflects Your love. Help me to live in such
a noble way, to be such a reflection of
You that people will know me to be a
blessing wherever I go. Amen.

THINK ABOUT IT:

*How do you want to be remembered?
How can you become more of a
blessing—to God and others?*

Evening
TONIGHT, I AM
THAT WAVE

*But when you ask, you must believe
and not doubt, because the one
who doubts is like a wave of the sea,
blown and tossed by the wind.*

JAMES 1:6 NIV

Oh dear Lord, tonight I confess that I am
that wave You talk about in James 1:6.
Forgive me. My doubts are causing me to
get hammered and hurled by the wind.
When this occurs, why is it usually in the
night? Is it because there is no light or
warmth from the sun? Is it because Satan
works harder to discourage us because
he knows we feel more vulnerable in the
darkness? Or do we think that slumber
seems like a form of death, and secretly, it
frightens us? Whatever the reason, Lord,
I ask You to calm those waves of doubts
and fear right now with Your supernatural
power. In Jesus' name I pray. Amen.

THINK ABOUT IT:

*When do doubts plague you,
and how do you handle them?
What scripture might you memorize
to help you fend off uncertainties?*

Morning
FEELING USED UP

Jesus replied: " 'Love the Lord your God with all your heart and with all your soul and with all your mind.' This is the first and greatest commandment."

MATTHEW 22:37–38 NIV

I admit, God, that there are days I don't feel loved by my family. They come to me for requests—a mother lode of them. They come to me for help, cash, new toys, cash, clean socks, cash. I feel used up at times. I recently had this niggling thought: Is this what my prayer time looks like? You know, when I ask for more and more stuff to make my life smoother, healthier, better—and maybe a little richer? Sometimes I forget to be Your child. To just love You as *I* always dream of being loved by others. Forgive me, Lord. Remind me to run into Your loving arms. To be still at times and know You are God. To love and be loved by You. Amen.

THINK ABOUT IT:

What ways can you show God how much you love Him?

Evening
TIME IN ETERNITY

You make known to me the path of life; you will fill me with joy in your presence, with eternal pleasures at your right hand.

PSALM 16:11 NIV

From a young age, Lord, we realize that somewhere a clock is ticking, ever counting time, reminding us of closure. Although I find joy in a blossoming fragrant rose, I watch it fade all too quickly. And as I relish an achingly beautiful passage of music, I know with lingering sadness that it too must end. All the memorable, beautiful moments come to a close. But I thank You, Lord, that there is life beyond this transitory earth! I choose You, Jesus, as my Lord of all; and in doing so, I choose eternity with You, where beauty, delight, and wonder will never fade or end. So I'm going to stop obsessing over that clock now, because You and I have forever together. Amen.

THINK ABOUT IT:

Have you chosen Christ as your Savior? Do you celebrate your eternal heritage?

Morning
THE EPIC BATTLE

For our struggle is not against flesh and blood, but against the rulers, against the authorities, against the powers of this dark world and against the spiritual forces of evil in the heavenly realms.

EPHESIANS 6:12 NIV

All is quiet in the house, Lord, as I come before You. My heart content, I take joy in Your presence and feel Your everlasting peace. But I sense an epic battle raging around us in the spiritual realm. So I pray for me and my family members, Lord, that You would place Your divine protection around each of us: physically, mentally, and spiritually. Please watch over us so that we might go out into the world—to fulfill our calling, to delight in Your wondrous creation, and to proclaim Your good news—but without giving in to the temptations of this world or surrendering to the enemy! Amen.

THINK ABOUT IT:

What are some earthly manifestations of this spiritual battle, and in what ways has it influenced your family? What scriptures can you memorize to keep you and your thoughts in God's light?

Evening
YOU DELIGHT IN ME?

"The LORD your God is with you, the Mighty Warrior who saves. He will take great delight in you; in his love he will no longer rebuke you, but will rejoice over you with singing."

ZEPHANIAH 3:17 NIV

That's a mind-boggling thought, Lord—that You take delight in me. I know I take merry pleasure in my kids. In their funny peekaboo antics under their makeshift tent made of blankets. Their crayon masterpieces, which are currently on exhibit, taped to the refrigerator door. Their giddy, skipping runs as they make a kite lift off the ground and fly into the wild blue yonder. I love it. Is that the way You see me, Lord? With genuine delight? Hard to imagine, and yet my spirit longs to understand this truth and celebrate it. Praise You, Lord, for Your love. It inspires me, woos me, comforts and sustains me. Amen.

THINK ABOUT IT:

What are some of the ways you bring God delight?

Morning
YOU ARE MINDFUL OF ME

*When I consider your heavens,
the work of your fingers, the moon
and the stars, which you have set
in place, what is mankind that
you are mindful of them, human
beings that you care for them?*

PSALM 8:3–4 NIV

Thank You, Lord, that You are mindful of me and my family. That You care for us deeply. When I think of the vastness of Your heavens, I am filled with profound awe, and I wonder how it is that You can love us all so dearly—as if we are each a priceless treasure. Thank You for humbling Yourself to be born into our world, to live among us, and then to sacrifice everything for our good. Thank You for Your precious gift. . .Your unfathomable love. Amen.

THINK ABOUT IT:

*What are the various ways you
experience God's love for you?
How does His love change your life?*

Evening
WITH ALL YOUR HEART

*Whatever you do, work at it with
all your heart, as working for the
Lord, not for human masters.*

COLOSSIANS 3:23 NIV

One of the many things our society needs is balance, Lord—even in the area of work. Some people choose to work so little they aren't able to feed their families, while others make their careers such a top priority that they hardly get to *see* their families! Neither one of those ways is going to work properly. Please help me to be an example of Your biblical teachings. Show me how to encourage my children to live by working with all their heart for *You*, not their overseers, that they might know the pleasure that comes from pleasing You! In Jesus' name I pray. Amen.

THINK ABOUT IT:

*What is a chore that you can do
together with your children that
could create a teachable moment
concerning this topic of how you,
as God's children, should view work?*

Morning
INDEED, JUST PASSING THROUGH

For our light and momentary troubles are achieving for us an eternal glory that far outweighs them all.

2 CORINTHIANS 4:17 NIV

I am so weary, Lord. My burden seems too heavy, the pain too intense, and the grief and loss too much to bear. Be very near me, Jesus, in all I am going through. Tenderly remind me that we are merely sojourners in this life. We are indeed just passing through. As a Christian, I have the assurance that after these dusty travels are finally done, my home is in heaven. "Home, sweet home" will have a new, profound meaning, beauty beyond belief, and there will be an eternity of joy unspeakable! Thank You for that promise, Lord, and the peace it brings. In Jesus' name I pray. Amen.

THINK ABOUT IT:

What are you looking forward to most about heaven?

Evening
THE STONES WILL CRY OUT

"Blessed is the king who comes in the name of the Lord!" "Peace in heaven and glory in the highest!" Some of the Pharisees in the crowd said to Jesus, "Teacher, rebuke your disciples!" "I tell you," he replied, "if they keep quiet, the stones will cry out."

LUKE 19:38–40 NIV

When I think of Your creation, Lord, and Your miracles, Your unfailing love, and Your death on the cross for my redemption, I want to raise my hands in praise. All of creation exalts You, and so should I! When I get the spiritual nudge to do so, let me raise my voice to praise You, Lord. May I sing a new song and even dance before You as David did. For You are the King of kings and Lord of lords. May all glory and honor and praise be Yours. Hallelujah! Amen.

THINK ABOUT IT:

What are some ways you can praise God for all He has done for you and your family?

Morning
HOLY EXPECTATIONS

He has told you, O man, what is good;
and what does the Lord require of you
but to do justice, and to love kindness,
and to walk humbly with your God?

MICAH 6:8 ESV

Life is full of expectations, Lord. Personal expectations on who to be and what to achieve. The expectations of others. How easy it is to feel as though I'm not living up to expectations, especially as a Christian. Am I *enough* for You, Lord? When Satan leads me to doubt myself, remind me of Your desire for my life. You want something deeper than an outward display of righteousness. You require a willing heart, a commitment to do Your will. All good works flow from a heart dedicated to You. May my expectation always be to remain humbly by Your side. Amen.

THINK ABOUT IT:

When you think about pleasing God,
does your mind go to outward behavior
first or to the state of your heart?

Evening
MIDDLE GROUND

Give me neither poverty nor riches;
feed me with the food that is needful for
me, lest I be full and deny you and say,
"Who is the LORD?" or lest I be poor and
steal and profane the name of my God.

PROVERBS 30:8–9 ESV

Father, how often do I pray for just enough? Not as often as I should. While I don't pray for poverty, I have prayed for better. More. Whether more work or more friends or more security. . .I forget that what You provide is enough. I don't desire to be in want, Father, but I also know that having more than enough can lead me to bypass the one who daily showers provision on me. Keep me humbly reliant upon Your care. Be my sufficiency. Turn this heart toward contentment in the "just enough" that You provide. Amen.

THINK ABOUT IT:

Do the words of the proverb make
you rethink your requests of God?

Morning
COUNTING THE COST

"For which of you, desiring to build a tower, does not first sit down and count the cost, whether he has enough to complete it?"

LUKE 14:28 ESV

Lord, thank You for the free gift of salvation! But remind me, Lord, that while salvation is through faith alone, saving faith is more than a prayer and then continuing on in the same way as before. It requires a total commitment to You—a giving up of me for Your sake. As Your disciple, I should not harbor sin—but come to You in genuine repentance. I should not cling to what this earth offers—but center my security on what You promise. I must be willing to follow where You lead. Impossible? Through my own efforts, yes; but through the sovereign work of Your Holy Spirit, I am saved! Amen.

THINK ABOUT IT:

What might discipleship cost you?

Evening
ASK FOR IT

If any of you lacks wisdom, let him ask God, who gives generously to all without reproach, and it will be given him. But let him ask in faith, with no doubting, for the one who doubts is like a wave of the sea that is driven and tossed by the wind.

JAMES 1:5–6 ESV

Wisdom, Father, can be elusive. What is Your will for my life? How do I handle the trials this world throws at me with joy and grace? My lack of wisdom draws me ever closer to You. You have all the answers because You have written my life's story. Today I want to ask for wisdom, Father. But before I do, I need a boost in faith. In my head, I say I trust You; please root out any doubt residing in my heart. Let greater wisdom begin with realizing my need for You in all things. Amen.

THINK ABOUT IT:

Do you ever find yourself asking God for wisdom but doubting He'll supply it?

Morning
GOD IN GLORY

*But God forbid that I should glory,
save in the cross of our Lord Jesus
Christ, by whom the world is crucified
unto me, and I unto the world.*

GALATIANS 6:14 KJV

Father, it is so easy to focus on personal success, even when I'm serving You. It is so easy to rejoice in what I've done individually, what we've done as a church, when in reality all success comes from above. Keep us humble. Keep us centered on the cross. Gently remind us that success is for You, through You alone. A boost in attendance or a friend led to Jesus. Increased giving and new opportunities. In our worship services. In my path in life. For me and for my church, Father, may our successes always point to You. May I shout with joy in response to all *You've* done. Amen.

THINK ABOUT IT:

*To whom is your applause directed
when an individual or your church
family accomplishes something?*

Evening
SPIRITUAL TRAINING

*Train yourself for godliness; for while
bodily training is of some value,
godliness is of value in every way,
as it holds promise for the present
life and also for the life to come.*

1 TIMOTHY 4:7–8 ESV

A body in motion is a good thing, Father. You designed us for movement. I want to be healthy, but I don't want to make physical fitness alone my goal. I should care for my body while recognizing the limits. My body can only do so much. And the rewards of physical training only last on this earth, and illness and injury can quickly sweep them away. Training in Your ways provides strength and stamina to withstand the marathon of life and to serve You fully. One day this earthly body will become a heavenly body adorned with the rewards of a life lived for You. Amen.

THINK ABOUT IT:

*Do you see fitness or godliness
as having greater value?*

Morning
WITHOUT SIGHT

Jesus said to him, "Have you believed because you have seen me? Blessed are those who have not seen and yet have believed."

JOHN 20:29 ESV

Lord Jesus, we can all be Thomas at times. We ask for signs. We want proof. If only we could touch Your nail-pierced hands. . . The truth is believing without seeing is hard. You knew this. You knew that many believers would come to faith without seeing You, the proof of Your resurrection, until heaven. So You spoke words of encouragement. By believing without seeing, I am blessed. And You have not left me without the help of Your Spirit. You "show" Yourself to me in countless ways. Through Your provision. Through Your faithful presence in my life. Through the beauty of Your creation. Through answered prayers. Lord, You are undeniable. Amen.

THINK ABOUT IT:
How do you believe without physically seeing Christ?

Evening
GOD THE GARDENER

"I am the true vine, and my Father is the vinedresser. Every branch in me that does not bear fruit he takes away, and every branch that does bear fruit he prunes, that it may bear more fruit."

JOHN 15:1–2 ESV

Father, every day is a chance to grow as a Christian and to bear fruit for You. It can be frustrating when I don't seem to make as much progress as I want to or think I should make. Remind me that You are always working, pruning me to become more like Your Son, Jesus. Often the pruning isn't pretty at first, but in time the branch will grow, the buds will appear, and my life will bear more fruit. Thank You for Your loving care, that You do not settle for what is but guide me toward fullness and beauty in You. Amen.

THINK ABOUT IT:
In what areas of your life is God the vinedresser working?

Morning
EVER THE SAME

*Jesus Christ is the same
yesterday and today and forever.*
HEBREWS 13:8 ESV

Lord, change is a natural and often necessary part of life. From the moment of our conception, we grow. From day to day, year to year, life stage to life stage, we change. Change can bring new perspectives; it can clear paths to new experiences. But also inherent in change is uncertainty. Not knowing can be scary, Father. When the changes in my life cause me to shrink back, stand close by my side. You are there even now! I can rely on Your presence and unchanging nature amid the uncertainty. Thank You for remaining constant. I don't have to wonder what Your future character will be. I already know. Amen.

THINK ABOUT IT:

*Which of God's traits (His love,
His faithfulness, His power,
His omniscience, His goodness. . .)
steady you when you face
life's upheavals?*

Evening
THE WALLS CAME TUMBLING DOWN

*By faith the walls of Jericho
fell down after they had been
encircled for seven days.*
HEBREWS 11:30 ESV

Lord, Your military strategy to conquer Jericho probably seemed crazy to the Israelites. But as they followed Your command and the walls fell down, they had no doubt that You were the strength behind their victory. I desire to follow Your will for my life, Lord. But when following means meeting with barriers, remind me that You are able to do wondrously more than I can imagine, even when the obstacles seem insurmountable and Your ways crazy. Your wisdom is beyond comprehension. You see the beginning and the end, and You desire only the best for me. May I trust You completely in faith. Amen.

THINK ABOUT IT:

*Do you believe that God's instructions
for living life and His plan for
you will yield the best results—
better than you can imagine?*

Morning
HE ALREADY KNOWS

*All my longings lie open
before you, Lord; my sighing
is not hidden from you.*

PSALM 38:9 NIV

Father, You see my heart, don't You? You know every thought, every fear, every anxiety. When I sigh, You hear. When I cry, You feel every tear. You know how I struggle with worry. Lord, I want to give things to You. I want to let go and trust You with everything, but those thoughts just keep coming back. Help me to breathe in Your peace, breathe out my fear and anxiety. When worry takes over my thoughts, remind me that You've got it all under control. I know the struggle may continue, but right now, in this moment, I give it all to You. I trust You, Father. I lay it all down, open before You.

THINK ABOUT IT:

*What worries plague you right now?
God already knows. Give them to Him.*

Evening
DO NOT WORRY

*"Therefore I tell you, do not worry
about your life, what you will eat or
drink; or about your body, what you
will wear. Is not life more than food,
and the body more than clothes?"*

MATTHEW 6:25 NIV

The command not to worry is a hard one for me. I wish there were an on/off switch. I'd gladly turn off my anxiety permanently if I could. But every time I think I have a hold on my anxious thoughts, worry sneaks back in. The truth is I know You'll take care of me. You always have. Even when bad things happen, You work them out for my ultimate good. I know the worry-free life is a discipline, and I have to work at it. Have patience with me, Lord, and teach me to let go. Teach me to soak in the peace You give to those who trust You completely.

THINK ABOUT IT:

*What physical things, such as food
and clothing, do you worry about?*

Morning
BLESSABLE

"Now therefore, if you will obey my voice and keep my covenant, you shall be my own possession among all peoples; for all the earth is mine."

EXODUS 19:5 RSV

That little word *if* holds such power. Here, You made a promise, but a condition is attached. You said You'd take care of things if Your people obeyed You. In other words, You'd bless them if they chose to be blessable. Sometimes I worry and fret about why things aren't going my way, when I should really be asking if I'm upholding my end of things. I know salvation doesn't come by works, but that does not negate my responsibility to obey You in all things. Thank You for Your promises and Your blessings, Lord. Help me to be obedient. I want to be blessable.

THINK ABOUT IT:

How can you become more blessable today? In what areas can you obey God better?

Evening
DWELL AMONG US

"I will dwell among the people of Israel, and will be their God. And they shall know that I am the Lord their God, who brought them forth out of the land of Egypt that I might dwell among them; I am the Lord their God."

EXODUS 29:45–46 RSV

Dear Father, as I read this promise You made to dwell among the people of Israel, I want my family to be included. Please dwell among my people. Be our God. Just as You brought the Israelites out of bondage, You've brought us through so much. Keep my family, my friends, and all my loved ones close to You, Lord. Walk with us, stay in our thoughts, and guide us. For all the people in my circle who don't know You or aren't walking with You, draw them in, Father. Be our God. Mark us as Yours, and don't let us go.

THINK ABOUT IT:

Who are you worried about today? Call them by name, and ask God to stay close to them.

Morning
LITTLE LIES

Do not lie to each other, since you have taken off your old self with its practices.
COLOSSIANS 3:9 NIV

Lies slip out of my mouth so easily sometimes, Lord. Not big lies. Not lies that would hurt anyone (or at least that's what I tell myself). Just the little lies that make a conversation go a little easier—or that make a story more interesting. All people tell those sorts of lies, don't they? And yet, Lord, when I read the Bible, I can't help but notice that You take the truth seriously. Dishonesty may be common in the world, but it's not Your way. So teach me to guard my tongue. Remind me that the truth matters. Show me the ways my little lies spring from my old self, the version of me that cared more about herself than she did God or anyone else. I want to be true to You and to the person You created me to be.

THINK ABOUT IT:

Why do you think honesty is so important to God? Do even "little lies" have the potential to do harm?

Evening
BUTTERCUPS AND DANDELIONS

"If God gives such attention to the wildflowers, most of them never even seen, don't you think he'll attend to you, take pride in you, do his best for you?"
LUKE 12:28 MSG

I know the Bible promises that You will take care of Your people, Lord. It promises that You love me and that You will never leave me. It promises so many wonderful things! But right now, I'm having a hard time believing that those promises mean anything. They seem like wishful thinking. They're too good to be true. And then I look at the beauty of an ordinary flower, a buttercup or a dandelion, and I see how intricate the petals are, how perfectly designed, each one a tiny miracle of loveliness. That flower is just one small evidence of Your love at work in the universe. It's a reminder to me that You are present everywhere, Your love constantly on the move to bring beauty and hope into our world. My doubts are just clouds in my head; they don't represent reality. You always keep Your promises.

THINK ABOUT IT:

When do doubts multiply in your mind? Is there anything you can do that will help you remain more confident in God's love and care?

Morning
HEAVY BURDENS

"Come to Me, all who are weary and burdened, and I will give you rest."
MATTHEW 11:28 NASB

Oh God, my life is just so *hard* lately. Work is a constant stress, my family has been sick, I can't seem to shake this cold, my friend and I had an argument, and the dog ate my best pair of shoes I was planning to wear to a wedding. All those things may sound so small, I know, but together they pile up. They make a heavy load on my shoulders. I'm so tired of lugging it around. Every morning, I wish I didn't have to get up and deal with so many challenges. I wish instead I could just curl up and sleep a little longer. But I can't—so, Lord, help me out. Take the many challenges of my life into Your capable hands, I pray. Thank You that You are big enough to carry them all.

THINK ABOUT IT:

Are you willing to let God carry your burdens? What would you need to do to release them into His hands?

Evening
A CROWN OF LIFE

God blesses those who patiently endure testing and temptation. Afterward they will receive the crown of life that God has promised to those who love him.
JAMES 1:12 NLT

Thank You, loving Father, that I never have to be ashamed to bring my temptations to You. You understand that I'm weak, and You don't condemn me. You are always there at my side, waiting to help me. So once again, Lord, here I am, asking for Your help. I don't want to rely on alcohol to get me through life; I just want You. So show me how to endure the temptation to drink (without giving in to it). Remind me that I want Your crown of life far more than I want to drink.

THINK ABOUT IT:

What does the phrase "crown of life" mean to you? In what ways does God crown you with life?

Morning
DEEP SECURITY

The LORD is my light and my salvation; whom shall I fear? the LORD is the strength of my life; of whom shall I be afraid?

PSALM 27:1 KJV

You know my past, Lord. You know how hard it is for me to trust people. Even with the people I love most, I'm always half expecting them to let me down. I'm always waiting for the little signs that will tell me they've stabbed me in the back in one way or another. God, I know my distrust is coming between me and the people I want to be close to. It's even coming between me and You. Deep down inside, I'm just plain scared. Remind me, I pray, that it doesn't matter what other people do—You are the one who will keep me safe. I don't need to be scared about other people letting me down, because You never will.

THINK ABOUT IT:

If trust comes hard to you because of your past, can you ask God to give you a deep security that's rooted in Him?

Evening
GOD'S PROTECTION

Even when I walk through the darkest valley, I will not be afraid, for you are close beside me. Your rod and your staff protect and comfort me.

PSALM 23:4 NLT

I'm tired of being hurt, Lord. I'm sick of being criticized. I feel so small, so broken. This man I love says he loves me, and I believe he does—but he also hurts me. He's robbed me of my confidence in myself. He's forced me to live a secret life, hiding my bruises from the people who love me. I feel ashamed, afraid, angry, and just so hurt, right down to my bones. How can the person who says he loves me most be the person who hurts me most? Is this my fault, God? Do I deserve his anger? But no, I hear Your gentle voice whispering to my heart: I did nothing to deserve this. You don't want me to be hurt like this. Oh God, help me. I am in the darkest valley I've ever known; lead me out into the light. I'm afraid; stay close beside me. Protect me and guide me; show me what steps to take. Give me the courage to walk into the freedom and safety You want for me.

THINK ABOUT IT:

A shepherd's rod and staff were used to protect the sheep from dangers. Can you imagine the Good Shepherd using His rod and staff as you seek help for your situation?

Morning
GOD NEVER GETS TIRED

The Lord is the everlasting God,
the Creator of the ends of the earth.
He will not grow tired or weary, and
his understanding no one can fathom.
He gives strength to the weary and
increases the power of the weak.

ISAIAH 40:28–29 NIV

I feel utterly helpless, Lord. I don't know what to do to fix this situation—and if I *did* know what to do, I'm not sure I'd have the strength to follow through. These circumstances are simply too big and too complicated for my abilities. So I'm glad, God of power and might, that I can turn to You. If You created the world, You can certainly handle the situation I'm facing. Thank You that You are never too tired to help me. Thank You that Your wisdom is infinite. Lead me, I pray. Give me the strength and insight I need to address this problem. I know I can't do it without You.

THINK ABOUT IT:

When you look at creation, does
that give you greater confidence in
God's ability to act on your behalf?

Evening
ENEMIES OF LOVE

For I am persuaded, that neither death,
nor life, nor angels, nor principalities,
nor powers, nor things present, nor
things to come, nor height, nor depth,
nor any other creature, shall be able
to separate us from the love of God,
which is in Christ Jesus our Lord.

ROMANS 8:38–39 KJV

I took a stand for justice, Lord. I spoke out for love, and I stood firm, believing You stood with me. But now people are angry with me. They feel threatened by my words. They don't like the company I keep. I've made enemies—real enemies who would harm me physically if they could. Their threats scared me. But God, I know they can do nothing to separate me from Your love. No matter what happens, my spirit is safe with You. Your love wraps around me and holds me close. Please continue to use me to speak Your truth.

THINK ABOUT IT:

Do you trust God enough to stand
with Him even when it's dangerous?

Morning
BRINGING GOOD CHEER

*Anxiety weighs down the heart,
but a kind word cheers it up.*
PROVERBS 12:25 NIV

I love kind people, Lord! They usually come along at just the right time with a cheerful word. Just one pat on the back, one positive, affirming word, and my entire situation seems to change. Even if the circumstances don't, my attitude does—and that's half the battle. There is great power in the spoken word.

I want to be that kind of person, Father—one who goes around giving pats on the back and speaking encouraging, uplifting words. Stresses will disappear if the world is flooded with encouragers. Help me as I set out on a path to minister to others in this way, I pray. May I penetrate people's hearts with kindness. Amen.

THINK ABOUT IT:

*Who can you cheer up
today with a kind word?*

Evening
SUCH LOVE

You have searched me, LORD, and you know me. You know when I sit and when I rise; you perceive my thoughts from afar. You discern my going out and my lying down; you are familiar with all my ways. Before a word is on my tongue you, LORD, know it completely. You hem me in behind and before, and you lay your hand upon me. Such knowledge is too wonderful for me, too lofty for me to attain.
PSALM 139:1-6 NIV

Oh Lord, when I read Your love note to me in Psalm 139, I can't contain my delight— that You could love me so dearly. You not only created me but continue to know every detail surrounding my life. And You still love me and want to be with me! Yes, such knowledge is too wonderful for me to understand, but oh, how I love to hear it. Thank You, Lord. Amen.

THINK ABOUT IT:

What are some ways God has shown His love for you and your family?

Morning
I WILL LISTEN

"Then you will call on me and come and pray to me, and I will listen to you."
JEREMIAH 29:12 NIV

Oh Lord, I am weary from the clamor and chatter of this world. Everyone seems to be shouting these days, desperate to be heard. They want us to listen, to understand, to empathize. . .all day, every day. I am about to collapse from all the appeals and demands, but then I see Your divine words: "I will listen." Those have to be three of the most beautiful words ever put together. Imagine, You, the Creator of the universe, are willing to listen to me, whether I'm having a fine day or a foul one. Thank You, Lord, for this most precious blessing called "listening." Amen.

THINK ABOUT IT:

Why do you think God wants to listen to His children? What are some of the things you need to talk to Him about today?

Evening
GOD'S WORD

And after fasting forty days and forty nights, he was hungry. And the tempter came and said to him, "If you are the Son of God, command these stones to become loaves of bread." But he answered, "It is written, 'Man shall not live by bread alone, but by every word that comes from the mouth of God.' "
MATTHEW 4:2–4 ESV

I know I can overcome temptation by filling my mind with Your Word. The more of the Word of God I know, the easier it is to recall scripture at times when I'm tempted. One of my weakest areas is the temptation to worry and not trust You. Satan tempted Jesus with bread when He was hungry, and he tempts me with worry when I'm stressed, anxious, and weak. Help me as I discipline myself to spend time in Your Word. Bring appropriate scriptures to my mind when I'm tempted to worry.

THINK ABOUT IT:

How much time do you spend reading God's Word? Plan today to read it regularly.

Morning
YOU'VE OVERCOME THE WORLD!

"I have said these things to you, that in me you may have peace. In the world you will have tribulation. But take heart; I have overcome the world."

JOHN 16:33 ESV

In this world, I have had trouble. In this world, I have had heartache. Pain. Confusion. Turmoil. In this world, I've been tempted, tried, and wounded.

But You, Lord? You have overcome the world. I don't have to be stressed when trouble comes. I don't have to give in to fear. There's no reason for me to panic when things don't go my way, because You have overcome all of it. There's no problem I will face that You haven't already overcome. So today I reaffirm my trust in You. I place my hand in the hand of the ultimate overcomer! Amen.

THINK ABOUT IT:

Jesus said these things specifically so that you would have peace. Can you sense His love for you?

Evening
DEAD MAN WALKING

After Jesus said this, he cried out in a loud voice, "Lazarus, come out!" The dead man came out, his hands and feet wrapped with pieces of cloth, and a cloth around his face.

JOHN 11:43–44 NCV

Why do I waste time worrying about things, Lord? If You could raise Lazarus from the dead, if You could lift sick people off their sickbeds, then why would I think You wouldn't lift me too?

In so many ways, I can relate to the Lazarus story. I've never been physically dead, but there have been times when I felt like everything had come to an end for me. When I wondered if there was hope. But You're a hope-giver! You roll away stones. You lift my weary head. You turn situations around.

Today I'm "coming forth"—from my worries, my anxieties, my fears. I'm coming forth to new life, new hope in You. How I praise You for new beginnings, Lord! Amen.

THINK ABOUT IT:

Has Jesus ever raised you from the dead?

Morning
AUNT GERTRUDE

*"But I tell you, love your enemies and
pray for those who persecute you."*
MATTHEW 5:44 NIV

Life can be sailing along so beautifully,
Lord, and I'm thinking I'm a pretty good
Christian woman—then along comes Aunt
Gertrude. Honestly, she is a barrel of terrible, and she rolls right over me! I guess
everybody has an Aunt Gertrude in their
lives. No matter how hard it is, I will trust
You are working out our relationship for
good. Perhaps I am to learn the lesson
of humility. Or I'm to rely on Your divine
patience and discover the art of loving the
unlovable. Or maybe You want me to pray
for Aunt Gertrude. Thank You for Your
gentle reminder to love those who seem
to be my enemies and persecute me. And
may my children see their mother taking
all her cares—even Aunt Gertrude—to You,
Lord. Amen.

THINK ABOUT IT:

*Do you have someone in your life
who is like Aunt Gertrude? If so, how
do you deal with the strife? What is
God teaching you in this situation?*

Evening
I LOVE STUFF

*When you ask, you do not receive,
because you ask with wrong
motives, that you may spend what
you get on your pleasures.*
JAMES 4:3 NIV

I love stuff, Lord. Doesn't everybody?
We're told by some very knowledgeable
advertising folks that we won't live well
without a certain quantity of merchan-
dise. Of course, later that same stuff
ends up on a high shelf so I can't see the
mental stamp of SILLY all over it. Maybe
the reason some of my prayers don't get
answered the way I hope is because my
motives aren't always right. That is, I'm
too busy asking for more stuff for my own
pleasure. My children are watching me!
Help me, Lord, to bring my prayer life into
alignment with Your will, not mine. And
allow my children to learn this important
lesson—that sometimes we don't get what
we ask for because we're asking with the
wrong motives—along with me. Amen.

THINK ABOUT IT:

*Do you have the right motives
when you pray? If not, how can
you improve with the Lord's help?*

Morning
CHEER UP, SELF!

When the cares of my heart are many,
your consolations cheer my soul.
PSALM 94:19 ESV

I remember when I was a kid, Lord, how my schoolteacher would say, "Turn that frown upside down!" It only takes a second or two to change a scowl into a smile, and when the edges of my lips tip up, so does my attitude.

Today I'm asking for a lips-tipped-up sort of day. Even though my cares are many, You can still cheer my soul. I take refuge in You, in Your Word, and in Your care. You've got me covered, so why should I fret?

Cheer up, self! That's my motto of the day. Thanks for shifting my attitude, Lord! Amen.

THINK ABOUT IT:

When was the last time you had to cheer yourself up (spiritually and emotionally)?

Evening
I WON'T FAINT

If you faint in the day of adversity,
your strength is small.
PROVERBS 24:10 ESV

Okay, I'll admit it: I give up too easily! Sometimes I "faint in the day of adversity," as Your Word says, Lord. I see a mountain in front of me, and it looms larger than life. Scaling it seems impossible. Instead of speaking to it and expecting it to move, I cower in fear.

Increase my faith today, I pray! I don't want my strength to be small. I want it to be bigger than any mountain and stronger too! I want to be able to look at mountains and speak to them in Jesus' name then watch them tumble into the sea. Thanks for being a mountain-mover, Lord! Amen.

THINK ABOUT IT:

What are your near-to-fainting triggers?

Morning
REBUILDING

*I also told them about the gracious
hand of my God on me and what
the king had said to me. They
replied, "Let us start rebuilding."
So they began this good work.*

NEHEMIAH 2:18 NIV

Sometimes the tasks in front of me seem too big to take on, Lord. I get overwhelmed just thinking about all the work that needs to be done. I get stressed, which only complicates matters.

Then I'm reminded of the biblical greats, people like Nehemiah. They faced huge obstacles and encountered massive challenges, but they forged ahead and saw great rewards in the end.

When I read about the rebuilding of the wall, I begin to see things from Your perspective, Lord. You've given me big tasks, yes, but You've given me all the tools I need to accomplish what's in front of me to do. I'm so grateful You've made provision for the big things! Amen.

THINK ABOUT IT:
What has God rebuilt in your life?

Evening
THE ROCK

*"He is like a man building a house,
who dug deep and laid the foundation
on the rock. And when a flood
arose, the stream broke against
that house and could not shake it,
because it had been well built."*

LUKE 6:48 ESV

The wise man built his house upon the rock. I remember singing that song as a child, Lord. Those who are wise choose You as the foundation for their lives. Nothing has changed from childhood until now. If I want to be successful in any realm of life, then I need to keep my trust in You, not myself. When I hyperfocus on myself, I'm like the man building his house on sand. Everything is bound to crumble.

I'm done with crumbling. I'm done with a self-focused life. From now on, my house will be built on the Rock. Thank You for keeping my spiritual house standing strong, Lord! Amen.

THINK ABOUT IT:
Is your spiritual house well built?

DAY 137

Morning
IN ONE EAR

But be doers of the word, and not hearers only, deceiving yourselves. . . . The one who looks into the perfect law, the law of liberty, and perseveres, being no hearer who forgets but a doer who acts, he will be blessed for his doing.
JAMES 1:22, 25 ESV

Father, as I read my Bible, I pray that the words would penetrate deeper than hearing and begin to change me. As I meditate on Your holy Word, may the truths resonate in my heart and prompt action—to conform my ways to Your ways. You offer freedom from the bondage of sin. Oh, that I would not hear the good news and fail to thrive in total obedience to Your Word. When the Holy Spirit convicts, Father, may I be quick to respond. Your Spirit will strengthen me as I act, and through my obedience I am blessed. Amen.

THINK ABOUT IT:
How swift are you to apply the truths of God's Word to your life?

Evening
FRIEND OF GOD

Whoever wishes to be a friend of the world makes himself an enemy of God. Or do you suppose it is to no purpose that the Scripture says, "He yearns jealously over the spirit that he has made to dwell in us"? But he gives more grace.
JAMES 4:4–6 ESV

Father, You held back nothing to save me. Through the blood of Your beloved Son, You made a way for me to reach You. You *want* a relationship with me. My only response should be total commitment to You. How You must feel when I choose my ways over Your ways, even for a moment! Forgive me, Father. I owe my all to You, not just the parts that are easy to surrender. Show me where I am clinging to the world and not to my faith. Pour out Your grace as I learn to humbly follow You. You are worthy of nothing less and abundantly more. Amen.

THINK ABOUT IT:
Do you see God as deserving your entire being?

Morning
ACTIVE FAITH

But as for you, O man of God. . . .
Pursue righteousness, godliness,
faith, love, steadfastness, gentleness.
Fight the good fight of the faith.
Take hold of the eternal life to which
you were called and about which
you made the good confession in
the presence of many witnesses.

1 TIMOTHY 6:11–12 ESV

Father, I love Paul's words to Timothy. The faith that he describes is not idle. It is dynamic. Timothy should *pursue, fight, take hold of*. . . . He should not sit back and remain static in his life of faith but be actively involved in it. Father, remind me of these verses each morning. Keep me from complacency where I no longer seek to grow. May I chase after what You desire in my life. May I deepen my faith even in the darkness. May I always focus on heaven and what it means for me here on earth. Amen.

THINK ABOUT IT:
What action is God
calling you to in your life?

Evening
STILL REJOICE

Though the fig tree should not blossom,
nor fruit be on the vines, the produce
of the olive fail and the fields yield
no food, the flock be cut off from the
fold and there be no herd in the stalls,
yet I will rejoice in the LORD; I will take
joy in the God of my salvation.

HABAKKUK 3:17–18 ESV

Lord, most of us want some measure of predictability in our lives. We want the crops to yield in their time and for the harvest to be great. But prosperity is not a guarantee, and neither is a "normal" life. Hardship will happen; disruptions occur. Yet as the prophet declares, it does not need to leave us sapped of joy. You are still Lord and our salvation. We can rejoice in that fact, come what may. Amen.

THINK ABOUT IT:
Have challenging circumstances
in your life made it difficult
for you to rejoice in God?

Morning
LABOR SHORTAGE

Then he said to his disciples, "The harvest is plentiful, but the laborers are few; therefore pray earnestly to the Lord of the harvest to send out laborers into his harvest."

MATTHEW 9:37–38 ESV

Father, there is no shortage of souls in need of Your salvation. Every human being is unrighteous apart from Christ and the cross. You rescue us from sin and welcome Your saved ones into Your family. More than that, You have made every Christian an integral part of Your plan to reconcile lives to You. What a privilege! May I be a bold witness to Your grace. And may I persistently pray for others who share the good news. Father, You are Lord of the harvest; send out laborers that all may hear of You. Amen.

THINK ABOUT IT:

Are petitions for the spread of the gospel a regular part of your prayer life?

Evening
A GOD LIKE NO OTHER

Who is a God like you. . . ? He does not retain his anger forever, because he delights in steadfast love. He will again have compassion on us; he will tread our iniquities underfoot. You will cast all our sins into the depths of the sea.

MICAH 7:18–19 ESV

Lord, Your love is unimaginable. That You would send Your perfect, beloved Son to die for sinners. . . That You would sacrifice so much for those who can give so little in return. . . It seems incredible. Then I read the words in Micah about Your forgiveness toward Your people, and I am even more amazed. You have compassion *again*. Your love is steadfast. Your grace is forever. Thank You. May my life be living gratitude. As I kneel before You, may I be humbled by all that You are. You are unlike any other, Lord. Amen.

THINK ABOUT IT:

What comes to mind when you consider God's unwavering compassion toward you?

Morning
EVEN THERE

If I take the wings of the morning and dwell in the uttermost parts of the sea, even there your hand shall lead me, and your right hand shall hold me.

PSALM 139:9–10 ESV

Father, no matter where I go, You are with me. I cannot wander beyond Your reach. I cannot stray out of Your care. You are everywhere always, and You are here beside me. But You are more than present. Your Word says You lead me—guiding me in Your ways, directing me according to Your will for my life. You hold me. . . drawing me to Your side, supporting me. And when I drift, I never have far to go to return to You. You have not abandoned me; You long for me to rest in Your presence. Thank You for Your faithfulness. Thank You for remaining close. Amen.

THINK ABOUT IT:

Do you believe that God is present in your life even when you have waned in your relationship with Him?

Evening
HE IS PATIENT

But do not overlook this one fact, beloved, that with the Lord one day is as a thousand years, and a thousand years as one day. The Lord is not slow to fulfill his promise as some count slowness, but is patient toward you.

2 PETER 3:8–9 ESV

Lord, You see differently than we do. Even Your sense of time differs from ours. You have promised to return soon, but *soon* will be in Your perfect timing. In Your great love, You are patient, desiring all who will come to You to find salvation. As I wait for Christ's return, place a burden on my heart to pray for those who have not yet met You as their Lord and Savior. May I be a partner in Your waiting through prayer. Thank You for not losing Your patience toward us, Lord. Amen.

THINK ABOUT IT:

How can you best use this time to impact the world for God's kingdom?

Morning
LET US REJOICE

Let the heavens be glad, and let the earth rejoice; let the sea roar, and all that fills it; let the field exult, and everything in it! Then shall all the trees of the forest sing for joy before the Lord, for he comes.

PSALM 96:11–13 ESV

Lord, Your creation is marvelous. Just thinking of the vast night sky, the power of the oceans, and the beauty of the land fills my mind with wonder. But as astounding as the natural world is now, it is nothing compared with the wonder of all creation celebrating Your return. You reign, and the heavens and earth will shout before You. As Your creation—as Your child—let me shout in adoration of You. You are worthy. Fill my heart with such a deep understanding of Your greatness that I never fail to praise You. For Your might. For Your goodness. For Your grace. I worship You. Amen.

THINK ABOUT IT:

What words of praise can you bring before God today?

Evening
LOVE IN DEED

Suppose someone has enough to live and sees a brother or sister in need, but does not help. Then God's love is not living in that person. My children, we should love people not only with words and talk, but by our actions and true caring.

1 JOHN 3:17–18 NCV

Father, *loving others* is a principle I often hear in church and read in Your Word. Loving others is what I want to do in response to Your great love for me. But if I'm honest, it can be easier to talk about reaching out in love than it is to actually reach out. Fear, inconvenience, selfishness. . .all ugly parts of my old nature, Father, but ones You can help me overcome. When I feel the pull of Your love to help someone, may I respond as Your hands and feet on earth, providing out of the blessings You have lavishly given me. Amen.

THINK ABOUT IT:

What simple—or big—ways can you share God's love with others?

Morning
HIS WORD REMAINS

All flesh is grass, and all its beauty is like the flower of the field. The grass withers, the flower fades when the breath of the Lord blows on it; surely the people are grass. The grass withers, the flower fades, but the word of our God will stand forever.

ISAIAH 40:6–8 ESV

Lord, a change in seasons makes the words of Isaiah so clear. Come fall, the lush grass of summer withers and lies dormant in winter; then fresh spring flowers fade as summer's heat takes over. Humans too age with time, our beauty fading. What a comfort to know that despite the changes all creation is destined to undergo, Your Word remains unchanged. Your plans and Your promises will not alter as the years pass. They endure as a firm foundation to uphold Your children. Your Word is trustworthy, Lord, and You are just as faithful. Amen.

THINK ABOUT IT:

How does the everlasting nature of God's Word encourage you through life changes?

Evening
BE READY

"Stay dressed for action and keep your lamps burning, and be like men who are waiting for their master to come home from the wedding feast, so that they may open the door to him at once when he comes and knocks. Blessed are those servants whom the master finds awake when he comes."

LUKE 12:35–37 ESV

Father, we women prepare many times in our lives. We get ready to go out in the morning. We schedule, plan, create. We wait for loved ones to return home. In all our busyness, let us not forget to be ready for the most important event: the return of Christ. Remind us, Father, of the words of Your Son. We should dress for action. Keep the lamps burning. Anticipate His second coming. I don't want to be idle or caught unawares on that day. Help me prepare my heart and center on You first. Amen.

THINK ABOUT IT:

Do you approach each day as if it could be the day of Christ's return?

Morning
TOTALLY DEVOTED

Do not love the world or the things in the world. . . . For all that is in the world—the desires of the flesh and the desires of the eyes and pride of life— is not from the Father but is from the world. And the world is passing away along with its desires, but whoever does the will of God abides forever.
1 JOHN 2:15–17 ESV

Lord, this world is full of distractions, distractions that Satan can use to keep me from living fully for You. From the things in the world—all the *stuff* I chase after—to the world's beliefs on how I should live, there is so much that can lead me astray. These things are not from You, Lord. And they are not here to stay. Nothing in my life should take priority over You. May I love You entirely and be devoted to You exclusively. Amen.

THINK ABOUT IT:
What does loving the world mean to you? To God?

Evening
PART OF GOD'S FAMILY

Sing to God, sing praises to his name; lift up a song to him who rides through the deserts; his name is the LORD; *exult before him! Father of the fatherless and protector of widows is God in his holy habitation. God settles the solitary in a home.*
PSALM 68:4–6 ESV

God, You are almighty; You reign. You are our heavenly Father too. You care about orphans and widows. You care that Your children are in families. Whether biological, adopted, or a church family, I pray for all believers to find a place of belonging. May I reach out and be a sister to those I meet. You never meant us to live as solitary creatures. As our greatest example while He walked this earth, Your Son surrounded Himself with His disciples, a family of sorts. And He had You. I sing praises to You, my Father. Amen.

THINK ABOUT IT:
Do you need to seek out Christian brothers and sisters to walk alongside?

DAY 144

Morning
BEAUTIFUL FEET

How then will they call on him in whom they have not believed? And how are they to believe in him of whom they have never heard? And how are they to hear without someone preaching? And how are they to preach unless they are sent? As it is written, "How beautiful are the feet of those who preach the good news!"

ROMANS 10:14–15 ESV

Lord, may I take time today and every day to pray for missionaries around the globe. They have accepted Your high calling to spread the gospel. Relieve hardships, Lord. Provide out of Your boundless love. Draw hearts to You as Your disciples speak of Your salvation. Remind me too, Lord, that we are all missionaries in our own small spheres. Today and every day, I have the chance to testify to what an amazing, eternal effect Your grace can have on an ordinary woman. Amen.

THINK ABOUT IT:

Take time this week to choose one missionary and commit to pray for the fruitfulness of his or her work.

Evening
MORE IS MORE

But godliness with contentment is great gain, for we brought nothing into the world, and we cannot take anything out of the world. But if we have food and clothing, with these we will be content.

1 TIMOTHY 6:6–8 ESV

Father, with the abundance many of us enjoy, contentment should be easy. Somehow, it isn't. I lack nothing, yet so much of my time or energy goes to *things*. Contentment is a mindset I need to cultivate daily. When I want new, better, more. . .turn my heart toward contentment, Father. Open my eyes to the overflow of material blessings I already have. Fill my days with gratitude for Your lavish provision. Lead me to share with others who don't have as much. Teach me what is sufficient and what is excess. I desire to follow Your will for my life, even in what I own. Amen.

THINK ABOUT IT:

How can turning to God first before pursuing more keep you focused on contentment?

Morning
AWESOMELY AND WONDERFULLY

For You created my innermost parts;
You wove me in my mother's womb.
I will give thanks to You, because I am
awesomely and wonderfully made.

PSALM 139:13–14 NASB

Loving God, You make each person in Your image. Each individual is Your gift of love to the human race. I praise You, Lord, that each of us is unique and each is perfect in Your sight, "awesomely and wonderfully made." Remind me, Lord, to see You in all who live with different abilities. May I never reject them or create obstacles for them to overcome. May I work instead to facilitate access and welcome. I want to cooperate with You to create communities open to the gifts of each individual. May I never forget that Your body is incomplete whenever anyone is excluded or left behind.

THINK ABOUT IT:

Have your words or actions ever
excluded or failed to welcome
someone who is differently abled?

Evening
THE GENEROSITY OF GOD

Return to your rest, my soul, for the
LORD has dealt generously with you.

PSALM 116:7 NASB

Lord, I need Your peace to soothe my heart. Each time I find myself awake in the middle of the night, the pressing needs and worries I'm facing feel overwhelming. I ask for Your love to surround me. I lay my burdens before You, every single one, knowing they're much safer in Your hands than they are in mine. I surrender to You every anxious thought. Help me to trust You more. Thank You that through every weakness and difficulty I encounter, Your strength is displayed in my life. In the darkness of the night, when I'm at my lowest, I choose to hope in You. You have been very generous to me, Lord. Let me rest in You.

THINK ABOUT IT:

Instead of focusing on worries when
you can't sleep, can you count all the
ways God has been generous to you?

Morning
CONTENT WITH WHAT YOU HAVE

Keep your lives free from the love of money and be content with what you have, because God has said, "Never will I leave you; never will I forsake you."

HEBREWS 13:5 NIV

Lord, I surrender my financial affairs and concerns about money to Your divine care and love. Take my worries about money and replace them with faith in Your care. I commit to being grateful for all You have already given me. Help me to learn to manage my finances wisely, seeking help where needed. Remind me to be content with what I have instead of always wanting more. Thank You that You are always with me.

THINK ABOUT IT:

We usually think that more money is the answer to financial strain—but are there ways you could simplify your life that might decrease your financial worries?

Evening
ENOUGH FOR TODAY

"Don't worry about tomorrow, for tomorrow will bring its own worries. Today's trouble is enough for today."

MATTHEW 6:34 NLT

Oh Lord, I am wound up inside. I feel I cannot continue to meet the demands placed upon me. I worry that I am burned out. I worry about being worried! I fear I may buckle under the weight of all this anxiety. God, I am so tired of carrying this stress around. I desperately need Your peace. So I come to You, to rest in Your presence. May I find shelter from my worries. Lead me to a new state of mind, a fresh perspective—one that's grounded in trust. Remind me to stop borrowing trouble. Restore my heart.

THINK ABOUT IT:

When we worry, we fix our minds on the future instead of dealing with what is right in front of us. What might you have overlooked because of your worries?

Morning
PRAYER CHANGES THINGS

But Moses implored the Lord his God and said, "O Lord, why does your wrath burn hot against your people, whom you have brought out of the land of Egypt with great power and with a mighty hand? . . . Turn from your burning anger and relent from this disaster against your people."

Exodus 32:11–12 esv

Thank You for this reminder that prayer changes things. You were angry at Your people for their continued disobedience. Even though they deserved punishment, You listened to Moses' pleas and changed Your plans. When I'm tempted to worry about things, bring this story to mind. My time is much better spent praying, talking to You, and asking You to change the course of things. You are gracious and good, merciful and kind, and You're always willing to listen to our cries for help. Father, thank You for not giving us what we deserve. Thank You for dealing with us with compassion and love.

THINK ABOUT IT:
Have you talked to God about what concerns you today?

Evening
STEPPING BACK

"Go up to a land flowing with milk and honey; but I will not go up among you, lest I consume you in the way, for you are a stiff-necked people."

Exodus 33:3 rsv

Sometimes I get angry and upset about things, and I don't handle it well. I explode or I hold it all inside, causing my anxiety to grow. When I'm upset, help me follow Your example. You were angry at Your people, and You stepped away for a while. You withdrew Your presence to give Yourself time to cool off so You wouldn't consume them with Your anger. Teach me to take a step back and give myself time to process instead of acting out my anxiety and frustration, doing and saying things I'll regret.

THINK ABOUT IT:
What frustrations are building up inside you now? How can you take a step back to avoid doing something you'll regret?

Morning
WORK, NOT WORRY

According to all that the Lord had commanded Moses, so the people of Israel had done all the work. And Moses saw all the work, and behold, they had done it; as the Lord had commanded, so had they done it. And Moses blessed them.

EXODUS 39:42–43 RSV

Dear Father, I pray that at the end of my life, You'll survey all I've done and be pleased. When worry consumes me, I often become frozen. Anxiety keeps me from accomplishing the work You've planned for me. Set me free from the fear that paralyzes me, Father, so I can be a productive servant. I want to accomplish all the things You've set before me. With all that is in me, I want to please You.

THINK ABOUT IT:

How has worry prevented you from doing what God has called you to do? Ask God to deliver you from that fear.

Evening
WAITING FOR THE CLOUD TO LIFT

Throughout all their journeys, whenever the cloud was taken up from over the tabernacle, the people of Israel would set out. But if the cloud was not taken up, then they did not set out till the day that it was taken up.

EXODUS 40:36–37 ESV

So many of my fears increase when I move ahead of You. I decide how I want things to go, and I act without waiting for Your guidance. My actions often make things worse, not better, and my anxiety increases. Help me be like the Israelites, who waited for Your direction. The cloud being lifted from the tabernacle was Your sign that they should move forward. Oh, may I watch You that closely! May I never move at all until I'm sure You're showing me the way.

THINK ABOUT IT:

Have you moved in front of God lately? Ask Him to clearly show you how and when to act.

Morning
THE FIRE

"The fire on the altar shall be kept burning on it; it shall not go out. The priest shall burn wood on it every morning, and he shall arrange the burnt offering on it and shall burn on it the fat of the peace offerings. Fire shall be kept burning on the altar continually; it shall not go out."
LEVITICUS 6:12–13 ESV

The fire on the altar that never went out—that's a symbol of You, isn't it? It's a reminder that Your fire never goes out. No matter what's going on in my life, I can be confident that You're on it. Even when You seem distant, You're working on my behalf. Even when it looks like nothing is happening, You're changing circumstances, moving people's hearts, and making the way smooth for those who love You. Thank You for this reminder, Lord. Thank You that Your fire never ceases.

THINK ABOUT IT:
In what circumstances does it feel like God isn't doing much? Trust that He's working.

Evening
SHOW ME YOUR GLORY

And Moses said, "This is the thing that the LORD commanded you to do, that the glory of the LORD may appear to you."
LEVITICUS 9:6 ESV

I love this reminder that You love obedience. When we obey You, You show up. When we obey You, You make Your presence known. Instead of worrying about things, I can simply do what You've commanded. I can love others, show kindness and mercy, and follow Your statutes. When I obey You, You'll stay close to me, and I'll see Your glory all around me. Forgive me for thinking I need to be in charge of my circumstances and make things happen my own way. When I'm tempted to struggle for control, remind me to simply obey You and watch for You to appear.

THINK ABOUT IT:
How can you obey God in your circumstances? Make a plan to do that and watch for God to show up.

Morning
FOR ONE

"What man of you, having a hundred sheep, if he has lost one of them, does not leave the ninety-nine in the open country, and go after the one that is lost, until he finds it? And when he has found it, he lays it on his shoulders, rejoicing. . . . Just so, I tell you, there will be more joy in heaven over one sinner who repents than over ninety-nine righteous persons who need no repentance."

LUKE 15:4–5, 7 ESV

Lord, what a beautiful picture of salvation! You, the Great Shepherd, seek the lost—not only for a time, but until You find us. And then You bring the lost ones back to Your flock. You rejoice over our return. May our response be joy too and not pride, like the religious leaders of Jesus' day. We need Your guiding hand to bring us back to You. Lead us. Save us. Thank You for Your care. Amen.

THINK ABOUT IT:

How have you seen the Great Shepherd work in your life?

Evening
READY AND WILLING

And the angel answered her, . . . "Nothing will be impossible with God." And Mary said, "Behold, I am the servant of the Lord; let it be to me according to your word."

LUKE 1:35, 37–38 ESV

Father, what went through Mary's mind when she heard the angel's news that day, and then when she faced a radically changed life—one she would never have imagined—all the days that followed? Confusion? Fear? Dread? Joy? Your plans don't always make sense to Your children, Father. I want to learn from Mary. Whatever emotions she felt, she trusted You. She humbly submitted to Your will. You may ask me to do difficult things in my life, things that seem impossible. When doubt creeps in, remind me that nothing is impossible for You. You have great plans for me—ones I would never imagine apart from You. Ones I will accept with open arms. Amen.

THINK ABOUT IT:

When God leads you in an unexpected direction, what is your response?

Morning
BLESSED ARE. . .

"Blessed are the poor in spirit, for theirs is the kingdom of heaven. Blessed are those who mourn, for they shall be comforted. Blessed are the meek, for they shall inherit the earth. Blessed are those who hunger and thirst for righteousness, for they shall be satisfied. Blessed are the merciful, for they shall receive mercy. Blessed are the pure in heart, for they shall see God."
MATTHEW 5:3–8 ESV

Perhaps it is part of our culture, Lord, but the idea of "being blessed" often equals material or transitory things of this world. We are blessed with comfortable homes, full pantries, expendable income, beauty, health. . . . What You consider "blessed," though, goes much deeper than the physical. You shower us with so many intangible things, including relationship with You. Widen my perspective on blessing, Lord. I am blessed indeed! Amen.

THINK ABOUT IT:
What are the many ways God shows you blessing?

Evening
JUST PRAY

"And when you pray, don't be like those people who don't know God. They continue saying things that mean nothing, thinking that God will hear them because of their many words. Don't be like them, because your Father knows the things you need before you ask him."
MATTHEW 6:7–8 NCV

God, as I kneel before You in prayer, keep my words simple. May they have meaning and not be empty words, empty phrases. I don't need to fill Your ears with endless talk for You to hear, because You have promised to listen to me when I pray to You in faith. You are my heavenly Father; You want me to come to You as Your child. I'm calling out to You today in reverence but also with assurance that my Abba hears me and knows what I need even before I form the words on my tongue. Amen.

THINK ABOUT IT:
Do memorized prayers come easier to you than pleas to God as a child to her Father?

Morning
THE JOY OF THE LORD

Then he said to them, "Go your way. Eat the fat and drink sweet wine and send portions to anyone who has nothing ready, for this day is holy to our Lord. And do not be grieved, for the joy of the LORD is your strength."

NEHEMIAH 8:10 ESV

Lord, the nation of Judah had been through years of captivity and struggle and sin, yet they still had reason to celebrate. The joy of the Lord—their God, You—was their strength. I also have reason to celebrate, even in difficult times, because of Your presence in my life. I can experience joy to do life's hard tasks, life's mundane tasks, life's impossible tasks, because You are with me. You strengthen me. No matter what, I have Your gift of grace, and that alone is reason to rejoice. Amen.

THINK ABOUT IT:

What ways can you acknowledge and celebrate God's strengthening in your life?

Evening
LIVING SACRIFICES

So brothers and sisters, since God has shown us great mercy, I beg you to offer your lives as a living sacrifice to him. . . . Be changed within by a new way of thinking. Then you will be able to decide what God wants for you; you will know what is good and pleasing to him and what is perfect.

ROMANS 12:1–2 NCV

Lord, with the sacrifice of Your Son on the cross, we believers no longer need to offer animal sacrifices to You. The shed blood of the Lamb saves us. In response, I can offer my life as a living sacrifice. All that I do becomes worship and service to You. But doing so requires guidance, Lord. As I read and meditate on scripture, Your Holy Spirit will change me from the inside. I will see Your will for me, and my life will be a daily reflection of Your grace. Amen.

THINK ABOUT IT:

What comes to mind when you think of your life as a living sacrifice?

Morning
DAY BY DAY

So we do not lose heart. Though our outer self is wasting away, our inner self is being renewed day by day. For this light momentary affliction is preparing for us an eternal weight of glory beyond all comparison, as we look not to the things that are seen but to the things that are unseen.

2 CORINTHIANS 4:16–18 ESV

Father, our earthly bodies are not eternal bodies. Illness, fatigue, injury, aging. . .we are fragile creatures! Some days—when I am healthy—it's easy to ignore this truth. But when I am weak, I must turn to You. As I admit my weakness, though, the words of Paul remind me that I should not lose heart. You renew me day in, day out. You are making me strong for my forever home in heaven. Once I am there, Your glory will outshine any darkness I experience in this life. Amen.

THINK ABOUT IT:

How can you look at whatever afflicts you today—or tomorrow— through God's eyes?

Evening
WHAT'S ON YOUR MIND?

Finally, brethren, whatsoever things are true, whatsoever things are honest, whatsoever things are just, whatsoever things are pure, whatsoever things are lovely, whatsoever things are of good report; if there be any virtue, and if there be any praise, think on these things.

PHILIPPIANS 4:8 KJV

Father, as a woman, I tend to think a lot. I mentally list the tasks I have to accomplish on any given day and then feel the pressure of getting everything done. I worry about family, friends. I contemplate what I did or should have done in the past and what awaits me in the future. I labor over all that is going wrong in the world. . . . Please stop my churning thoughts, Father. Remind me of the things You would have me dwell on— things that are true, honest, just, pure, lovely. Positive things. Things worthy of praise. Refresh my mind today. Amen.

THINK ABOUT IT:

How can you begin to replace negative ways of thinking with God's prescription for your mind?

Morning
A ONE-OFF CREATION

Make a careful exploration of who you are and the work you have been given, and then sink yourself into that. Don't be impressed with yourself. Don't compare yourself with others. Each of you must take responsibility for doing the creative best you can with your own life.

GALATIANS 6:4–5 MSG

Father, You lovingly created me as an individual. From the way I look to who I am to what I do—my entire being is the work of Your hands. As I take on this life You've given me, keep me humble, focused on what You do *through* me. Guard my heart against comparison, Father. With the bombardment of social media, seeing what others are doing is a new normal. May I be bold to step away from that norm so I fulfill my calling and do not yearn for someone else's. Amen.

THINK ABOUT IT:
Have you taken time to discover who you—God's unique creation—are?

Evening
HOPE IS. . .

For in this hope we were saved. Now hope that is seen is not hope. For who hopes for what he sees? But if we hope for what we do not see, we wait for it with patience.

ROMANS 8:24–25 ESV

Lord, humans can hope for many things, and hope can mean many things. As a Christian, I find my hope in You. Hope gives me reason to face the day ahead. Hope says that despite the bad, good will ultimately triumph. Hope lifts me from the depths to heaven's heights. And even though I can't see what I hope for yet, it is certain. I don't have to hope in *maybe*; I hope in what is sure to come. My eternity is secure with You, and one day I will share in Your glory. Thank You for not leaving us without hope, Lord. Amen.

THINK ABOUT IT:
How does knowing that your future is safe with God change your definition of hope?

Morning
SEARCH ME

Search me, O God, and know my heart!
Try me and know my thoughts! And
see if there be any grievous way in me,
and lead me in the way everlasting!
PSALM 139:23–24 ESV

God, in the moment I chose to accept Jesus Christ as my Savior and Lord, I was saved. With nothing to offer in return, I became a child of God. But my life as Your daughter does not end at salvation. You want to transform me, to mold me. On my own, I could never change, so I invite You, just as David did, to search me. Know my heart, God. Test me and my thoughts. Root out any sinful tendencies, and guide me in the path of righteousness paid for by Jesus. May I always welcome Your tender leading in my life. Amen.

THINK ABOUT IT:

Is the thought of God probing
you scary or comforting?

Evening
PRESS ON!

Brothers and sisters, I know that I have
not yet reached that goal, but there is
one thing I always do. Forgetting the
past and straining toward what is
ahead, I keep trying to reach the goal
and get the prize for which God called
me through Christ to the life above.
PHILIPPIANS 3:13–14 NCV

Father, as I move toward my goal of Christlike-ness, remind me that the Christian life is more marathon than sprint. I will not reach perfection on this earth. At times, I will feel as though I'm bolting full speed ahead; at others, I may be crawling inch by inch. I'll have triumphs, and I'll make mistakes. In each of these moments, help me focus on You alone, not being burdened by the past but looking forward to the prize of complete Christlike-ness in my eternal home. Amen.

THINK ABOUT IT:

How does the promise of heaven
encourage you to persevere in
both the successes and stumbles
of your Christian journey?

Morning
ETERNAL JOY

"When a woman is giving birth, she has sorrow because her hour has come, but when she has delivered the baby, she no longer remembers the anguish, for joy that a human being has been born into the world. So also you have sorrow now, but I will see you again, and your hearts will rejoice, and no one will take your joy from you."
JOHN 16:21–22 ESV

Lord, Your crucifixion must have been a sorrowful time indeed for Your disciples. But You reminded them of the joy that would follow the anguish. Although You would see them again physically—after Your resurrection—You also left them with the promise of Your Holy Spirit. Their hearts would "see" You forever and rejoice. I share in that same joy. Despite the sorrowful circumstances of this life, Your Spirit is with me permanently, and that is cause for rejoicing. Thank You for being my joy. Amen.

THINK ABOUT IT:
Do you believe that the joy of knowing Christ can overshadow any sorrow in this life?

Evening
FOR MY GOOD

"For I know the plans I have for you, declares the LORD, plans for welfare and not for evil, to give you a future and a hope."
JEREMIAH 29:11 ESV

When circumstances in my world overwhelm me, Father, when I can't see my way out of another day, it is hard to trust in the goodness of Your plans. Maybe I find it difficult to see the good, the future, the hope because my focus is off. You see from above, a heavenly point of view. My view is so very limited. Help me see through Your eyes. You envision my life, and You want more than happiness; You want joy. You want more than "getting by"; You want abundance. You want the peace and security that only come from utter dependence on You. When my world crumbles, shift my focus, Father. Amen.

THINK ABOUT IT:
How will aligning your perspective on life with God's help allow you to rest in His sovereign care?

DAY 157

Morning
A CHECKLIST FOR LOVE

Love is patient and kind; love does not envy or boast; it is not arrogant or rude. It does not insist on its own way; it is not irritable or resentful; it does not rejoice at wrongdoing, but rejoices with the truth. Love bears all things, believes all things, hopes all things, endures all things.

1 CORINTHIANS 13:4–7 ESV

God, love is so central in Your Word. You loved us, so You sent Your Son. We are to love You and love others. As I live a life of love, may the words in 1 Corinthians be my guide. May my love be patient and kind. . .content with my lot; happy for others. . .humble. May it be mindful of others and not always seeking my own benefit. . .long-suffering and able to let go of grudges while holding on to and celebrating truth. May it bear all, believe all, hope, and endure. Amen.

THINK ABOUT IT:
What does love look like lived out?

Evening
PALMS HEAVENWARD

Humble yourselves, therefore, under the mighty hand of God so that at the proper time he may exalt you, casting all your anxieties on him, because he cares for you.

1 PETER 5:6–7 ESV

Lord, as I pray today, the cares of this world distract me. My mind wanders from praise and prayer to all the things left undone, to all the problems and concerns in my life right now. So I kneel before You with open hands, palms toward the sky. I let go of every thought that keeps me from precious communion with You. Where I am weak, You are more than capable of shouldering these burdens. I come to You humbly, submitting to Your omniscience and timing in caring for me. I believe You will exalt me above these difficult circumstances how and when You see fit. I release them to You, Lord. Amen.

THINK ABOUT IT:
What keeps you from handing over your cares to God?

DAY 158

Morning
ORDER MY STEPS

The heart of man plans his way,
but the LORD establishes his steps.
PROVERBS 16:9 ESV

Father, most of us do some planning in our lives. We make business plans, life plans, vacation plans, meal plans. Planning is useful, often necessary. Yet I can plan and plan and plan, then even the smallest thing gone wrong reminds me that, ultimately, I am not in control. This can send me into a panic, or it can push me toward You. While I am not in control, Father, You are! Always. I cannot see all the curves ahead, let alone around them, but You can. I cannot remain strong through the ups and downs, but You can hold me steady. When I don't know whether to turn left or right, You guide me. You establish my steps. Amen.

THINK ABOUT IT:
What planning in your life do you need to surrender to God before taking your first step?

Evening
WITH ONE VOICE

May the God of endurance and encouragement grant you to live in such harmony with one another, in accord with Christ Jesus, that together you may with one voice glorify the God and Father of our Lord Jesus Christ.
ROMANS 15:5–6 ESV

Father, Your children are part of Your family, united through the blood of Your Son. At times, like our earthly families, we argue. Where Your Word is silent on some issues, we have an opinion. We want to have our say, whether we speak softly in our small circles or shout loudly to the whole congregation. But Your desire is harmony, not discord. So we cry out with the apostle Paul, Father, that You grant us the endurance and encouragement we need to live in harmony. Our goal? To speak together of Your glory. Amen.

THINK ABOUT IT:
Where can you be a voice of unity in your church family?

Morning
NOT WHAT YOU'D EXPECT

But God chose what is foolish in the world to shame the wise; God chose what is weak in the world to shame the strong; God chose what is low and despised in the world, even things that are not, to bring to nothing things that are, so that no human being might boast in the presence of God.

1 CORINTHIANS 1:27–29 ESV

Lord, Your ways are higher than ours (Isaiah 55:9). And they are often the opposite. Where we would choose the beautiful, the powerful, the popular, You choose the plain, the lowly, the underdog. A baby born to be a Savior. The weak become strong. Humble ones inherit the kingdom. Sinners find forgiveness. All the glory belongs to You, Lord, for without You, we are nothing. Through You, we are children of the Most High. Amen.

THINK ABOUT IT:
When was the last time you were surprised by the amazing ways God works?

Evening
AN EMPATHETIC SAVIOR

For we do not have a high priest who is unable to sympathize with our weaknesses, but one who in every respect has been tempted as we are, yet without sin. Let us then with confidence draw near to the throne of grace, that we may receive mercy and find grace to help in time of need.

HEBREWS 4:15–16 ESV

Lord Jesus, You walked the earth as I do. You've known pain, hunger, weariness, emotion. You faced temptation in the wilderness for forty days and forty nights. There is nothing I can go through that You don't understand. Yet, unlike me, You are blameless. It is only through Your sinless life that I gain life eternal. I can come boldly to the throne seeking forgiveness, seeking grace, knowing that I will find an advocate in You. Help me walk this earth as You did. Amen.

THINK ABOUT IT:
When you are in life's wilderness, do you have confidence to approach Christ for the grace you need?

Morning
ON DRY LAND

Then Moses put out his hand over the sea. And the Lord moved the sea all night by a strong east wind. So the waters were divided.

EXODUS 14:21 NLV

Why do I forget so easily, Lord? It's as if I watch You perform miracle after miracle and then I walk away and forget what You've done. Do I have memory loss? Am I scatterbrained?

I don't want to forget. I want to be reminded every minute of every day that You're more than capable. On top of that, You care! You want the best for me. When I'm facing raging seas, You'll part the waters not to please Yourself but so I can pass over on dry land. I matter to You. My well-being is on Your mind.

I'm going to brush up on the miracles of old so that I have faith for miracles today. Then I'll come to You with a sense of expectation that mountains will move, seas will part, and walking on water really is a possibility. Amen.

THINK ABOUT IT:

When was the last time God intervened in your life in a miraculous way? Do you believe He'll do it again?

Evening
BELIEVING WITHOUT SEEING

Jesus said to him, "Have you believed because you have seen me? Blessed are those who have not seen and yet have believed."

JOHN 20:29 ESV

"I'll have to see it to believe it." How often have I used those words, Lord? (More than I can count!) I don't want to be a see-it-to-believe-it person any longer. I want to have such strong faith that I can believe something before I see it. I can make my requests with anticipation in my heart that You will come through for me, even when it looks absolutely impossible from all outward appearances.

There's no reason to doubt. You've done it before, and You'll do it again. You're consistent and faithful, even when I'm not. So I'll keep trusting, keep believing, keep hoping, even on the roughest days. Amen.

THINK ABOUT IT:

Are you the "gotta see it to believe it" sort?

Morning
A FRUITY RESPONSE

But the fruit of the Spirit is love, joy, peace, forbearance, kindness, goodness, faithfulness, gentleness and self-control. Against such things there is no law.
GALATIANS 5:22–23 NIV

When I read this scripture about the fruits of the Spirit, Lord, I wonder if it's possible to have all of them at the very same time. Sometimes I get so stressed out that all of the fruits seem to get tossed from the fruit bowl at once. I lose my joy, I lose my peace, I lose my patience with others, and I'm not kind to anyone.

Stress is a terrible thing! It causes me to say yes when I should say no and to give in to temptation or make wrong decisions. I'm so glad I don't have to live that way! Give me a fruity response, Lord! Amen.

THINK ABOUT IT:

Which fruit is the hardest for you to exhibit?

Evening
IN TIMES OF TROUBLE

The LORD is a stronghold for the oppressed, a stronghold in times of trouble.
PSALM 9:9 ESV

Trouble, trouble. . .everywhere! That's how I feel when I'm going through a stressful season. I turn to the right and bump into trouble. I turn to the left and there it is again. No matter where I go, trouble seems to follow. I often wonder if there's an escape from it or if I'll be plagued by it all my life.

But when I run to You, Lord? No trouble can be found in Your courts—only peace, love, forgiveness, and satisfaction. You truly are my stronghold when I'm feeling oppressed. Why would I ever turn to anyone or anything but You? Amen.

THINK ABOUT IT:

Looking back, would you change any of the troubles you've walked through?

Morning
FORGET ABOUT IT!

Now listen, daughter, pay attention, and forget about your past. Put behind you every attachment to the familiar, even those who once were close to you!

PSALM 45:10 TPT

You've asked me to pay attention, Lord, so I'm coming to You today with eyes wide open. Only when I keep my focus on You can I truly battle the temptation to look over my shoulder at the things in my past that still haunt me.

I'm grateful for the reminder that the attachments of yesterday need to be severed. Today I choose to do that. I break attachments with toxic relationships, bad attitudes, poor judgment, and apathy. May my only attachment be to You, Lord! Amen.

THINK ABOUT IT:

What comes to mind when you read the phrase "attachment to the familiar"?

Evening
YOU'RE MY SAFE PLACE

God, you're such a safe and powerful place to find refuge! You're a proven help in time of trouble— more than enough and always available whenever I need you.

PSALM 46:1 TPT

I love this scripture, Lord! There aren't a lot of places to feel safe in this world. I've tried relationships. I've tried money. I've tried climbing the economic ladder. None of those things actually led to long-term safety, though the promises were many.

When I come to You, though? You are truly safe. You are truly powerful. I find refuge in You, my help in time of trouble. Best of all. . .You're always there. I don't have to go searching for You because You are only a prayer away. How grateful I am! Amen.

THINK ABOUT IT:

How has God been a "proven help" in your times of trouble?

Morning
POWER FROM ON HIGH

"But you will receive power when the Holy Spirit has come upon you, and you will be my witnesses in Jerusalem and in all Judea and Samaria, and to the end of the earth."

ACTS 1:8 ESV

I'll admit it, Lord: I feel like a weakling sometimes. It's as if someone has pulled the plug and zapped me of all my strength, all my energy, all my want-to.

In moments like those, when I'm tempted to give up, I am reminded of the supernatural power that comes from Your Spirit. This holy power invigorates me for the tasks ahead, like letting others know about You and spreading joy to those in need. It also helps me face any challenges that come my way. I'm ready, Lord! Fill me today with Your power. Amen.

THINK ABOUT IT:

God can do in a moment what it would take us years to accomplish. How has He proven this in your life?

Evening
HARMONY

Live in harmony with one another. Do not be proud, but be willing to associate with people of low position. Do not be conceited.

ROMANS 12:16 NIV

Not everyone is easy to get along with, Lord. Of course, You know this. Some of the people in my world? I would rather avoid them altogether. They're tough cases, for sure.

Does anyone feel this way about me? I hope not. I don't want to be known as a contentious, difficult person. I don't want to be seen as arrogant or prideful. May I reflect You so that others will be drawn to You when they meet me. And please show me how to live with (and love) the tough ones, I pray. Amen.

THINK ABOUT IT:

What can you do today to make a tough relationship more harmonious?

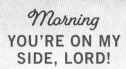

Morning
YOU'RE ON MY SIDE, LORD!

"And that all this assembly may know that the LORD saves not with sword and spear. For the battle is the LORD's, and he will give you into our hand."

1 SAMUEL 17:47 ESV

I'm so grateful for the promise that You are for me, not against me, Lord!

When my enemies dare to raise their heads against me, they are really raising their heads against You! If only they knew that the God of heaven and earth, the all-powerful author of all, is working on my behalf. Those Goliaths would run the other way if they knew how powerful You are! Prove Yourself today, I pray, so that others will know that You have given the battle into my hand. Amen.

THINK ABOUT IT:

When did God last prove Himself to your loved ones by moving on your behalf?

Evening
THOSE HARD-TO-LOVE PEOPLE

"But to you who are listening I say: Love your enemies, do good to those who hate you, bless those who curse you, pray for those who mistreat you."

LUKE 6:27–28 NIV

I won't lie, Lord. This verse? It's not my favorite. I would rather *not* love my enemies, thank You very much! This kind of love doesn't come naturally to me. And it certainly doesn't feel natural to do good to those who hate me or, worse yet, mistreat my loved ones.

I'm learning, though. This is the way You want me to live—not just for their benefit but for mine as well. You have a better way. You bless those who bless others. I'm going to give radical love my best shot, but I'll definitely need Your help. Amen.

THINK ABOUT IT:

How can you show love to your hardest-to-love person today?

Morning
RESTING IN HIM

Whoever dwells in the shelter of the Most High will rest in the shadow of the Almighty.

PSALM 91:1 NIV

I feel like I've stumbled through a lot of dark valleys lately, Lord. They've cast long, low shadows over me that have been hard to escape.

But You offer a different kind of shadow. Like a mother hen extending her wings for her baby chicks to take comfort, You extend Your arms to me.

Today I come. I come away from the stress. I come away from the negative feelings. I come away from the chaos. I come away from those who would seek to hurt me. I come to You and rest in the shadow of Your wings, Lord. Only there will I find comfort and peace. Amen.

THINK ABOUT IT:

Are you resting in His shadow today?

Evening
I WON'T GIVE IN TO FEAR

I sought the LORD, and he answered me and delivered me from all my fears.

PSALM 34:4 ESV

It's tempting, I'll admit. There are times when I allow myself to give in to fear and doubt. I begin to wallow, much like a pig in his pen. It becomes almost enjoyable to me. Self-pity becomes my best friend. Chaos rules the day.

Then I'm reminded that You never intended for me to live this way! You don't want me to give in to fear. You don't want me to wallow in that hole. You're standing nearby, arms extended, asking me to seek You so that You can deliver me once and for all. So today I seek You with my whole heart and thank You in advance for Your deliverance. Amen.

THINK ABOUT IT:

How can you spend more time seeking Him?

Morning
YOU KEEP YOUR PROMISES, LORD!

Now the Lord was gracious to Sarah as he had said, and the Lord did for Sarah what he had promised. Sarah became pregnant and bore a son to Abraham in his old age, at the very time God had promised him.
GENESIS 21:1–2 NIV

I love the story of Sarah and Abraham, Lord! It's such a wonderful reminder that even the things that feel completely impossible to me are more than possible for You.

If You could cause an elderly woman to conceive and then give birth to a son, then the dreams that You've placed in my heart are more than doable for You! If You could restore Sarah's faith by fulfilling Your promise to her, I know You will do the same in my situation. So I thank You in advance. I will not be found faithless. I won't give in to fear or stress. I put my trust in You and watch You move on my behalf. Amen.

THINK ABOUT IT:
What specific promises are you counting on God to keep?

Evening
I NEED TO LET IT GO

"For if you forgive others their trespasses, your heavenly Father will also forgive you, but if you do not forgive others their trespasses, neither will your Father forgive your trespasses."
MATTHEW 6:14–15 ESV

I'll be honest. . .I have a hard time letting things go, Lord. I latch on like a dog with a bone sometimes, and then I wonder why I have no peace in my life. The answer is so obvious, but I can't see it. Perhaps I don't want to.

Today's verse is the perfect reminder that there is a way to let go. But it's going to require something of me. If I can loosen my grip. . .if I can learn to forgive people for the things they've done, then You will forgive me. It's a win-win for all of us. I'm going to need Your help, for sure! Intervene in my heart today, I pray. Amen.

THINK ABOUT IT:
Are you holding unforgiveness in your heart toward anyone today?

Morning
A GREAT CATCH

He said, "Throw your net on the right side of the boat and you will find some." When they did, they were unable to haul the net in because of the large number of fish.

JOHN 21:6 NIV

I appreciate how practical You are, God. You always give good advice. To the fishermen, You said, "Throw your net on the right side." You spoke their language. And because You took the time to do that, they responded.

You speak just as practically to me. You're teaching me how to love those around me by casting a wide net. I want to be loving and patient with people just as You are with me. May I never be found guilty of pushing anyone away from You because of my harsh or bitter outlook. I want to be a true reflection of You in all I say and do. Amen.

THINK ABOUT IT:
Are you standing in the gap for a loved one?

Evening
ANXIETY, BE GONE!

So then, banish anxiety from your heart and cast off the troubles of your body, for youth and vigor are meaningless.

ECCLESIASTES 11:10 NIV

Today's verse reminds me of those stories about bad guys of old being banished to dungeons as a punishment for their crimes. There, in those deep, dark places, they were left to ponder their evil ways.

You're asking me to banish anxiety from my heart in much the same way—to send it to the pit where it belongs. It has tormented me long enough. The time has come to send it far, far away. I won't allow it to bog me down any longer. I have a lot of living to do, after all! So, anxiety, be gone in Jesus' name! Amen.

THINK ABOUT IT:
How has the Lord helped you banish anxiety in the past?

Morning
SOMETIMES I GET ANGRY

*Be angry and do not sin; do not let
the sun go down on your anger, and
give no opportunity to the devil.*

Ephesians 4:26–27 esv

I wish I was one of those people who didn't have to struggle with my temper, Lord. But I'll admit. . .there are days when I completely lose it. Stresses take me to the boiling point, and I'm like a teakettle erupting. I can't seem to control myself in those moments.

Your Word says that getting angry is not a sin. But acting on my anger in unhealthy ways? Therein lies the problem. I'm going to need Your help with my temper, for sure. I don't want to hurt those around me by exploding. And I never want the sun to go down on my anger. Give me Your peace to calm the storms inside my heart, I pray. Amen.

THINK ABOUT IT:
*How do you calm yourself
when your temper flares?*

Evening
RIVERS IN THE DESERT

*"Remember not the former things,
nor consider the things of old.
Behold, I am doing a new thing;
now it springs forth, do you not
perceive it? I will make a way in the
wilderness and rivers in the desert."*

Isaiah 43:18–19 esv

I have been through parched, dry seasons, Lord. When I look back on my past, I wonder sometimes how I made it through. Then I'm reminded: You made a way every time there seemed to be no way.

You provided rivers in the desert. You gave refreshment when I was weary and dry. You made a path for me to succeed even when it felt impossible. And because You have done this for me in the past, I know You will do it again and again and again. I trust You, Lord. I won't follow any path but Yours. Amen.

THINK ABOUT IT:
*When did God last carve a way
through the wilderness for you?*

Morning
I WON'T BE DISMAYED

Fear not, for I am with you; be
not dismayed, for I am your
God; I will strengthen you, I will
help you, I will uphold you with
my righteous right hand.

ISAIAH 41:10 ESV

Heavyhearted. Burdened. Weighed down. Stressed out by my emotions. These are all phrases that have described me at one point or another.

I'll confess, I have allowed my emotions to rule me at times. The heaviness feels like a cross I must bear. But You have called me to rise above my emotions. You tell me that You will strengthen me so that I don't have to be afraid or dismayed.

So today I choose Your way. I won't allow my emotions to dictate how this day plays out. I'm grateful for Your intervention in my heart and my actions. Amen.

THINK ABOUT IT:
When you're stressed, do you
tend to give in to dismay?

Evening
EVERYTHING I NEED

His divine power has given us
everything we need for a godly
life through our knowledge
of him who called us by his
own glory and goodness.

2 PETER 1:3 NIV

Some of the stress in my life comes from not trusting You for my provision, Lord. I'll admit it.

More often than not I get worked up over finances—whether there's enough money in the bank to cover the mortgage or adequate groceries in the pantry to feed the family today. You not only provide the tangible things I need, Lord, but also give me all that I need emotionally, spiritually, and psychologically to live a godly life.

Today I look to You for my total provision, inside and out. You've got me covered, so I place my trust in You and choose not to fret. Amen.

THINK ABOUT IT:
What are you asking God for today?

DAY 170

Morning
GOD NEVER GIVES UP

Being confident of this very thing, that he which hath begun a good work in you will perform it until the day of Jesus Christ.

PHILIPPIANS 1:6 KJV

Jesus, the world seems to be spinning out of control. Everywhere I look, I see chaos—and I don't see a way to restore order to the mess. I long just to throw in the towel and say, "Enough. I'm done. I give up." Give me a new perspective, Lord, and blow away the clouds that dim my vision. Remind me, whenever life seems hopeless, to turn my eyes to You. As I look back at history and at my own life, I see that Your hand was always working, even when things seemed the worst. Give me new confidence in You now, I pray. Thank You that You are still working—and You never give up.

THINK ABOUT IT:

Can you increase your hope for today by looking at what God has done in the past?

Evening
CONFESSION

If we claim we have no sin, we are only fooling ourselves and not living in the truth. But if we confess our sins to him, he is faithful and just to forgive us our sins and to cleanse us from all wickedness.

1 JOHN 1:8–9 NLT

God, I'm scared of people finding out who I really am. I'm scared of being seen as a fraud, a hypocrite. I'm scared that everyone will abandon me, and I'll be alone in my sin and shame. But, Lord, I'm also scared of my heart growing colder and colder toward You. I wish there was an easy way out of this situation, but I know the only way forward is to follow You. I'm done making excuses, done pretending. I need Your grace, Lord, to help me change. I come to You, confessing my sin, asking for cleansing, for forgiveness, and for redemption. I can't fix myself. Only You can make me clean again.

THINK ABOUT IT:

How does keeping a sin hidden allow it to grow even larger?

Morning
RELEASING GRUDGES

"When you are praying, first forgive anyone you are holding a grudge against, so that your Father in heaven will forgive your sins, too."

MARK 11:25 NLT

Jesus, thank You that You have forgiven all my brokenness, all my mistakes, all my pride and selfishness. I confess that I have not extended that same love and mercy toward others who have offended me. Instead, I have held anger, bitterness, and resentment in my heart. Now, though, I want to release this grudge that has held me in bondage. Set me free, I pray. Heal my wounded heart, and give me the courage to be vulnerable once again. I don't want anything to come between You and me.

THINK ABOUT IT:

How might unforgiveness keep you from a close relationship with God?

Evening
CRYING IN THE NIGHT

Arise, cry out in the night, as the watches of the night begin; pour out your heart like water in the presence of the Lord. Lift up your hands to him for the lives of your children.

LAMENTATIONS 2:19 NIV

Things always seem worse in the dark, Lord, when I can't sleep. Wrap Your arms around me, I pray, as I lie here, beset with fears and sorrows. Remind me to use this sleepless time to talk to You. Thank You that You are listening as I pour out my heart. I ask that You be with my children and all the people I love. I put them in Your hands now, and I'll do so again tomorrow night and the night after. Take my anxiety and sadness from me, and replace it with Your peace. Even if sleep still evades me, may I rest in Your presence. Let me relax in the knowledge that You have everything under control.

THINK ABOUT IT:

While you wait for sleep, can you take advantage of this time by praying?

Morning
BETRAYED BY A FRIEND

*Even my close friend, someone
I trusted, one who shared my
bread, has turned against me.*

PSALM 41:9 NIV

Betrayal, Jesus, has wounded my heart; but I pray that it would not keep me from sharing Your love with others. As I move forward with other relationships in my life, help me not to punish those who are innocent by assuming they too will betray me. Restore my ability to trust. Work in the heart of the friend who betrayed me, God, and show me ways to rebuild trust in this relationship if that is possible. Remind me that You too were betrayed by a friend, and yet You never stopped reaching out in love. May I follow Your example.

THINK ABOUT IT:

*Has betrayal changed the way
you think about other people in
general? How might God want
to heal you from this hurt?*

Evening
GOD-REALITY

"Steep your life in God-reality, God-initiative, God-provisions. Don't worry about missing out. You'll find all your everyday human concerns will be met."

MATTHEW 6:33 MSG

This burden I'm carrying at work, Lord, feels too heavy, too cumbersome to pick up and carry day after day. Please give me freedom from this weight. Change the circumstances of this situation, I pray, and free my heart and mind from the anxiety it causes. Guide me with Your Spirit so I can know how to resolve, manage, or walk away from this worry. Thank You that You are my comforter and my friend. You care about each detail of my life, and You are already working on my behalf to bring peace and restoration to this situation. Help me always to live in Your reality, trusting in Your initiative and provision.

THINK ABOUT IT:

*What does it mean to live in
"God-reality"? How might this
shift in perspective change how
you feel about your job?*

Morning
PERFECT PEACE

*You will keep in perfect peace
all who trust in you, all whose
thoughts are fixed on you!*
ISAIAH 26:3 NLT

Lord, I admit that I often forget that You are with me. I forget to think about You throughout the day. So it's no wonder, I suppose, that worry so often consumes my thoughts. I need to get to know You better. I need to become more familiar with Your Word and Your promises. Help me to put You first in every area of my life. Remind me to live one day at a time. Teach me not to worry about tomorrow but instead focus on what You're doing in my life right now. I know that You will take care of each of my needs—spiritual, financial, relational, physical, and emotional. Help me to trust You more and worry less.

THINK ABOUT IT:

How might fixing your thoughts on God be a good antidote for worry?

Evening
SWEET SLEEP

*When you lie down, you will not
be afraid; when you lie down,
your sleep will be sweet.*
PROVERBS 3:24 NASB

I'm having so much trouble sleeping, Lord, that I don't have the energy to function well during the day. Even worse, when I'm so tired, I can't experience the peace You want for me. As I prepare for sleep tonight, please relax my body. Send me thoughts that will quiet and calm my mind. Remind me when I can't sleep to pray about whatever is worrying me. Thank You for Your constant care and unconditional love. Take away all my fears so I can rest in You.

THINK ABOUT IT:

Have you asked God to show you what is causing your insomnia? Is it something spiritual, something emotional, or something physical? Have you talked to your doctor about the problem?

Morning
SAVED FROM DESTRUCTION

*He sent His word and healed them,
and saved them from their destruction.*

PSALM 107:20 NASB

Jesus, during Your time on earth, You ministered to all who came to You. You never judged or withheld Your healing touch. Look with compassion now upon all who, through addiction, have lost their health and freedom. Restore them to wholeness, I pray. Remove from them the fears that beset them, and strengthen them in the work of their recovery. Give patient understanding and persevering love to those who care for them. Send out Your Word to heal and save.

THINK ABOUT IT:

How might you reach out in love to someone who suffers from addiction?

Evening
THE PEACE OF JESUS

"Peace I leave you, My peace I give you; not as the world gives, do I give to you. Do not let your hearts be troubled, nor fearful."

JOHN 14:27 NASB

Dear Jesus, thank You for the calm and peace You promise to give me even when I'm at my most anxious, in the middle of life's chaos, when life is spinning out of control. Help me to remember that when I feel overwhelmed by what I can't predict or plan, You already know what will play out, and You'll be with me through the process. Help me, Lord, to trust You as I steady my mind and heart on Your promises. Remind me to care for my body in the ways it needs so that my thoughts can embrace Your peace more easily. Thank You, Jesus, for sharing Your own peace with me.

THINK ABOUT IT:

How is the peace of Jesus different from any peace the world can give?

Morning
LOVE INSTEAD OF FEAR

"Do not fear them, for the LORD your God is the One fighting for you."
DEUTERONOMY 3:22 NASB

Lord Jesus, I know that You told us to pray for our enemies, and so I'm doing that right now. I ask first that You would saturate my life with Your Spirit's power and might. Take away my fear and replace it with trust in Your love. Send that love flowing through me, and forgive me for holding on to any resentment, self-righteousness, or hatred. I release into Your hands all thoughts of revenge. May I have the strength I need to bless my enemies. Thank You that You will protect me. Free me from fear and hatred, and give me a spirit of love and power. Bless these individuals with Your grace.

THINK ABOUT IT:

How does fear interfere with the love God wants you to show to everyone, even your enemies?

Evening
THE UNITY OF THE SPIRIT

Be completely humble and gentle; be patient, bearing with one another in love. Make every effort to keep the unity of the Spirit through the bond of peace.
EPHESIANS 4:2–3 NIV

God, You made us in Your own image and redeemed us through Jesus, Your Son. You call us to join together in love and service so that the world may see You through us. Take away the arrogance and impatience that have infected our church. Break down the walls that separate us; unite us in bonds of love; and work through our struggles and confusion to accomplish Your purposes. Remind me that I am far from perfect, and make me patient with others' imperfections. Restore our bond of peace, I pray.

THINK ABOUT IT:

When you look at the discord in your church, what is the biggest factor that has broken your unity in the Spirit?

DAY 176

Morning
JOB STRESS

*Moses said to the Lord, "Pardon your
servant, Lord. I have never been
eloquent, neither in the past nor since
you have spoken to your servant.
I am slow of speech and tongue."
The Lord said to him, "Who gave
human beings their mouths? Who
makes them deaf or mute? Who gives
them sight or makes them blind? Is it
not I, the Lord? Now go; I will help you
speak and will teach you what to say."*

EXODUS 4:10–12 NIV

God, Moses didn't think he could do the
job You'd given him to do. I understand
that feeling. Like Moses, I'm all too aware
of all the ways I'm not skilled enough, all
the ways I don't know enough, and all the
mistakes I've made in the past. Remind
me, God, as You reminded Moses, that
You are the one working through me as I
do my job. Help me to rely on You rather
than on my own abilities.

THINK ABOUT IT:

*Moses sounds like he's being humble,
but it's clear that God has a bone to
pick with him. Do you ever let false
humility hold you back from the
work God is calling you to do?*

Evening
ENCOURAGEMENT
FOR THE DOUBTING

Be merciful to those who doubt.

JUDE 22 NIV

Lord, I know that all of us have times of
doubt. Help me never to look down on
anyone who is doubting. Instead, may I
reach out in love and support, as others
have so often supported me. I know,
Jesus, that You are the author of our faith.
Faith isn't something we have to muster
up out of sheer determination; it's something You give to us. Empower us to let
go of the way we idolize the visible and
the known in our lives so that You can
replace our doubts with faith. Remind
us not to sit and stew in our fear and
doubt, but instead may our days overflow
with prayer. Teach us to encourage one
another and be patient with each other's
doubts.

THINK ABOUT IT:

*Is there someone in your
life today who may need
your encouragement to
rise above her doubt?*

Morning
GOD TO THE RESCUE

*The righteous person faces many troubles, but the L*ORD* comes to the rescue each time.*

PSALM 34:19 NLT

Give me the courage, Lord, to face these challenges that have come into my life. Help me to persevere and not give up, knowing that You will always come to my rescue when I need You. Instead of blaming You or looking elsewhere for the answers, remind me to look to You and trust completely in You. Help me surrender everything to You—the circumstances as well as my emotions, my thoughts, my actions, my control—knowing that You are already working to bring a resolution to this situation. Thank You, God, for hearing and answering my prayer.

THINK ABOUT IT:

As you face this set of challenges, ask yourself: Am I willing to turn my control over to God? Or am I still trying to handle things on my own?

Evening
MAKE THINGS RIGHT

"If you enter your place of worship and, about to make an offering, you suddenly remember a grudge a friend has against you, abandon your offering, leave immediately, go to this friend and make things right. Then and only then, come back and work things out with God."

MATTHEW 5:23-24 MSG

You are a God of relationships, Lord. Again and again throughout Your Word, I see how important our connections with other humans are to You. You even make it clear that we can't be right with You if we're not right with others. And so, Lord, I bring to You this relationship that I've been forced to realize is no longer healthy. Forgive me for my part in what went wrong. Show me how to make things right. Make our relationship pleasing to You once again.

THINK ABOUT IT:

When you examine your life, do you see any relationships that need your attention? What steps can you take to restore them to health?

Morning
SPOILED CHILDREN

Where do you think all these appalling wars and quarrels come from? Do you think they just happen? Think again. They come about because you want your own way, and fight for it deep inside yourselves. . . . You're spoiled children, each wanting your own way.

JAMES 4:1–3 MSG

It's easy for me, Lord, to think of violence as something that happens "out there," committed by "bad people," while I am innocent and removed from such behaviors. And yet, God, I realize that I live in a society that privileges some people while it oppresses others—and violence too often arises from this. Before I put the blame on other people, help me to look at my own heart. May I be willing to surrender my privilege so that Your peace and justice may have room to spread throughout our society.

THINK ABOUT IT:

Sometimes when we read Bible verses, it's easy to apply them to others rather than ourselves. What might God be saying to you through these verses from James?

Evening
READY TO LET GO

We brought nothing into this world, and it is certain we can carry nothing out.

1 TIMOTHY 6:7 KJV

God, You have blessed me with so many wonderful things—a family, a career, a home, friends. I am grateful for all Your gifts, but I also ask that You remind me not to cling to them too tightly. May I love all You have given me while holding them in my heart lightly, ready to let them go so that I can move on into eternity with You. I possessed nothing when I was born, and I will possess nothing when I die—nothing except Your love, which has always been mine and always will be mine. Help me to face death without fear, knowing that even in death You will be with me. Make me ready to let go.

THINK ABOUT IT:

When you think about your death, what frightens you most? Can you give this fear to the one who loves you?

Morning
YOUR BODYGUARD

Is anyone crying for help? God is listening, ready to rescue you. . . . If you're kicked in the gut, he'll help you catch your breath. Disciples so often get into trouble; still, God is there every time. He's your bodyguard.
PSALM 34:17–20 MSG

Lord God, Your Word tells me that You are always listening to me, ready to help. I pray today that You would wrap me in Your love. I ask for Your guidance and protection. Wherever I go today, guard me. So many things can go wrong during the day, but I know that no matter what happens, You'll be there. You'll hear me when I cry. You'll wrap Your arms around me if events take me by surprise. I don't know what this day may hold; I can't predict what accidents might befall me; but You, Lord, know the future. Your love is my bodyguard, going before me, sheltering me from harm.

THINK ABOUT IT:

One of the worst things about unexpected crises is that they upset our plans; they make us realize we are not in control of our lives. Can you trust God's plan for your life, no matter what happens?

Evening
OUR FOREVER HOME

This world is not our permanent home; we are looking forward to a home yet to come.
HEBREWS 13:14 NLT

I hate the thought of leaving this world, Lord. I don't want to lose all the familiar things I love: a cup of coffee in the morning, the pleasure of a good book, my children's smiles, the warmth of a loved one's arms, the scent of freshly mown grass, fireflies on a summer evening, the wind in the trees—and so many other countless lovely things. But I have to believe, God, that if this world is full of beauty, heaven will be even more amazing. So dying won't mean leaving everything behind that I love—instead, it will mean finally having the fullness of everything, the complete shebang, with absolutely nothing missing. And best of all, it will mean that I finally come home to You, to live in Your presence forever.

THINK ABOUT IT:

What scares you most about dying? Can you take comfort from verses like this that speak of heaven as home?

Morning
A SPIRITUAL LIFELINE

*One of those days Jesus went out
to a mountainside to pray, and
spent the night praying to God.*

LUKE 6:12 NIV

Lord, when I read about Your prayer life while You were on this earth, I'm deeply humbled. You spent a great deal of time in fellowship with the Father. Modern-day men and women tend to think of prayers in minutes or even seconds, hence the phrase "breathing a prayer." Then we're off and running again with our hectic schedules. But You made prayer a fundamental part of Your life. May I always take the time for prayer, whatever amount of time it takes for fellowship, guidance, support, requests, encouragement, repentance, thanksgiving, and praise. May I see prayer not as a quick fix, but as a spiritual lifeline—to You. Amen.

THINK ABOUT IT:

*What prayers do you put off
because you're too short on time?
What can you do to strengthen
prayer as your spiritual lifeline?*

Evening
HOW I WANT TO LIVE

*"Watch and pray so that you will
not fall into temptation. The spirit
is willing, but the flesh is weak."*

MATTHEW 26:41 NIV

When it comes to temptation, Lord, many people aren't worried about it—they just give in to it! But I have also seen those same people as they deal with the aftermath of their choices. Not good. Sometimes, there would be a season of elation and amusement as they gave in to sin, but when it was over, some kind of injury, grief, or destruction followed in its wake. That is not how I want to live my life, Lord, nor how I want my family to live. When we are enticed by temptations—no matter what kind—may we learn to rush to You in prayer and allow You to give us the courage and strength to flee from them! Amen.

THINK ABOUT IT:

*What temptations have been enticing
to you? Have you asked God to help
you overcome those temptations?*

Morning
FALLING INTO PLACE

Jesus replied: " 'Love the Lord your God with all your heart and with all your soul and with all your mind.' This is the first and greatest commandment."

MATTHEW 22:37–38 NIV

When I read the above verses, Lord, I see how simple our relationship really can be. Simple and beautiful. It's easy for me to buy into the idea that our relationship is complicated and unattainable when considering all the opposing opinions and theologies out there. But I understand these verses so well, since they go right to the heart of our father-daughter bond. If I love You—*really* love You—then I wouldn't want to do anything to harm our intimate fellowship. Everything would fall into place, just as it was supposed to in the Garden of Eden. What verses. Simply beautiful! Amen.

THINK ABOUT IT:

Do you love God with all your heart and soul and mind?

Evening
NOT THE END
OF THE STORY

But mark this: There will be terrible times in the last days. People will be lovers of themselves, lovers of money, boastful, proud, abusive, disobedient to their parents, ungrateful, unholy, without love, unforgiving, slanderous, without self-control, brutal, not lovers of the good, treacherous, rash, conceited, lovers of pleasure rather than lovers of God—having a form of godliness but denying its power. Have nothing to do with such people.

2 TIMOTHY 3:1–5 NIV

Lord, I know You are returning, and we may be living in the last days, so help me to always be watchful and ready for You whenever that day of Your second coming may be. Please don't let me be swayed by people who are described in the verses above. May I train up my children so they will want to become lovers of You and not lovers of the world! Amen.

THINK ABOUT IT:

Are you and your family ready for the Lord's return?

Morning
LOVE SONGS

The Lord appeared to us in the past, saying: "I have loved you with an everlasting love; I have drawn you with unfailing kindness."

JEREMIAH 31:3 NIV

People love tender love stories and love songs because they show just how deeply and passionately the human heart can be touched. Perhaps in the verse above we see a bit of a love song, sung to Israel, but also sung to me, to my family, and all of mankind. May I always share Your Word with my loved ones, Lord, so that they might know how You draw them near with unfailing kindness and how You love them with a love that is never ending. May their hearts embrace Your tender kindness and love always! In Jesus' name I pray. Amen.

THINK ABOUT IT:

Do your children know just how much God loves them? What are some ways to share that good news?

Evening
A HOT MESS OF WORRY

Do not be anxious about anything, but in every situation, by prayer and petition, with thanksgiving, present your requests to God.

PHILIPPIANS 4:6 NIV

From a very young age, Lord, we learn to worry about our troubles. But then we read in Your Word that though there will be trouble in this life, we *shouldn't* worry (John 16:33). Since this means *no one* will escape tests and trials, how can I stay calm? Especially now that I have children—wee ones who never stop running headlong into peril—my ability to imagine what can go wrong at any given moment has skyrocketed! And, given that we live in a world that is getting darker spiritually, I've become a hot mess of worry! Yet, again, Your Word says we're to be anxious for nothing. And by that You mean absolutely *nothing*. Please show me, Lord, how I can live that way. I need Your divine help right now. In Jesus' name I pray. Amen.

THINK ABOUT IT:

What are a few worries you can bring before God right now?

DAY 183

Morning
ANOTHER GIFT FROM GOD

Then God blessed the seventh day and made it holy, because on it he rested from all the work of creating that he had done.

GENESIS 2:3 NIV

Lord, I confess that I've used most of my Sundays to get caught up on all the miscellaneous "other work" that I couldn't get done during the week, and in doing so, I've only made myself even more bleary-eyed tired. Because Sunday was made for man, not the other way around, Lord, I know You mean for this special day to be given to us not as an impossible rule to follow, but as a gift to receive. It's to be a wonderful refreshment for our bodies, minds, and spirits. Please help me and my family learn how to use our Sundays as You see fit, so together we can start the new week with eagerness and joy! Amen.

THINK ABOUT IT:

What are some ways you can rest on Sunday and be refreshed for the new week? If you can't rest on a Sunday, on what day can you be refreshed?

Evening
MAKE ME READY FOR MORE

I gave you milk, not solid food, for you were not yet ready for it. Indeed, you are still not ready.

1 CORINTHIANS 3:2 NIV

Lord, I want to grow spiritually. I sense that my soul has been stuck in a rut for a long time. Maybe it's because I didn't want to change. After all, change can be scary! But I want to please You in all I do, so give me courage to become the woman You created me to be. Even if the process is painful, help me to be open to moving beyond the baby-milk phase, and make me ready for solid spiritual food. I'm excited about a deeper understanding of Your Word, growing up as a Christian, and a closer relationship with You! In Jesus' name I pray. Amen.

THINK ABOUT IT:

What are some of the ways you can know you're moving beyond the milk phase as a Christian?

Morning
LOVE HURTS

Have mercy on me, Lord, for I am faint; heal me, Lord, for my bones are in agony. My soul is in deep anguish. How long, Lord, how long?
PSALM 6:2–3 NIV

Oh God, it hurts so much to love people sometimes. I give so much, care so much, and it takes so much out of me. Lord, my heart is breaking for my dear ones. They are aching, and I am aching. They are in turmoil, and I am in turmoil. I haven't caused this pain. No one has. But still, it's there. As real and as sickening as a punch in the gut. Sometimes when I think about it, I can't even breathe. "My bones are in agony. My soul is in deep anguish." But, Lord, You know this kind of pain. You know every inch of the hurt we are feeling. You know what it's like to hurt for the ones You love. God, help me get through this. Help me be strong for my loves. Amen.

THINK ABOUT IT:

What good can come through hurting for others? How can you increase your God-given strength during those times?

Evening
NOT LEFT BEHIND

"I will not leave you as orphans; I will come to you."
JOHN 14:18 NIV

Jesus, I'm sitting here in the night, awake again. I'm just awake, thinking about this little life You have placed in my hands, and I feel so unworthy, so in awe, so alone. But You have promised that You will come, so I know You are here, even now in this darkness. Even here in this mess of a nursery, rocking back and forth with me, breathing in, breathing out. Your Spirit comforts me, Jesus, like the soothing of a mother's hand on a baby's warm back. Thank You, Lord. I'll keep breathing and rocking and depending on You. Amen.

THINK ABOUT IT:

Do you live as if you fully believe Jesus is with you in every moment? If not, what can you do to breathe Him into your life?

Morning
NOT THE OLD DAYS ANYMORE

Do not say, "Why were the old days better than these?" For it is not wise to ask such questions.
ECCLESIASTES 7:10 NIV

God, I used to do so many things. I used to have hobbies, read books, and do crafts. I used to go out with friends, have dinner parties, and go on spur-of-the-moment trips. There is so much of me that I don't recognize anymore, Lord. Much of my life has become so routine, so scheduled, and so full of things I do for other people. They are my people. And I love them, God. But sometimes I wonder if I've gotten a little lost in the middle of it all. Sometimes I feel a little bit sad about losing part of who I am. Lord, can You help me find a better balance? Can You help me find me? Amen.

THINK ABOUT IT:
What can you do to find a better balance between responsibilities and the rest of who you are— in God's eyes and your own?

Evening
WHEN I NEED UNDERSTANDING

Great is our Lord and mighty in power; his understanding has no limit.
PSALM 147:5 NIV

Lord, I need Your clarity. I need Your understanding. I need the wisdom of Solomon and the patience of Job. I need to be able to explain things clearly. I need to have courage to face my own fears about this. And I need to have the determination to stick to it, even when things get tricky. Because I know things will get hard, Lord. I just know there will come a time when one or both of us want to chuck it all out the window and go get ice cream. But I also know that with You, we can do this. Together, we can get it done. Amen.

THINK ABOUT IT:
What's something hard that you have faced for someone else's benefit? How did God and His Word help you?

Morning
TOUGH DECISIONS

*Give careful thought to the
paths for your feet and be
steadfast in all your ways.*

PROVERBS 4:26 NIV

God, it's time. I have been dreading this day and this decision. But now it's here. And I want so much to be doing the right thing, Lord. I have prayed and prayed about this. You know how often I have come before You and laid this struggle at Your feet. And yet still a voice of doubt creeps into my head. Lord, I ask You one more time—if this is the right thing to do for me and my loved ones, please let me know that. Please let me feel Your peace. And if, even after all this time, I've got it wrong, then please let me know that too. Let Your will be done. And let me see it clearly. Amen.

THINK ABOUT IT:

*What's your process for making tough
decisions? How easy is it for you to
leave the results in God's hands?*

Evening
ENOUGH TROUBLE

*"Do not worry about tomorrow, for
tomorrow will worry about itself. Each
day has enough trouble of its own."*

MATTHEW 6:34 NIV

Lord, can I please have a few more hours in the day? I know that's a lot to ask. It seems like an impossible request. Yet I feel like I am constantly being asked to do the impossible. How in the world am I supposed to pick up one kid from practice and attend the concert of another on the other side of town at the same time? How am I supposed to feed my family and pets, fill the prescriptions, iron the uniforms, and help with the littlest one's book report? How am I supposed to remember to wash the dog and walk the laundry? There just isn't enough time, Lord. There isn't enough *me*. Help me do what I can and be content with that. Amen.

THINK ABOUT IT:

*What do you do when you feel
stretched? What Bible verse
can you cling to for relief?*

Morning
MY STRENGTH

The LORD is my strength and my shield; my heart trusts in him, and he helps me.
PSALM 28:7 NIV

God, I know I'm supposed to be the strong one. I'm supposed to hold us together. I'm supposed to put on a brave face and act like I have it all together. I'm supposed to have the answers. But God, You know I don't. I just don't have it in me today. And I feel so weak, uncertain, and afraid. Lord, I am depending wholly on You. I place my mouth, my mind, and my spirit in Your hands. Give me words of comfort and hope. Grant me clarity and peace. Fill me up with Your courage and power. I have no idea how to get through this day, Lord, but I know I can do it with You beside me. Amen.

THINK ABOUT IT:
How do you feel when you are fully dependent on God?

Evening
CALL ON HIM

I love the LORD, because he has heard my voice and my pleas for mercy. Because he inclined his ear to me, therefore I will call on him as long as I live.
PSALM 116:1–2 ESV

I do love You. I love You with all that is in me. I know You don't get angry at me when I worry about things. Instead, You invite me to share my thoughts, my fears, and my anxieties with You. You listen to every word, and You encourage me with reminders of Your love. I know my cries don't stop at the ceiling, but they reach Your ears the moment they escape. I call on You right now. You know my thoughts. You know every worry, every concern. Thank You for listening. Thank You for sending Your Holy Spirit as a comforter. And thank You for never getting tired of my pleas for mercy.

THINK ABOUT IT:
Do you call on God every single day? He wants you to.

Morning
GOOD ANGER
AND BAD ANGER

Go ahead and be angry. You do well to
be angry—but don't use your anger as
fuel for revenge. And don't stay angry.
Don't go to bed angry. Don't give the
Devil that kind of foothold in your life.
EPHESIANS 4:26 MSG

Whenever I lose my temper, Lord, I feel guilty—but this verse reminds me that anger is not a sin. Psychology also tells me that anger can be a healthy emotion, one that pushes us to work for justice in the world. It can impel us to speak up when things aren't right. Even You got angry, Jesus! But I know that if I nurse my anger, clinging to it and refusing to let it go, it can turn sour inside me. When that happens, instead of inspiring acts of justice, it can lead to acts of violence. It can turn into hate. So, Lord, thank You for the gift of anger—but remind me always to release it into Your hands. I don't want to use anger as an excuse for sin.

THINK ABOUT IT:

When you look back at your life,
can you see an instance when your
anger led to something good? Can
you also see a time when you held
on to your anger too long, and it
ended up hurting someone?

Evening
THE PRISON
OF ADDICTION

Remember them that are
in bonds, as bound with them.
HEBREWS 13:3 KJV

God, may I never look down on those who suffer from addiction. Teach me to see with Your eyes of love, realizing that addiction is like a prison cell—it puts bars around a person's life, bars that can seem impossible to escape. May I feel the suffering of those who are trapped by addiction. Give me ways and opportunities to express Your love to them. Show me anything I can do to help open their prison doors so that they can go free. May I always hold them in my prayers.

THINK ABOUT IT:

The author of this verse from the book
of Hebrews was talking about literal
bonds, but he makes clear that we
are to identify with those who are
not free, whatever those bonds may
look like. Can you see that addiction
is as much a prison cell as if it put
actual bars around its victims?

Morning
COURAGE!

Energize the limp hands, strengthen the rubbery knees. Tell fearful souls, "Courage! Take heart! GOD is here, right here, on his way to put things right and redress all wrongs. He's on his way! He'll save you!"
ISAIAH 35:3–4 MSG

Father, lately we are living in an atmosphere of fear. We're afraid of germs and disease; we're afraid of violence and war; we're afraid of natural disasters and climate change. We're even afraid of each other. Use me, I pray, to dispel this atmosphere of fear. May I speak words of courage and hope to everyone I encounter (whether in person or on social media). I don't want to spread complacency, Lord, but I do want to fight the apathy that comes from fear. Teach me to encourage others to take action rather than be paralyzed by fear. Remind me always to point to You, the one who is ever ready to work with us to put the world to rights. Thank You that You are here with us in the midst of our troubled world.

THINK ABOUT IT:

Can you pray for an opportunity today to spread active courage in place of paralyzed fear?

Evening
DOUBTS FOR THE WORLD'S FUTURE

With God nothing shall be impossible.
LUKE 1:37 KJV

Oh God, I'm so filled with doubts about the future. I know that You've promised never to leave me, and I know You always seek to bless me. But when I look at the world today, I can't see how things are going to work out. Every time I read the news, I hear about another disaster, another threat to our safety and well-being. Will there still be a world for my children and grandchildren—or will we destroy our planet and ourselves along with it? Lord, take my fears and doubts. I know that You are still working in our world. I know that nothing is impossible for You. Please work miracles in our broken world. Restore us and make us whole.

THINK ABOUT IT:

Have you tried praying each time you read bad news? Turn each new threat over to the one who loves you.

Morning
BE HOLY

"For I am the LORD your God. Consecrate yourselves therefore, and be holy, for I am holy. . . . For I am the LORD who brought you up out of the land of Egypt to be your God. You shall therefore be holy, for I am holy."
LEVITICUS 11:44–45 ESV

Why do I so often forget that I was made in Your image? Though I have a sin nature, I also have Your image running through my veins. I was created to be like You, to be in fellowship with You. The word *holy* means to set apart for a high calling. When I allow fear and anxiety to rule my thoughts, I'm not reflecting Your image or Your holiness. When I'm tempted to worry, remind me that You've called me to be holy, and worry isn't part of that picture.

THINK ABOUT IT:

In what ways can you reflect God's holiness in your life today?

Evening
LIKE THE ISRAELITES

"Yet you would not go up, but rebelled against the command of the LORD your God. And you murmured in your tents and said, 'Because the LORD hated us he has brought us out of the land of Egypt, to give us into the hand of the Amorites, to destroy us.' "
DEUTERONOMY 1:26–27 ESV

When I read about how ungrateful the Israelites were for all You did for them, it's easy to be judgmental. But I'm no different than they were, am I? When I think back over my life, I recall so many ways You've shown Your love. You've poured out Your mercy, Your compassion, Your kindness, and still I worry. Worry is really just complaining in my head, isn't it? Worry says that I don't trust Your goodness. Forgive me, Lord. Today, right now, in this moment, I set aside my fear, knowing You will take care of things in the best possible way.

THINK ABOUT IT:

What have you complained about recently? Can you trust God with it?

Morning
IN THE WILDERNESS

"For the Lord your God has blessed you in all the work of your hands. He knows your going through this great wilderness. These forty years the Lord your God has been with you. You have lacked nothing."
DEUTERONOMY 2:7 ESV

Dear Father, You have blessed me just as You blessed the Israelites. When I think back through my life, Your blessings are too many to count. You know all about the wilderness I'm going through, and You've never left me for a moment. You know every detail of every circumstance, and You've felt every tear I've cried. Every day, every hour of my life, You've been with me. Truly, I've never lacked a thing that I needed. Thank You, Lord, for Your constant, tender care over me. I love You. I trust You. I know You are good.

THINK ABOUT IT:

In what ways has God blessed you? How have you felt His presence in your own wilderness?

Evening
YOU SHALL NOT FEAR

"You shall not fear them, for it is the Lord your God who fights for you."
DEUTERONOMY 3:22 RSV

If anyone had reason to worry, it was Joshua. His job was to bring the Israelites into a hostile land, and he knew they'd have to fight to possess the land You had promised them. But instead of worrying, he chose to recall all You'd done for Your people in the past. He knew You wouldn't bring them this far just to abandon them. He told the people not to worry for You were fighting for them. Help me follow Joshua's example, Lord. Help me make gratitude a daily practice, for I know recalling Your goodness is a key to overcoming worry. You've brought me through so much. Help me know, deep in my heart, that I have nothing to fear. I know You are fighting for me even now.

THINK ABOUT IT:

In what ways has God fought for you in the past? Trust that He's still fighting your battles.

Morning
TELL OF HIS GOODNESS

"Only take care, and keep your soul diligently, lest you forget the things that your eyes have seen, and lest they depart from your heart all the days of your life. Make them known to your children and your children's children."

DEUTERONOMY 4:9 ESV

Recalling Your goodness in my life is a key to not worrying, isn't it? When I tell others about all the great things You've done for me, it helps everyone. It helps the listener to know and understand Your character. And it helps me by building my faith and renewing my confidence in Your great love. When worry claims my heart, remind me to talk about the things You've brought me through in the past. Thank You for Your unchanging, unfailing love, Father.

THINK ABOUT IT:

What are some stories you can tell about God's goodness? To whom can you tell them?

Evening
HIS STEADFAST LOVE

"For I the LORD your God am a jealous God, visiting the iniquity of the fathers on the children to the third and fourth generation of those who hate me, but showing steadfast love to thousands of those who love me and keep my commandments."

DEUTERONOMY 5:9–10 ESV

I'm so honored to be a member of Your family, to be called Your child. I do love You, Lord, and I try to keep Your commandments. Because of this, I know I have nothing to fear. Even though I'm not perfect, You know my heart, and You promised to show steadfast, unfailing love to those who love You (that's me) and those who keep Your commandments (that's also me, to the best of my ability). Help me to rest in the confidence of Your never-ending, all-consuming love.

THINK ABOUT IT:

How can you demonstrate your love for God today?

Morning
A HEART LIKE THIS

"Oh that they had such a heart as this always, to fear me and to keep all my commandments, that it might go well with them and with their descendants forever!"
DEUTERONOMY 5:29 ESV

Give me a heart like this, Lord. Instead of fearing my circumstances or my future or even other people, I only want to fear You. A better word for fear, in this case, is *reverence*. I want to be a God-fearing person. Help me to show You reverence, Lord, by keeping Your commandments and honoring You in all I do. I want to be counted among those who truly love You. I know You take care of those who sincerely obey and respect You. More than anything, I want to please You. Give me that kind of heart.

THINK ABOUT IT:
In what ways can you show God honor, reverence, and respect today?

Evening
IMPERFECT LOVE

"For you are a people holy to the LORD your God. The LORD your God has chosen you to be a people for his treasured possession, out of all the peoples who are on the face of the earth. It was not because you were more in number than any other people that the LORD set his love on you and chose you, for you were the fewest of all peoples."
DEUTERONOMY 7:6–7 ESV

I know You don't bless us because we're righteous or because we deserve blessing. Our righteousness is like filthy rags to You (Isaiah 64:6). Instead, You bless those who love You—imperfect as that love may be—because You are good. You bless us because You keep Your promises. You bless us because You chose us. Help me to stop worrying, focus on loving You the best I can, and trust in Your goodness.

THINK ABOUT IT:
How can you show God you love Him today?

Morning
CONFIDENCE

"But blessed is the one who trusts in the LORD, whose confidence is in him."
JEREMIAH 17:7 NIV

When I worry, I don't feel blessed. I guess that's because when I worry, I'm not blessable. I can't always choose the thoughts that enter my mind, but I can choose the thoughts I dwell on. From now on, instead of pausing on worry, fear, and anxiety, I will force those thoughts to the side and focus instead on Your goodness and power. I will set my mind on Your faithfulness, and I'll trust in Your love for me. To the best of my ability, I won't concern myself with anything but pleasing You. I know You will take care of me, and You'll handle my concerns in a far better way than I can imagine. You have my full confidence. Thank You for the freedom that comes with that kind of trust.

THINK ABOUT IT:

Do your thoughts dwell on your fears? Force those thoughts aside, and focus on God's great love for you.

Evening
MADE FOR POWER

For the Spirit God gave us does not make us timid, but gives us power, love and self-discipline.
2 TIMOTHY 1:7 NIV

Dear Father, You didn't make me timid or fearful. You didn't create me to be dominated by worries and anxiety. You created me to be powerful, loving, strong, and self-disciplined. If these worries aren't from You, they must be from the enemy. He wants me to live a defeated, fear-filled life, so he plagues me with thoughts that keep me from being my best self. I've been ruled by worry for so long, I don't know what it feels like to not be afraid. Teach me, Father. Show me what it means to be powerful and in control of my thoughts. Teach me to love You and others with a fierce, unmatchable love. I want to be strong, just as You made me to be.

THINK ABOUT IT:

Do you consider yourself a strong person? Picture yourself wearing God's power everywhere you go.

Morning
GOD IS FOR US

If God is for us, who can be against us?
He who did not spare his own Son,
but gave him up for us all—how
will he not also, along with him,
graciously give us all things?
ROMANS 8:31–32 NIV

Father, this tells the whole story, doesn't it? You love me more than my mind can comprehend. It's a passionate love, a fierce love. You gave Your own beloved Son, Jesus. You traded His life for mine. He was the only one who could suffer death and conquer it in the end, so You sent Him to stand in my place. If You did that, how can I doubt Your love and care for me? How can I worry about trivial, temporary things, when You've already poured out Your bountiful, sacrificial love? My cares are minor in comparison. I know You're more than able to handle every trial I face. Thank You for that kind of love.

THINK ABOUT IT:

What fears dominate your thoughts?
Do you believe God can handle them?

Evening
FOR WHAT IS RIGHT

But even if you should suffer for what
is right, you are blessed. "Do not fear
their threats; do not be frightened."
1 PETER 3:14 NIV

I've often suffered for my own poor choices. That's no fun, but I recognize my role in those trials. But sometimes I do my best to please You, to honor You, to live for You, and I suffer because of it. When that happens, it can feel like You've forsaken me, though You promised You wouldn't. It's hard to equate suffering with blessing, but I guess that's where faith comes in—faith in Your goodness. And faith in knowing You haven't finished my story yet. I know that despite my current hardships, my final chapter will be filled with blessings beyond measure. Give me courage through the fire, Lord. I trust You.

THINK ABOUT IT:

Have you ever suffered for doing
what is right? God knows. He sees.
And He will bless you for it.

Morning
NO FEAR

*Fear of man will prove to be
a snare, but whoever trusts
in the LORD is kept safe.*
PROVERBS 29:31 NIV

When I worry about other people and what they can do to me, when I'm afraid of what others may think of me, that shows a lack of trust in You. In Romans 8:31, I'm reminded that if You are for me, who can be against me? I don't know why I care so much about others when I should only care about what You think. I don't know why they make me so anxious when I have You on my side. Today, right now, I trust in You alone. I will not fear; I'll only trust. I am Your child. You have promised never to leave me or forsake me. I know as long as I stay close to You, You will take care of me.

THINK ABOUT IT:

*Is there a person in your life
who causes you anxiety?
Trust God, and let Him handle it.*

Evening
SETTING MY HEART

*Set your hearts on things above,
where Christ is, seated at the right
hand of God. Set your minds on
things above, not on earthly things.*
COLOSSIANS 3:1–2 NIV

All too often, I do the opposite of what this verse commands. I set my heart on earthly things, and I get stuck there. That's Satan's plan, isn't it? He places worries right in my line of vision, hoping I'll take the bait and get hooked. And so many times, I bite. When those earthly fears and anxieties enter my mind, help me avoid the trap by setting my thoughts on You alone. Instead of worrying, I'll think about Your goodness. I'll praise You. I'll thank You for all the wonderful things You've done. Instead of setting the hook, help me set my heart on You.

THINK ABOUT IT:

*What is Satan's most common
bait in your life to distract you
from focusing on Christ?*

Morning
I SHALL SEE GOD

"For I know that my Redeemer lives, and He shall stand at last on the earth; and after my skin is destroyed, this I know, that in my flesh I shall see God."

JOB 19:25–26 NKJV

Why do I spend so much time thinking about temporary things, when this verse carries such truth? I know You live, Father. You've existed from the beginning of time, and You will be King for all eternity. Your presence is as real—and far more eternal—than my most pressing problems, my most worrisome fears. I can say this with confidence: one day, I will stand before You. I'll see You in the flesh. I'll hug You, and You'll hug me, and we'll spend all eternity loving each other. That's what I want to think about from now on.

THINK ABOUT IT:

How do you think you'll feel when you see God in the flesh for the first time? Bask in His love right now, for you're already in His presence.

Evening
FOR ETERNITY

Then Job arose, tore his robe, and shaved his head; and he fell to the ground and worshiped. And he said: "Naked I came from my mother's womb, and naked shall I return there. The Lord gave, and the Lord has taken away; blessed be the name of the Lord."

JOB 1:20–21 NKJV

Thank You for this reminder that my problems are only temporary. All my fears and doubts, my worries and anxieties will one day melt away in Your presence. Even now, You've sent me Your peace. It's mine for the taking; I only have to accept it as I focus on Your great love. This life will soon pass away, and none of the things that seem so important now will matter at all. I want to live a life that matters for eternity. Blessed is Your name, O Lord!

THINK ABOUT IT:

What things seem important now but won't matter in eternity?

Morning
FOREVERMORE

And I heard a loud voice from heaven saying, "Behold, the tabernacle of God is with men, and He will dwell with them, and they shall be His people. God Himself will be with them and be their God. And God will wipe away every tear from their eyes; there shall be no more death, nor sorrow, nor crying. There shall be no more pain, for the former things have passed away."

REVELATION 21:3–4 NKJV

Thank You for this reminder that the last chapter hasn't played out yet. You've already written the story in advance, but the plot is still happening. You wrote these words so I wouldn't worry. In the end, everything will be okay. Everything will be better than okay as You wipe every tear, right every wrong, and pour out Your love and peace and grace and mercy on Your children forevermore.

THINK ABOUT IT:
Can you picture that day when God will heal all your pain and wipe all your tears?

Evening
SEED AMONG THORNS

"Now he who received seed among the thorns is he who hears the word, and the cares of this world and the deceitfulness of riches choke the word, and he becomes unfruitful."

MATTHEW 13:22 NKJV

I don't want to be like the person in this parable. I've heard Your Word. I've been shown Your way. But the things I worry about are like a thick veil over my eyes. They blind me to Your truth. They push me to forget what I know about You and cause me to lose my faith. I don't want to be a seed among thorns, Father. I want to be planted in the rich, fertile soil of Your truth. Worry and fear are not from You. When my focus strays to my worries, pull my gaze back to You. I love You, and I know You are more than able to take care of all my needs.

THINK ABOUT IT:
How have you been like a seed among thorns? How can you find more fertile ground?

Morning
WHAT TO SAY

"But when they arrest you and deliver you up, do not worry beforehand, or premeditate what you will speak. But whatever is given you in that hour, speak that; for it is not you who speak, but the Holy Spirit."

MARK 13:11 NKJV

I've never had to worry that I'd be thrown in jail or lose my life because of my faith. But I have been in positions where I worried I'd say or do the wrong thing and be judged harshly for it. In those moments, quiet my spirit, and help me listen to You. Let it be Your words that come out of my mouth so others will know You are God. And please be with the people around the world who are in more dire circumstances for their faith. Give them peace, and give them the right words to say.

THINK ABOUT IT:

What conversation are you worried about? God will provide the words if you trust Him and follow His prompting.

Evening
TEMPORARY OR ETERNAL?

Therefore remove sorrow from your heart, and put away evil from your flesh, for childhood and youth are vanity.

ECCLESIASTES 11:10 NKJV

This passage is all about focus. Solomon encourages young people to push aside the follies of this world, because those things that provide pleasure right here, right now, are only temporary. He even calls lustful things "sorrow," because he knows seeking after temporary pleasures will bring sorrow in the end. When I worry about things, in a way, I'm seeking temporary pleasure. Whatever I worry about, if the problem is fixed, I'll have a short-lived relief until another issue comes along for me to worry about. Help me stop wasting my time on those issues that won't matter in ten, twenty, or one hundred years. I want to focus on the permanent joy and peace that come from seeking You.

THINK ABOUT IT:

What are you most worried about? Does it have eternal significance, or is it only temporary?

Morning
AND THE WALLS CAME TUMBLING DOWN!

When the trumpets sounded, the army shouted, and at the sound of the trumpet, when the men gave a loud shout, the wall collapsed; so everyone charged straight in, and they took the city.

JOSHUA 6:20 NIV

They're a safety mechanism, Lord—these walls I've put up. I've fixed them in place so that others can't break through. Unfortunately, I've often built walls between the two of us as well, Lord. I didn't mean for that to happen, but it did. I can sense them in my heart.

Like Joshua, when he faced the walls of Jericho, I come to You today in faith, asking for those walls to be torn down once and for all. I want to charge straight into the promised land of Your peace, victorious and fully set free. No matter how long or how far I have to march, those walls will come down in Jesus' name. Amen.

THINK ABOUT IT:

What walls need to come down in your life?

Evening
YOU'LL TEACH ME ALL THINGS

"But the Helper, the Holy Spirit, whom the Father will send in my name, he will teach you all things and bring to your remembrance all that I have said to you."

JOHN 14:26 ESV

With You, Lord, I feel like I'm getting a college education all over again. I'm on a forever learning curve, but You are teaching me things that no professor could possibly know. You give wisdom and insight and understanding. You offer discernment and peace and joy in place of confusion and frustration.

You are the best teacher around, Lord! Even the things I don't realize I need to know are mine for the taking with You leading the way. I will turn to Your Word, Your way, and Your heart so that I can walk in the fullness of joy You have called me to. Amen.

THINK ABOUT IT:

Are you still on a learning curve? What lessons are you struggling to learn?

Morning
BLIND EYES OPENED

*Therefore the Pharisees also asked
him how he had received his sight.
"He put mud on my eyes," the man
replied, "and I washed, and now I see."*
JOHN 9:15 NIV

I love the story about the blind man
receiving his sight. In some ways I feel
like I have walked a mile in his shoes.
Too many times the enemy has blinded
me to Your love, Your compassion, Your
direction. He's tricky!

But those blinders have fallen off
now! You've given me supernatural 20/20
vision so that I can see things the way
You see them, respond to others as You
would respond to them. When I'm using
this vision, it puts my stresses in perspective. I see them as what they really are—
stepping-stones to something better.

Thank You for making blind eyes see,
Lord. Amen.

THINK ABOUT IT:

*Has God ever given you supernatural
sight to see things as He does?*

Evening
EVERY HIDDEN THING

*Fear God and keep his commandments,
for this is the duty of all mankind.
For God will bring every deed into
judgment, including every hidden
thing, whether it is good or evil.*
ECCLESIASTES 12:13–14 NIV

They think they can get away with it, Lord.
Those things they do in secret? They're
sure You won't notice. The way they've
hurt me. The way they've wounded my
loved ones. They think their actions
are fine and good, that there will be no
price to pay.

But You are exacting a price even
now. You're drawing evil deeds out of
the darkness and into the light. Today
I pray for deliverance for my enemies,
the very ones who hurt me. As You deal
with them, may I learn to forgive so that
I can be set free—and ultimately so that
they can be set free as well. Thank You,
Lord. Amen.

THINK ABOUT IT:

*When did God last deliver
you from your enemies?*

Morning
I WON'T WEAR MY SHAME

Instead of your shame there shall be a double portion; instead of dishonor they shall rejoice in their lot; therefore in their land they shall possess a double portion; they shall have everlasting joy.

ISAIAH 61:7 ESV

Some of the people I know wear their shame on their sleeves, Lord. I can sense it, feel it when I'm around them.

I don't want to be like that. You've taken my shame. You've taken my past. There's no reason to let my yesterdays add any stress to my todays. In place of shame, You've given me a happy heart. You've blessed me with everlasting joy in place of sorrow over past indiscretions.

I love the way Your plan works, Lord. You swap out my bad for Your good. I will never understand such love, but I'm grateful all the same. Amen.

THINK ABOUT IT:
How can you let go of stress-inducing shame today?

Evening
STRESSING OVER A FRIEND IN NEED

Some men took a man who was not able to move his body to Jesus. He was carried on a bed. They looked for a way to take the man into the house where Jesus was. But they could not find a way to take him in because of so many people. They made a hole in the roof over where Jesus stood. Then they let the bed with the sick man on it down before Jesus.

LUKE 5:18–19 NLV

You know who she is, Lord. You know how much I care about her, how worried I've been about her. You know how many sleepless nights I've spent wondering if she will make it through this. Her situation seems too far gone, and I'm fretting over it.

Today I ask that You take charge, not just of her circumstances but of my heart and any role I play in this. I give this situation and this loved one to You, once and for all. Amen.

THINK ABOUT IT:
How do you decide when to help a friend. . .and when not to?

Morning
I'M NOT HELPLESS

Strengthen the feeble hands, steady the knees that give way; say to those with fearful hearts, "Be strong, do not fear; your God will come, he will come with vengeance; with divine retribution he will come to save you."
ISAIAH 35:3–4 NIV

Okay, I'll admit it, Lord: sometimes I act like I'm totally helpless. I allow myself to give in to defeat and despair instead of reminding myself that I have the best helper ever ready to come out swinging on my behalf.

You are the best, after all! You helped David take down Goliath. You helped Joshua take down the walls of Jericho. You remind me through Your Word that I can cross the sea on dry land. Why would I ever doubt Your ability or Your love for Your children, Lord? Thank You, my Lord and helper. I lean on You today. Amen.

THINK ABOUT IT:

How can you remind yourself today that God really will come to save you, that He won't leave you utterly helpless?

Evening
YOU REJOICE OVER ME

"The LORD your God is with you, the Mighty Warrior who saves. He will take great delight in you; in his love he will no longer rebuke you, but will rejoice over you with singing."
ZEPHANIAH 3:17 NIV

Oh, how I love the image this verse presents! I'm down here on Planet Earth, feeling stressed out and worried. And what are You up to, Lord? With joy, You are singing and dancing over me. You haven't got a care in the world! (Or the universe, as the case may be.) You haven't given up on my situation. You're already in celebration mode. That perspective changes everything. Today, may I rejoice—may I praise and sing and celebrate—even before I see the victory. Give me Your heavenly perspective, I pray. Amen.

THINK ABOUT IT:

Does it thrill your heart to know that God is singing over you?

Morning
I WON'T DOUBT

*But when you ask, you must believe
and not doubt, because the one
who doubts is like a wave of the sea,
blown and tossed by the wind.*

JAMES 1:6 NIV

When I come to You, Lord, I must confess that I don't always have sufficient faith to believe You're actually going to do what I'm asking You to do. My requests are huge at times, but my faith is very small.

I don't want to be like a wave blown and tossed by the wind. I want to be firm, steady, like a rock. Today, please take my doubts. Take my fears. Take away that nagging feeling that things are going to get worse instead of better. Replace those feelings with confidence, not in myself but in You. Amen.

THINK ABOUT IT:

*What can you do to remain
steady when the winds blow?*

Evening
PATIENCE IS A VIRTUE

*Love is patient, love is kind. It does
not envy, it does not boast, it is not
proud. It does not dishonor others,
it is not self-seeking, it is not easily
angered, it keeps no record of wrongs.*

1 CORINTHIANS 13:4–5 NIV

Love is patient. I could stop right there while reading this verse, because I know that I'm not always the most patient person around, which must mean I'm not showing adequate love at times, Lord. This has been a shortcoming in my life, I admit.

You've been so patient with me, heavenly Father! So many times You could have scolded or rebuked, but instead You chose to love me through the situation, in spite of my mistakes. Now it's time for me to start showing that same kind of patience to others, even those who stumble and fall more than their fair share. Show me how to exhibit patience to the difficult ones, I pray. Amen.

THINK ABOUT IT:

*Love is patient. Do you exhibit God's
patience in showing love to others?*

Morning
YOU GO ABOVE AND BEYOND!

They all ate and were satisfied, and the disciples picked up twelve basketfuls of broken pieces that were left over.
MATTHEW 14:20 NIV

Average has never been good enough for You, Lord! You created giraffes with elevator-length necks. You created flamingos with long, skinny legs. You created mountain peaks so high we can't possibly climb them.

You're an "above and beyond" sort of God. And because You've always been willing to go above and beyond with Your children, I want to learn to do the same for others. That same generosity, that same exuberance to do more. . .may it be mine as well. May no one ever accuse me of being normal or average! Amen.

THINK ABOUT IT:

When was the last time God surprised you by going above and beyond?

Evening
ABUNDANT LOVE

And God is able to make all grace abound toward you, that you, always having all sufficiency in all things, may have an abundance for every good work.
2 CORINTHIANS 9:8 NKJV

Abundance. One dictionary defines it as an extremely plentiful supply; overflowing fullness; affluence; wealth. This verse promises that You'll make sure I have an abundance of whatever I need for every good work You've planned for me. Sometimes I long for abundance for my own selfish needs. You didn't promise to supply that. But You, in Your grace, will provide an overflowing amount of the things I need to help others, to be kind and generous, to work hard, to encourage the people around me. You'll supply everything I need to love like You love. Thank You for loving me abundantly so I can love others.

THINK ABOUT IT:

How has God loved you abundantly? How can you show that abundant love to others?

Morning
TRUE LIFE

Then He said to His disciples,
"Therefore I say to you, do not worry
about your life, what you will eat;
nor about the body, what you will
put on. Life is more than food, and
the body is more than clothing."

LUKE 12:22–23 NKJV

These words seem so simple when I read them. Yet they're hard to put into practice. I worry about what I eat, what I wear, how I'll pay my bills, what people think of me, and so many other things. Yet life is more than food, which will only satisfy me for a few hours. Life is more than clothing, which will get ripped and stained and eventually destroyed. True life is found only through a relationship with You. My focus should be on the eternal, not on the temporary. Help me shift my thinking to my relationship with You and trust You to take care of the rest.

THINK ABOUT IT:

What do you worry about most?
Can you trust God to take care of it?

Evening
ONLY YOU

For in much wisdom is much
grief, and he who increases
knowledge increases sorrow.

ECCLESIASTES 1:18 NKJV

This verse, written by King Solomon, seems kind of depressing. But when I think about its context, I understand what he was saying. Solomon spent much of his life seeking earthly knowledge and the wisdom of man, but in the end, it was all folly. He had all the riches he could desire, but it didn't bring him peace. I can relate. So much of my life is spent striving after things that, in the end, don't satisfy. Whether it's earthly wisdom, education, money, relationships, or health, none of it brings me the results I long for. Only You, Father, only You can bring me peace and serenity and joy. Help me learn from Solomon's mistakes and stop seeking things that won't quench my inner thirst. I only want to seek You.

THINK ABOUT IT:

What have you thought would
bring you peace only to find
you were wrong? Jesus Christ
will never let you down.

Morning
A GOOD WORD

*Anxiety in the heart of man
causes depression, but a good
word makes it glad.*
PROVERBS 12:25 NKJV

My anxiety does tend to plunge me into depression. It causes me to not be my best self, to avoid other people, and to focus my thoughts on the negative. The second part of this verse—a good word—can come from a number of sources. Sometimes I wait for others to encourage me, but that's hit or miss. But Your Word is a constant source of encouragement for me. I don't know why I don't spend more time reading it. When I'm feeling worried, anxious, and depressed, bring Your Word to mind. Your words always bring me peace, comfort, and joy. In the same way, help me to always speak "good words" to other people as I seek to uplift them the way You uplift me.

THINK ABOUT IT:

*What "good word" is God sending to
your mind right now? He loves you,
and that's always a good place to start.*

Evening
FINDING PEACE

*"Peace I leave with you, My peace I
give to you; not as the world gives
do I give to you. Let not your heart
be troubled, neither let it be afraid."*
JOHN 14:27 NKJV

Peace is a wonderful gift, but it seems just out of reach. Each time I think I've grasped it, it slips through my fingers. Perhaps that's because I'm looking to the wrong source. I seek that calm through my job, my relationships, my health, or my money. According to this verse, Your peace is already mine. You've already given it. And You don't give money or health or even earthly relationships as the source of peace because those things are temporary. The peace You give is in You alone, and You will never leave, never change. That's why I don't need to be troubled or afraid. Your love, Your peace is a permanent fixture in my life. All I have to do is hold on to You.

THINK ABOUT IT:

Who or what is your source of peace?

Morning
WHO'S IN CONTROL?

"Let not your heart be troubled;
you believe in God, believe also in Me."

JOHN 14:1 NKJV

"Let not your heart be troubled." That command indicates I have control over whether or not my heart is troubled. It suggests I can govern the worries and fears that plague me. I think that's a lot of my problem, Lord. Instead of controlling my thoughts, I let my thoughts control me. Anything that flits through my mind becomes the boss of me, dictating my mood and even my actions. My lack of control indicates a lack of faith in You. Forgive me, Father. I believe in You. I trust You. I have faith in You alone. Today and every day, when anxious thoughts enter my mind, give me the strength and discipline to send them packing.

THINK ABOUT IT:

What is your foremost concern right now? What can you do to keep that concern from dictating your thoughts and actions? God is waiting to take them from you if you'll just hand them over.

Evening
JOY IN THE MIDST

In the multitude of my anxieties within
me, your comforts delight my soul.

PSALM 94:19 NKJV

I'm so glad the psalmist wrote that he had a multitude of anxieties. Though I'm not happy for anyone to feel the way I do, it does make me feel less alone in my worries. The writer shared that even in the midst of all his worries and cares, he found comfort. Even more than comfort, he found delight. Can I really find joy in the middle of my fears? I believe I can, but only through You. Only when I totally and completely submit myself to You can I experience that kind of gift. Today, Father, I am Yours. I leave all my worries in Your hands. Thank You for Your comfort, which delights my soul.

THINK ABOUT IT:

Have you ever felt joy and delight in the middle of, or in spite of, your worries? Ask God to help you experience that today.

DAY 209

Morning
HUMILITY

Therefore humble yourselves under the mighty hand of God, that He may exalt you in due time, casting all your care upon Him, for He cares for you.

1 PETER 5:6–7 NKJV

I love it when You give recipes. This passage provides a recipe for success. If I humble myself before You, You will exalt me in Your time. Much of my worry stems from wanting to exalt myself instead of waiting on You. I want that job, that promotion, that success—either for myself or for those I love. Worry stems from focusing on myself and my circumstances instead of focusing on You. Teach me what humility looks like. I know I can start by casting all my worries on You, leaving them in Your capable hands, and not thinking about them anymore. Thank You for Your tender, loving care over all my circumstances.

THINK ABOUT IT:
How can humility help alleviate your anxiety?

Evening
FEAR NOT

"Fear not, for I am with you; be not dismayed, for I am your God. I will strengthen you, yes, I will help you, I will uphold you with My righteous right hand."

ISAIAH 41:10 NKJV

As I read these words, I can almost hear a parent speaking to a small, frightened child. *"Shush! Don't be afraid. I'm right here. I've got you. See? I'm holding on to you."* The difference is any earthly parent is flawed. An earthly parent is limited in power and influence. If an imperfect earthly parent will do all in their power to protect their cherished child, how much more will You, the Almighty God, do to protect me? You gave the ultimate sacrifice—Your Son. Why do I question Your motives or Your desire to take care of every need in my life? Thank You for holding on to me, Father.

THINK ABOUT IT:
Can you picture God holding you right now? He loves you, and He will never let you go.

Morning
WITH EQUAL MEASURE

The point is this: whoever sows sparingly will also reap sparingly, and whoever sows bountifully will also reap bountifully. Each one must give as he has decided in his heart, not reluctantly or under compulsion, for God loves a cheerful giver.

2 CORINTHIANS 9:6–7 ESV

God, You have given me so much. You gave Your Son for my redemption. You fill my life with Your blessings. I thank You for Your overwhelming generosity toward me. As I budget, help me give out of such a generous heart. Open my eyes to see the good that comes from pouring Your resources into others. And just as You give out of love, may my giving flow from love, not with a sense of obligation but with joy in witnessing Your hand at work. The blessings will be plentiful. Amen.

THINK ABOUT IT:

Do you believe that God will pour into your life as much as you pour out?

Evening
ANCHORED

So when God desired to show more convincingly to the heirs of the promise the unchangeable character of his purpose, he guaranteed it with an oath, so that by two unchangeable things, in which it is impossible for God to lie, we who have fled for refuge might have strong encouragement to hold fast to the hope set before us. We have this as a sure and steadfast anchor of the soul.

HEBREWS 6:17–19 ESV

God, when You make a promise, You keep it. Unlike people, who have let me down, You are faithful. I do not have to wonder if what You said is true. You, almighty God who cannot lie, guarantee that it is. I can run to Your promises as refuge; I can rest in Your promises as an anchor for my soul. May I never waver in my trust, I pray. Amen.

THINK ABOUT IT:

What truths from God's Word help you when you begin to doubt His promises?

DAY 211

Morning
CONTENT NO MATTER WHAT

I have learned in whatever situation I am to be content. I know how to be brought low, and I know how to abound. In any and every circumstance, I have learned the secret of facing plenty and hunger, abundance and need. I can do all things through him who strengthens me.

PHILIPPIANS 4:11–13 ESV

Lord, there's no telling what this life will bring. Much like what Paul described, I will experience good times and bad, be brought low and abound, face plenty and need. But whatever my current state or the future holds, I know the key to living successfully in contentment—total reliance on You. It is not only in the difficult times that I need You, Lord. I need You every day, good or bad. You strengthen me to live according to Your will, come what may. Amen.

THINK ABOUT IT:
How is Christ strengthening you to face today?

Evening
IF ONLY

And behold, a woman who had suffered from a discharge of blood for twelve years came up behind him and touched the fringe of his garment, for she said to herself, "If I only touch his garment, I will be made well." Jesus turned, and seeing her he said, "Take heart, daughter; your faith has made you well."

MATTHEW 9:20–22 ESV

Oh, to have the faith of this woman! Lord, she believed that Your power was so great that even touching the fringe of Your clothes would heal her. And she was right; You are almighty. As I face the difficult times in my life, remind me that You are able to heal, to save, with just a word. So much of the fear and doubt I experience comes from a faulty view of You. What appears impossible is possible under Your mighty hand. May I never limit my faith by underestimating You, Lord. Amen.

THINK ABOUT IT:
How does an inadequate conception of God keep you from living fully in faith?

Morning
READY TO HEAR

And the LORD came and stood, calling as at other times, "Samuel! Samuel!" And Samuel said, "Speak, for your servant hears."

1 SAMUEL 3:10 ESV

Lord, four times You called Samuel. You didn't stop when he didn't hear You. You called again. And You kept calling until he understood. Then Samuel was ready to listen, ready to obey. Throughout my life, You call to me. Sometimes I'm slow to hear, or I think I hear and then act when I really don't understand yet. Be patient with me, I pray. As I hurry to do what's in my mind, draw me back to You, to a place where I can listen for Your voice. Never give up calling my name until I hear—really hear—and obey. I want to be a willing servant, ready to follow Your leading. Amen.

THINK ABOUT IT:

Do you pause in your prayers to leave space for the Holy Spirit to "call" to your heart?

Evening
LIGHT UP THE WORLD

Do all things without grumbling or disputing, that you may be blameless and innocent, children of God without blemish in the midst of a crooked and twisted generation, among whom you shine as lights in the world, holding fast to the word of life.

PHILIPPIANS 2:14–16 ESV

Father, may I be ever mindful of the impression I leave with others about my faith. If I am downcast and complaining about Your will in my life, how will others see Your loving care despite difficult times? If I constantly question Your sovereignty, who will turn to You as Lord? I want to reflect Your love, the joy of being Your child, and the peace that only flows from You. As I shine as a light in the darkness, let others see and draw close to life. Amen.

THINK ABOUT IT:

How do others see Christ and a life of faith when they look at you?

DAY 213

Morning
OUR DELIVERANCE

For we were so utterly burdened beyond our strength that we despaired of life itself. . . . But that was to make us rely not on ourselves but on God who raises the dead. He delivered us from such a deadly peril, and he will deliver us. On him we have set our hope that he will deliver us again. You also must help us by prayer.

2 Corinthians 1:8–11 esv

Father, Your children face many difficult, sometimes frightening, times. Natural disasters, terrorism, persecution. . . In those times, You are our hope and rescue. You have the power to deliver us—from danger, evil, even death. As we face what seem to be insurmountable circumstances, guard our hearts. Draw us close so that we depend only on You. Remind us also to pray for those who are burdened beyond what they are able to bear alone. May they find relief in relying on Your strength. Amen.

THINK ABOUT IT:
Do you believe God can use despair to deepen our faith?

Evening
FREE IN CHRIST

For freedom Christ has set us free; stand firm therefore, and do not submit again to a yoke of slavery. . . . You were running well. Who hindered you from obeying the truth? This persuasion is not from him who calls you.

Galatians 5:1, 7–8 esv

Lord, believers in the early church encountered those who added works to grace. While good flows from a heart of faith, it is not what grants salvation. Christ sets us free. The grace that brings redemption allows us to live lives unburdened by guilt over past sin and strengthened through the Holy Spirit to reject present sin. May I never be led astray from a life rooted in faith alone, Lord. May I be free from the shackles of legalism and sin, and free to live for You. Amen.

THINK ABOUT IT:
What burdens of legalism are keeping you from thriving under God's grace?

Morning
DIRECT FROM GOD

All Scripture is breathed out by
God and profitable for teaching,
for reproof, for correction, and
for training in righteousness, that
the man of God may be complete,
equipped for every good work.

2 Timothy 3:16–17 esv

Lord, Your Word is amazing! It is a part of You, Your very breath, and through it You speak softly to my heart. You did not leave me to try and learn Your righteous ways on my own; that would be impossible for me. So You left Your Word, holy and unchanged through history, to reveal Your truth. With it, You convict me of sin and point me toward repentance and healing. Your sweet words buoy me in difficulty. They lead me back to You when I stray. They whisper wisdom in times of greatest need. What can Your Word not do? Amen.

THINK ABOUT IT:

Do you approach reading the Bible as a chore or as a chance to hear God speak into your life?

Evening
DEATH VANQUISHED

"Death is swallowed up in victory."
"O death, where is your victory?
O death, where is your sting?"
The sting of death is sin, and the
power of sin is the law. But thanks
be to God, who gives us the victory
through our Lord Jesus Christ.

1 Corinthians 15:54–57 esv

Father, nothing on this earth strikes quite as much fear as death. Even the thought of it is like a painful sting. Death, spiritual and physical, is what every person faces—apart from You. When You sent Your precious, perfect Son to die in our place, You broke the power of death. You provided a way to righteousness, a way to life with You. Even in the pain of this world, we have victory. We need not fear but can hold on to hope of eternity with You in heaven. Thank You, Father! Amen.

THINK ABOUT IT:

How does your view of death change when you focus on Jesus?

Morning
PRAISE HIM

Blessed be the name of the Lord from this time forth and forevermore! From the rising of the sun to its setting, the name of the Lord is to be praised! The Lord is high above all nations, and his glory above the heavens! Who is like the Lord our God, who is seated on high, who looks far down on the heavens and the earth?

Psalm 113:2–6 esv

God, You are like no other. In this world or out of it, You are high above all. As I come to You in prayer, may my first thoughts be praise to You for everything You do, for everything You are. Forever. So many times my focus is on me when I should lift my eyes to You and raise my hands in worship. Blessed is Your name, God. Worthy are You of my praise. Amen.

THINK ABOUT IT:

How can you make praise a daily part of your prayers and your life?

Evening
JOY JUST AHEAD

Weeping may tarry for the night, but joy comes with the morning. . . . You have turned for me my mourning into dancing; you have loosed my sackcloth and clothed me with gladness, that my glory may sing your praise and not be silent. O Lord my God, I will give thanks to you forever!

Psalm 30:5, 11–12 esv

Father, we all face dark nights in this life. Whether financial strain, sickness, or the loss of a loved one. . .hard times can sap our energy and leave us weeping. When I face difficulty, be with me to dry my tears. Hold me tight until the morning dawns. Then I will dance with joy. I will sing of Your power to transform me, to transform what once seemed an endless darkness into bright glory. I cry out with David: my God, I will give thanks to You forever! Amen.

THINK ABOUT IT:

How has your faith helped you endure trying times with the hope of joy to come?

Morning
THIRSTY FOR THE WORD

So put away all malice and all deceit and hypocrisy and envy and all slander. Like newborn infants, long for the pure spiritual milk, that by it you may grow up into salvation—if indeed you have tasted that the Lord is good.

1 PETER 2:1–3 ESV

Father, when I first came to You, I was like an infant, and like an infant who grows day by day, I am to grow in my faith. But spiritual growth can't happen if I'm harboring sin. Help me clear sin from my life and instead thirst for Your Word. Like milk for my soul, it has all that I need to mature in my Christian walk. You are good, Father, and Your goodness toward me propels me to seek Your truth. May I never stop growing. Amen.

THINK ABOUT IT:

Do you long for the spiritual milk of God's Word, or do you need to pray for renewed thirst?

Evening
HOLY CORRECTION

For the moment all discipline seems painful rather than pleasant, but later it yields the peaceful fruit of righteousness to those who have been trained by it. Therefore lift your drooping hands and strengthen your weak knees, and make straight paths for your feet, so that what is lame may not be put out of joint but rather be healed.

HEBREWS 12:11–13 ESV

Heavenly Father, when a loving parent disciplines a child, it is for the child's good, to teach her and keep her safe. You do the same for Your children, for me. You guide me toward holiness; You keep me from harm. While the discipline is unpleasant, it flows from Your immense love. I don't want to become discouraged or bitter. I want to yield, opening my eyes and ears to what You would have me learn. You see the end result: a healed me. Amen.

THINK ABOUT IT:

Would God's love for us be complete without His divine discipline?

Morning
JESUS, MOST HIGH

He is the image of the invisible God, the firstborn of all creation. For by him all things were created, in heaven and on earth, visible and invisible, whether thrones or dominions or rulers or authorities—all things were created through him and for him. And he is before all things, and in him all things hold together.

COLOSSIANS 1:15–17 ESV

Jesus, may I never forget the miracle that You are—God in flesh. In every attribute You are creator God, yet You walked the earth side by side with Your creation. You are above all, yet You humbled Yourself to seek lost souls and bring them to Your throne of grace. As one of Your created beings, I exist to give You glory. I praise You for holding everything together—from the vast universe to my individual life. Amen.

THINK ABOUT IT:

In seeing Christ as a baby born and a man crucified, do you worship Him also as holy God?

Evening
LOYAL WOMAN

But Ruth said, "Do not urge me to leave you or to return from following you. For where you go I will go, and where you lodge I will lodge. Your people shall be my people, and your God my God."

RUTH 1:16 ESV

God, You prize loyalty; You honor it. Ruth, burdened by the grief over losing her husband, could have sought solace by returning to her homeland, her people. But Ruth knew where she belonged—beside Naomi. She knew her role—to offer support to her family and worship to You. Despite the prospect of difficult times ahead, Ruth remained loyal, and You rewarded that loyalty. May my life display such faithfulness, God. May I never abandon my loved ones or You for the safe path. However rocky or clear the road ahead may be, You, ever loyal, will remain by my side. Amen.

THINK ABOUT IT:

What blessings might Ruth have lost had she chosen comfort over faith?

Morning
EVERY NEED

Then Jesus called his disciples to him and said, "I have compassion on the crowd because they have been with me now three days and have nothing to eat. And I am unwilling to send them away hungry, lest they faint on the way."

MATTHEW 15:32 ESV

Jesus, while You lived on earth, You did many amazing acts. You healed the sick and cast out demons. You walked on water and calmed storms. You lived a sinless life to rescue a sinful world. Along with all the miraculous, You were still Lord of the everyday too. You knew the crowd gathered to hear You would be hungry; You had compassion and provided for their need. Still today, You know what I need. You anticipate my weakness and have a plan to see me through. You watch out for me when I can't see the trouble ahead. Thank You for Your compassion for even the smallest care. Amen.

THINK ABOUT IT:

Why has God preserved these words of Jesus for us to read today?

Evening
PAY ATTENTION

Therefore we must pay much closer attention to what we have heard, lest we drift away from it. For since the message declared by angels proved to be reliable, and every transgression or disobedience received a just retribution, how shall we escape if we neglect such a great salvation? It was declared at first by the Lord, and it was attested to us by those who heard.

HEBREWS 2:1–3 ESV

Lord, Your gospel is an anchor for our lives. It is the truth that saves, proven without doubt over the centuries. The writer of Hebrews warns us to pay attention—close attention—to what we've heard. We are not to hear and move on but make the message the center of us. Impress on me the importance of Your words, Lord, that I may remain close, anchored to Your salvation as the direction for my life. Amen.

THINK ABOUT IT:

Do you need to re-center the gospel message in your life?

Morning
FOR ETERNITY

Of old you laid the foundation of the earth, and the heavens are the work of your hands. They will perish, but you will remain; they will all wear out like a garment. You will change them like a robe, and they will pass away, but you are the same, and your years have no end.

PSALM 102:25–27 ESV

Lord, just looking through my closet, I can see the truth of this psalm. No matter how well made and beautiful they were when new, clothes wear out. The seams weaken; the fabric thins and tears over time. Eventually, I toss them away. Your creation is just the same. No matter how well made and beautiful it may have been when You spoke it into existence, this earth and all in it will come to an end. But You remain eternal, God. Praise to You forever. Amen.

THINK ABOUT IT:

Because change is such a normal part of this life, is it difficult to see God as unchanging?

Evening
HELP OR HINDER

From that time Jesus began to show his disciples that he must go to Jerusalem and suffer many things. . . . And Peter took him aside and began to rebuke him, saying, "Far be it from you, Lord! This shall never happen to you." But he turned and said to Peter, "Get behind me, Satan! You are a hindrance to me. For you are not setting your mind on the things of God, but on the things of man."

MATTHEW 16:21–23 ESV

Lord, You loved Peter. He was one of Your trusted disciples and a part of building the early church. But he was human and susceptible to Satan's schemes. Anyone and anything not in line with Your divine plan is a hindrance. I don't want to get in Your way, Lord. I want to be a part of forwarding Your plans—in my life and the world. Shift my thoughts toward You, I pray. Amen.

THINK ABOUT IT:

Is your mindset making you a stumbling block or a stepping-stone in God's plan?

Morning
LITTLE CHILDREN

*"Let the little children come to me,
and do not hinder them, for
the kingdom of God belongs
to such as these."*

MARK 10:14 NIV

Lord, help me to remember—when my life is busy, my work demanding, and people at every turn asking me for help—that I can learn from children. I can slow down. I can focus intently on one tiny thing at a time. I can laugh easily. I can love with a big heart and big hugs. I can smile at everyone I see. I can dance with abandon. I can run barefoot. I can sing loud. I can make up stories. I can sit and listen too. I can be Your child, Lord. I can come to You. Now and forever. Amen.

THINK ABOUT IT:

*Imagine you are one of the children
in the crowd, coming to see Jesus.
What would you like to ask Him?*

Evening
NURSING

*Just as a nursing mother cares for her
children, so we cared for you. Because
we loved you so much, we were
delighted to share with you not only
the gospel of God but our lives as well.*

1 THESSALONIANS 2:7–8 NIV

The beautiful thing about nursing is not just the act itself, but it is in what the mother gives besides milk from her body. The milk is the symbol of all the many small and large sacrifices to come. Sacrifices of time and money, of energy and will, of gifts and achievements. Lord, let me remember this act of love as a symbol of how we are to feed and care for others—not just providing the facts or the gospel message, but giving from our hearts as well. When we share our lives with others, we show them what living in Your kingdom is really like. Please open my heart to share my life with Your children, Lord. Amen.

THINK ABOUT IT:

*In what ways can you share your
life—and the gospel—with others?*

Morning
A PURE HEART

*Create in me a pure heart, O God,
and renew a steadfast spirit within me.*
PSALM 51:10 NIV

Lord, I get weighed down by the list of sins that seems to grow every day. I know You don't keep a record of wrongs. I know that once You have forgiven me, I am indeed forgiven. But Lord, I keep falling back into my old ways. I keep losing my patience. I keep saying harsh words to my children. I keep relying on deception instead of just holding on to the truth. Lord, please make my heart pure. Make my desires be like Yours. Make my spirit strong and constant so I can stick to Your plan for me and my family. I know I am responsible for teaching my children Your ways. Help me, Lord, to live up to all You ask of me. Amen.

THINK ABOUT IT:

What will it take for your heart to be pure today? What words of God can help renew your spirit?

Evening
LIKE WAX

The mountains melt like wax before the LORD, before the Lord of all the earth. The heavens proclaim his righteousness, and all peoples see his glory.
PSALM 97:5–6 NIV

God of glory, I see Your hugeness, the enormity of Your strength, and the might of Your hand. I know You are bigger than the mountains and fiercer than the molten core of this planet. You are to be feared. Lord, help me show my child that the God we serve is bigger, better, stronger, wiser, and more full of love for us than any other god that people may claim. As I lie on my back and gaze at the heavens, let the massiveness of Your creation fill my mind with awe. Let Your creativity dazzle my thoughts. Amen.

THINK ABOUT IT:

What leads you to be filled with awe of God?

Morning
PROPER RESPECT

*Show proper respect to everyone,
love the family of believers,
fear God, honor the emperor.*

1 PETER 2:17 NIV

Lord, we are living in such a time when I don't even know if people recognize what proper respect looks like! People openly scoff and speak with contempt about our leaders, and our leaders in turn twist words and devise messages meant to cut others down and sow seeds of discord instead of promoting harmony and peace. God, it is easy to love the family of believers when everyone is getting along well. But when we are all so different, with such varied goals and perspectives, it can get tricky. Lord, help me to talk with people I trust and respect about the best way forward. Amen.

THINK ABOUT IT:

Do you know someone who speaks with respect toward others, no matter who they are? What might God want you to learn from him or her?

Evening
GOD OF GLORY

*The voice of the LORD is over the waters;
the God of glory thunders, the LORD
thunders over the mighty waters.*

PSALM 29:3 NIV

Lightning flashes across the sky, making the room glow for just a moment. Then with a low rumble, the thunder rolls through the house, rattling the windows. Thunder seems so big—too big for us to understand. You are big, Lord. Big and powerful and strong and glorious. I tell my child that sometimes You speak like the thunder—in a voice that rumbles and rages. And sometimes You speak like the spring rain—softly pattering on our paths. But what we can be sure of, and what can calm our fears, is that You always speak. And You are always in control. Thank You, Lord, God of glory, God of thunder. Amen.

THINK ABOUT IT:

What is something in nature that reminds you of a quality of God?

Morning
CALLED TO BE
A DISCIPLE

When Jesus had called the Twelve together, he gave them power and authority to drive out all demons and to cure diseases, and he sent them out to proclaim the kingdom of God and to heal the sick.

LUKE 9:1–2 NIV

I'll admit it, Lord: I'm not always the best at playing along in a group setting. Sometimes I like to be the one in charge. I enjoy dishing out instructions, but I'm not so keen on taking them.

Being Your disciple, however? I am more than happy to submit to Your authority, God! You offer me something that no other leader does—power to pray with faith, to believe for miracles. Authority to overcome even the biggest adversities. Best of all, You give me joy for the journey. I can always trust in You. Being Your disciple is a privilege, an honor, a challenge, and a joy! Amen.

THINK ABOUT IT:

God has given you authority just as He gave the first disciples authority. When was the last time you used it?

Evening
YOU COME THROUGH
FOR YOUR OWN

"My God sent his angel, and he shut the mouths of the lions. They have not hurt me, because I was found innocent in his sight. Nor have I ever done any wrong before you, Your Majesty."

DANIEL 6:22 NIV

Daniel in the lions' den. The three Hebrew men in the fiery furnace. David facing down the giant. Your Word is filled with stories of people who faced great trials and seemingly impossible situations.

Time and again You've come through for Your own! You delivered Daniel from the mouths of the lions. He wasn't harmed at all by those ferocious beasts. What a miracle! So why do I fret? Why do I forget that the same God who delivered Daniel stands ready to deliver me?

Thank You, my miracle-working God. Amen.

THINK ABOUT IT:

Has God shut the mouths of lions for you?

DAY 224

Morning
I'M BRINGING IT TO YOU, LORD

"This, then, is how you should pray: 'Our Father in heaven, hallowed be your name.'"
MATTHEW 6:9 NIV

How many times have I run to others with my problems, Lord? Too many to count! I go to friends. I go to loved ones. I whine and complain to my best friend or take my gripes to social media for the masses to share.

Sometimes You're the last one on my list. I wonder why I'm so stressed out, and then I realize I haven't connected with the only one who can actually transform the situation for me. So, Lord, I come to You today. I bring my grievances and my woes to You, along with my joys and celebrations.

May I never forget to come to You first. Amen.

THINK ABOUT IT:
Have you ever run to friends or an addiction instead of going to Jesus?

Evening
FRIENDS WHO HAVE MY BACK

Then Jonathan made a covenant with David, because he loved him as his own soul.
1 SAMUEL 18:3 ESV

I love the story of David and Jonathan, Lord! It's so wonderful to have a bosom friend, someone you can confide in. She not only keeps your secrets; she prays for you, encourages you, and is always there when you need her.

I long to be that kind of friend to others, one who is trustworthy and true. Speaking of amazing friends. . .You are the best, Jesus! When I can trust no other, I can put my faith in You. When others let me down, I know You never will. You are the best friend I could ever have, and I'm overwhelmed with gratitude! Amen.

THINK ABOUT IT:
Which friends do you "love as your own soul"?

Morning
YOUR PROMISES
ARE SURE

"I am putting my rainbow in the clouds as the sign of the agreement between me and the earth."

GENESIS 9:13 NCV

You hung a rainbow in the sky to remind Noah of Your promise that You would never again flood the earth, Lord. All I have to do is look up on a rainy day and see those brilliant colors shimmering overhead to be reminded that You always keep Your word. If You say it, You will do it. Your promises are sure.

My promises? Not so much. I often fall short of doing what I say I will do. I need reminding. You, Lord? I never have to remind You. You provide, and at just the right time. How grateful I am for the assurance of Your promises. Amen.

THINK ABOUT IT:
Are you the kind of person who needs and likes reminders?

Evening
I'M PUTTING YOU FIRST

"But seek first the kingdom of God and his righteousness, and all these things will be added to you."

MATTHEW 6:33 ESV

I need to keep You in Your rightful place, Lord! I don't always do that, I confess. Many times I put my own wants and wishes, my own hopes and dreams, above my passion for You. Sometimes I even put the wants and wishes of others above the things You have clearly called me to do.

I'm so sorry for all of the times I didn't put You first. You are Lord of all and deserving of Your rightful place in my heart and my life. When I put things in the proper order, the storms quiet, the seas grow still, and my heart is at peace. How I praise You for the peace You bring! Amen.

THINK ABOUT IT:
What does it mean to put God first?

Morning
YOU'RE A GOD WHO SUPPLIES

"For this is what the Lord, the God of Israel, says: 'The jar of flour will not be used up and the jug of oil will not run dry until the day the Lord sends rain on the land.' "

1 Kings 17:14 niv

Oh, how I love the stories of Your provision! You fed the multitude with five loaves of bread and two fish. You fed the prophet Elijah with a near-empty jar of flour and oil. You made sure the Israelites had manna and quail in the desert.

You always provide. In fact, You go above and beyond. So why would I doubt that You would do the same for me?

Today, I will trust You for my provision—the needs in my bank account, my pantry, even my heart. You're going to pour out blessings on me above what I could ask or think, Lord, and I'm ready with hands extended! Amen.

THINK ABOUT IT:
Has the Lord ever provided for you in a supernatural way?

Evening
DISTRESSED

Out of my distress I called on the Lord; the Lord answered me and set me free. The Lord is on my side; I will not fear. What can man do to me? The Lord is on my side as my helper; I shall look in triumph on those who hate me.

Psalm 118:5–7 esv

Father, I could have written this psalm. Right now I'm in distress over so many things. Here, in the middle of my mess, I call to You. I know You are on my side, always working for my good. I know with You in my corner, I have nothing to fear. . . and yet I'm afraid. So here I am, talking to You, knowing You hear me. This simple act of prayer puts me in a better state of mind. Thank You for always being there for me. I love You, I trust You, and I know You have good things in store for my life.

THINK ABOUT IT:
What distresses you right now? Talk to God about it.

Morning
I'M LEARNING FROM YOUR CREATION

"But ask the beasts, and they will teach you; the birds of the heavens, and they will tell you; or the bushes of the earth, and they will teach you; and the fish of the sea will declare to you. Who among all these does not know that the hand of the Lord has done this? In his hand is the life of every living thing and the breath of all mankind."
JOB 12:7–10 ESV

Caterpillars that morph into butterflies. Ocean waves that pound against the shore and then return to the sea to begin the process all over again. Mountain peaks that stand jagged and strong. I marvel at Your creation, Lord! These things delight me for they all point to You. Even the harshest things, like storm winds or fierce animals, are a reminder of Your grandeur.

You didn't miss a thing when You created the universe, Lord. So why would I ever think You would overlook the details of my life? You know. . .and You care. If You cared enough to make a giraffe's neck long enough to nibble from the trees above, surely You can take care of me. Amen.

THINK ABOUT IT:
What's your favorite part of God's creation?

Evening
YOUR FACE SHINES UPON ME

"The Lord bless you and keep you; the Lord make his face shine on you and be gracious to you; the Lord turn his face toward you and give you peace."
NUMBERS 6:24–26 NIV

I'll admit it, Lord. There are seasons when I feel overlooked. Forgotten. I wonder if the people in my world even remember I'm here at all. The stresses of my everyday life add up, but no one is around to share the load. No one seems to have time.

Then I remember this verse, and I can't help but smile. You're blessing me even during the stressful seasons. You're keeping me in good times and bad. You're making Your face shine upon me.

Wow! I could pause right there and lift my hands in celebration! The radiant blessing of Your holy presence brings peace to my soul, Lord. Thank You for shining down on me. Amen.

THINK ABOUT IT:
How do you sense God's face shining upon you?

Morning
HOPE FOR THE FUTURE

There is surely a future hope for you,
and your hope will not be cut off.
PROVERBS 23:18 NIV

Sometimes I'm fickle. I lose hope so quickly. I forget the marvelous blessings of yesterday (or even five minutes ago) and give up before the battle has even begun.

You're not a "giving up" sort of God. No, You're always reminding me that there's hope, no matter how bleak things look. And You're not keen on letting me give up either, are You, Lord? You nudge me to keep going even when my feelings dictate otherwise.

There is surely a future hope for me. So I really don't have anything to worry about, do I? If it's sure, if it's certain. . .then I have nothing to fear. Today, I lay down my worries and ask for faith to believe that my tomorrows are already in Your hands. Amen.

THINK ABOUT IT:

How does the word surely *drive home the point of today's verse?*

Evening
A GOOD TRADE

Be anxious for nothing, but in
everything by prayer and supplication,
with thanksgiving, let your requests
be made known to God; and the
peace of God, which surpasses all
understanding, will guard your hearts
and minds through Christ Jesus.
PHILIPPIANS 4:6–7 NKJV

Be anxious for nothing. Really? I feel like I'm anxious for everything. Anxiety gets in my skin, in my bones. It acts like a filter, coloring everything I view. Good thing You offer the solution to this problem. In everything, I should pray. In everything, I should give thanks. In everything, I should tell You what I want—the deepest desires of my heart—and You will give me peace. This doesn't say You'll give me everything I ask for. But You'll exchange my worries for peace. Thank You for Your tender love that trades my worst for Your best.

THINK ABOUT IT:

How would your days be
different if they were filled
with peace instead of worry?

Morning
CALMING THE STORM

And he awoke and rebuked the wind and said to the sea, "Peace! Be still!" And the wind ceased, and there was a great calm.

MARK 4:39 ESV

Right now, I feel like there's a great storm in my life. It feels dangerous and out of control, and I want it to end. Everything is turbulent, and I feel I'll be tossed overboard at any moment. I worry with every breath, and I cry myself to sleep at night—if I sleep at all. I need You to say, "Peace! Be still!" to the storms in my heart, Father. Even as I pray, I feel Your power taking control of the tsunami, calming the winds, bringing peace to my thoughts and emotions. Thank You for quieting the hurricane inside my heart.

THINK ABOUT IT:

What hurricane is blowing inside your heart right now? Listen closely for God to say, "Peace! Be still!"

Evening
STANDARD OF GRACE

And the Pharisees were saying to him, "Look, why are they doing what is not lawful on the Sabbath?" . . . And he said to them, "The Sabbath was made for man, not man for the Sabbath. So the Son of Man is lord even of the Sabbath."

MARK 2:24, 27–28 ESV

Dear Father, legalism is such a nasty trap. It causes me to compare myself to others and to some high standard I'll never be able to reach. This comparison, this high standard, is the root cause of much of my anxiety. It forces me on a hamster wheel of good works and unreachable goals and leaves me feeling like a failure. But that's not Your way, is it, Father? You have grace and mercy and compassion. You look at my heart rather than my abilities or even my actions. When You look at me, I hope You see someone who loves You and wants to please You.

THINK ABOUT IT:

What impossible standard have you tried to live up to?

Morning
SELF-EXAMINATION

"This is what the Lord says:
Be fair-minded and just. Do what
is right! Help those who have been
robbed; rescue them from their
oppressors. Quit your evil deeds! Do
not mistreat foreigners, orphans, and
widows. Stop murdering the innocent!"
JEREMIAH 22:3 NLT

Sometimes, God, we act as though You only care about people's souls, not their bodies. But again and again, Your Word tells us that's not the case. Scripture insists that we work to build a world where injustice no longer kills, oppression no longer robs, and prejudice no longer limits the lives of some people while other people are thriving. Lord, make me willing to see where I have contributed to injustice. Give me courage to speak out. Give me wisdom to act. Use me to build a safer, more just world for all Your people.

THINK ABOUT IT:

Injustice isn't something that only exists "out there"; it also exists in our own hearts. Are you willing for God to show you any areas where you harbor prejudice, any ways that you have allowed oppression to continue in our world?

Evening
TRUST BUSTERS

Let all bitterness, and wrath, and
anger, and clamour, and evil speaking,
be put away from you, with all malice.
EPHESIANS 4:31 KJV

Lately, Jesus, I'm finding it harder to trust other people. I suspect everyone around me of harboring evil in their hearts. I didn't used to be like this—so what changed? As I think about it, Holy Friend, I realize that more and more my friends and I focus on negative things when we talk. We're bitter and angry, and the more we talk about our bitterness and anger, the worse we feel. Together we've created a mindset by which we look at the world and everyone in it with distrust. Instead of seeing goodness, we see only evil. So it's no wonder that I don't trust people anymore. I'm always expecting the worst of them. Cleanse my heart of this negativity, I ask You, Jesus. May I see once more with Your eyes, perceiving the goodness in people rather than the evil.

THINK ABOUT IT:

How do your conversations affect the way you view others around you? Remember, distrust is contagious.

Morning
PEACE-LOVING

But the wisdom from above is first of all pure. It is also peace loving, gentle at all times, and willing to yield to others. It is full of mercy and the fruit of good deeds. It shows no favoritism and is always sincere.

JAMES 3:17 NLT

I know my family loves me, Lord—but lately the people who love me most are stressing me out! I'm so tired of trying to be a peacemaker. And I'm tired of feeling like I always have to defend myself. It's hard to hold on to my patience when some days I just feel like screaming at them all! Give me Your wisdom, I pray, so that I can see ways to relieve the tension in my family. Teach me to be gentle. Remind me that I don't have to be right all the time. Give me mercy and sincerity in all my interactions. Show me opportunities to perform small acts of love. Remind me never to play favorites. Transform my heart so that I can be a vehicle of Your peace.

THINK ABOUT IT:

When James said that "wisdom from above" is pure, he meant that it's not distorted or diluted by the selfishness that so often tinges our thoughts and actions. It's completely free of self-interest. How can you avail yourself of this heavenly wisdom today?

Evening
PERFECT LOVE

Such love has no fear, because perfect love expels all fear. If we are afraid, it is for fear of punishment, and this shows that we have not fully experienced his perfect love.

1 JOHN 4:18 NLT

I confess, God, that I'm still afraid of so many things in life. I'm afraid of sickness and disease. I'm afraid of what the future may hold. I'm afraid of getting old. I'm afraid of change. I'm afraid of death. My fear tells me, Lord, that I still don't completely believe in Your love. Part of me still thinks You're not strong enough to keep me safe; part of me wonders if You really care about my life. Thank You for being patient with my fears. Draw me closer to You. Teach me that Your love is real. Help me to rest in You, knowing that Your perfect love surrounds me and I have no need to fear.

THINK ABOUT IT:

How can you get to know God better so that you will trust Him more?

Morning
TRUST INSTEAD OF DISAPPOINTMENT

Trust in the LORD with all your heart and do not lean on your own understanding.

PROVERBS 3:5 NASB

I don't understand, Lord, why You keep letting me be disappointed. Why can't You answer my prayers with a yes? Why do You always say no? The things that I've asked for aren't bad things; they're things I believe would make the world a better place, things that would be a blessing. And yet You still say no. Wise Lord, help me to trust You more. Remind me that You know far more than I do; You can see the entire scope of time and eternity. You do all things at the right time. So I'll stop talking about what makes sense to me, and I'll start leaning on You more. You know how I long for wishes to come true—but I'll trust Your love to do what's right for me.

THINK ABOUT IT:

How might disappointment be connected to a lack of trust?

Evening
MOUNTAIN WALKING

The Sovereign LORD is my strength! He makes me as surefooted as a deer, able to tread upon the heights.

HABAKKUK 3:19 NLT

From the moment I get up, God, the possibility of an accident is always there with me. I could trip on the stairs and break my neck; I could slip on the sidewalk and break a bone; I might get in a car accident on the way to work; the next time I take a flight, the plane might crash. Maybe it sounds silly to worry about all those things—except that I know people who have experienced each of those accidents. And then, once I start thinking about all the accidents that *might* happen, I work myself up so much that I'm nearly too anxious to get out of bed in the morning. Remind me, Lord, that You are my strength in life. With Your help, I can rise above even the most dangerous situations. No matter how steep the mountain, I do not need to fear, for You make me nimble and light-footed.

THINK ABOUT IT:

What are the "heights" you have had to walk in life, thanks to an accident that disrupted your life? During that time, did you sense God's presence with you?

Morning
UNBROKEN

We've been surrounded and battered by troubles, but we're not demoralized; we're not sure what to do, but we know that God knows what to do; we've been spiritually terrorized, but God hasn't left our side; we've been thrown down, but we haven't broken.

2 CORINTHIANS 4:8–9 MSG

Dear Jesus, help me to claim these verses as my own during this time when I'm beset with challenges. You know that I'm surrounded on all sides; You know that my heart and body feel battered and exhausted. Despite this, do not let me be demoralized, I pray. I'm confused about what to do next, but You know the way I should go. I feel spiritually oppressed, anxious, and fearful, but I feel Your presence with me. I've fallen flat on my face more than once during this time, Lord (and I probably will again), and yet You keep me whole. You have never abandoned me in the past, and I know You won't now.

THINK ABOUT IT:

When we follow Jesus, He doesn't remove all challenges from our lives. Can you use these difficult times as opportunities to lean that much harder on God?

Evening
VIOLENT WORDS

"Count yourselves blessed every time people put you down or throw you out or speak lies about you to discredit me. What it means is that the truth is too close for comfort and they are uncomfortable."

MATTHEW 5:11 MSG

Not all violence is physical. Sometimes violence is verbal. It's people speaking lies about me, people rejecting me, people insulting me and criticizing me. Lord, I ask that You cloak me in Your love so that the violence aimed at me never reaches my heart. Let me not hesitate to speak the truth, no matter what is said to me. Show me how to bring Your peace to every situation. Bless me as I take a stand for You and Your kingdom—and use me, I pray, to bless others, even those whose words are violent.

THINK ABOUT IT:

Why do you think the truth can impel some people to resort to violence? Does fear ever hold you back from speaking truth?

Morning
PERSECUTION

"You're blessed when your commitment to God provokes persecution. The persecution drives you even deeper into God's kingdom."
MATTHEW 5:10 MSG

I don't like to offend people, Lord. I like to keep a low profile. I don't want to upset people. I especially don't want to make them angry with *me*—so when I hear people speaking in hateful ways, I just keep my mouth shut and walk away. I don't want to risk getting myself in trouble. But God, show me when You want me to speak out for Your kingdom. Don't let my fear hold me back from taking a stand against injustice. Give me the courage I need to stand firm against hate. I want my commitment to You to be greater than any discomfort I might feel. And if people don't like what I say and do—well, God, You can handle that. Just draw me closer to You.

THINK ABOUT IT:

As Christ's follower, you're not likely these days to be thrown to the lions or burned at the stake—but are you willing to speak out against injustice, even if it means you will face disapproval, anger, even hatred?

Evening
COOPERATION

"You're blessed when you can show people how to cooperate instead of compete or fight. That's when you discover who you really are, and your place in God's family."
MATTHEW 5:9 MSG

It's easy, God, just to dig in my heels and claim my position of righteous superiority. I *know* I'm right, and I *know* they're wrong. Why should I try to make peace when they won't listen to me? The more I argue with them, trying to persuade them to see the light, the angrier they get with me. You wouldn't want me to compromise my principles, would You? I didn't choose to be their enemy, but if that's what they want, I can't stop them. Oh, but God, now that I've put my feelings into words, I realize this isn't Your way. Your Word never says, "Stick to your principles at the cost of all else." Instead, it tells me to reach out my hand to my enemies, to seek common ground, to find ways we can cooperate instead of fight. Remind me to make love my priority.

THINK ABOUT IT:

What might you do today to find a way to cooperate with the people who disagree with you?

Morning
APPROACH IN FAITH

But she came and knelt before him, saying, "Lord, help me." And he answered, "It is not right to take the children's bread and throw it to the dogs." She said, "Yes, Lord, yet even the dogs eat the crumbs that fall from their masters' table." Then Jesus answered her, "O woman, great is your faith! Be it done for you as you desire."

MATTHEW 15:25–28 ESV

Lord, Your message was first for Israel, Your covenant people. But that did not stop this Canaanite woman from seeking You. She approached You with great faith, determined to receive even a scrap of blessing from You, knowing it would be more than enough. Persistence and confidence paid off. May I approach You in prayer with such persistence and confidence, knowing that You are able to do the miraculous. You respond to humble expressions of faith, Lord. Hear my cry today. Amen.

THINK ABOUT IT:
Do you approach God with faith that He will answer?

Evening
OUR GOOD SHEPHERD

"The sheep hear his voice, and he calls his own sheep by name and leads them out. When he has brought out all his own, he goes before them, and the sheep follow him, for they know his voice. . . . I am the good shepherd. The good shepherd lays down his life for the sheep."

JOHN 10:3–4, 11 ESV

Lord, what a beautiful picture of how You care for us! You call to us—Your own sheep—by name and lead us, as a personal, caring shepherd. You go before us, showing us the way to take. And in the ultimate expression of Your love, You laid down Your life that we might live. As one of Your sheep, I know Your voice when You call. Call to me now so that I follow You and learn from Your way. Amen.

THINK ABOUT IT:
What does Jesus' name of Good Shepherd mean to you?

Morning
SELF-DENIAL

"If anyone would come after me, let him deny himself and take up his cross and follow me. For whoever would save his life will lose it, but whoever loses his life for my sake and the gospel's will save it. For what does it profit a man to gain the whole world and forfeit his soul?"

MARK 8:34–37 ESV

Lord, as a follower of You, my life will not look like a nonbeliever's. What I chase after, what I model my ways after, will be different. Following You means sacrifice, just as salvation meant Your sacrifice on the cross. The sacrifice is not in vain! I can spend my energy, my time, my resources—my life—seeking to gain comfort and security and happiness in this world; but when death comes, it will amount to nothing. If, instead, I spend my energy, my time, my resources—my all—for Your sake, I will gain so much more. Amen.

THINK ABOUT IT:
What does denying self look like in your life?

Evening
THE GREEN GOD

"How difficult it will be for those who have wealth to enter the kingdom of God!" And the disciples were amazed at his words. But Jesus said to them again, "Children, how difficult it is to enter the kingdom of God! It is easier for a camel to go through the eye of a needle than for a rich person to enter the kingdom of God."

MARK 10:23–25 ESV

Money. God, why is it so important to us? We idolize it. We pursue it. We hoard it, protect it, invest it, dream about what we can do with it. If only we had enough money. . . We would be no better off than if we were paupers apart from You. Nothing in this world can secure what we need most—salvation. The riches of eternity begin and end in You. May I loosen my hold on money, God, and cling to You instead. Amen.

THINK ABOUT IT:
Why does the "security" of money keep people from turning to God?

Morning
MISSING THE POINT

"O you of little faith, why are you discussing among yourselves the fact that you have no bread? Do you not yet perceive? Do you not remember the five loaves for the five thousand, and how many baskets you gathered? Or the seven loaves for the four thousand, and how many baskets you gathered? How is it that you fail to understand that I did not speak about bread?"

MATTHEW 16:8–11 ESV

Lord, how often I am like the disciples! When I fixate on earthly concerns, I fail to grasp the wisdom You offer. When I focus only on the problems, I forget how You are able to take care of me in miraculous ways. Deepen my faith, Lord. Open my heart to Your truth. I pray for eyes and ears to understand so that I will never miss out on all You have to give. Amen.

THINK ABOUT IT:

Is a misplaced perspective preventing you from taking hold of something important?

Evening
NO FEAR

But he was in the stern, asleep on the cushion. And they woke him and said to him, "Teacher, do you not care that we are perishing?" And he awoke and rebuked the wind and said to the sea, "Peace! Be still!" And the wind ceased, and there was a great calm. He said to them, "Why are you so afraid? Have you still no faith?"

MARK 4:38–40 ESV

Lord, at first glance, Your words to Your disciples seem harsh. Tossed in a tiny boat on the sea, waves crashing overhead, no hope in sight. . .the situation looked dire. Because they weren't looking to You in faith. With You as Lord, what do I have to be afraid of? Pain—You will comfort me. Loneliness—You are with me. Need—You will provide. Uncertainty—You see ahead. Inability—You will see me through. Safety—You hold my life in Your hands. You are God. May I always have faith in You. Amen.

THINK ABOUT IT:

Why are you afraid?

Morning
COMFORT:
PASS IT ALONG

Blessed be the God and Father of our Lord Jesus Christ, the Father of mercies and God of all comfort, who comforts us in all our affliction, so that we may be able to comfort those who are in any affliction, with the comfort with which we ourselves are comforted by God.

2 CORINTHIANS 1:3–4 ESV

God, everyone needs someone to come beside them, to walk hand in hand during difficult times. You have not left us alone to withstand the battles; You come alongside us in hardship, offering strength and courage to continue. When I would wilt under pressure, You uphold me. And You call me to be a fellow comforter. Just as I experience the comfort of knowing I am not alone, I will extend a hand to others and be a witness to Your care. Amen.

THINK ABOUT IT:
*Who needs God's comfort—
via you—today?*

Evening
ALL IN GOOD TIME

For everything there is a season, and a time for every matter under heaven. . . . What gain has the worker from his toil? I have seen the business that God has given to the children of man to be busy with. He has made everything beautiful in its time.

ECCLESIASTES 3:1, 9–11 ESV

God, how much there is to do, how many things to accomplish! Remind me that just as You order nature, You appoint the seasons of my life—in Your perfect timing. Sometimes I rush ahead; sometimes I lag behind. But You, God, know exactly where I should be. Help me surrender my goals to You. Only when I'm in step with Your timing will I find satisfaction. I have confidence that You will make every season of my life beautiful in its time. Amen.

THINK ABOUT IT:
How can you find contentment in this season of your life— whether ugly or beautiful?

Morning
OLD AND NEW

To put off your old self, which belongs to your former manner of life and is corrupt through deceitful desires, and to be renewed in the spirit of your minds, and to put on the new self, created after the likeness of God in true righteousness and holiness.

EPHESIANS 4:22–24 ESV

Lord, You hear us say it—"Time for a change!" From our hairstyle, to our wardrobe, to the paint color on our walls, to our jobs, change can bring a new perspective, a feeling of beginning anew with fresh possibilities. The difference between old and new. When we come to You, Lord, You change us. We're able to shed the old self, which is full of sin, and don a new self. I need Your help in the process. Remove the hardened, dull layers until You reveal the gem underneath. Renew my mind with Your Word so I reflect from within Your holiness. Amen.

THINK ABOUT IT:
What does your new self look like in Christ?

Evening
THE DEVIL, WITHSTOOD

Your adversary the devil prowls around like a roaring lion, seeking someone to devour. Resist him, firm in your faith, knowing that the same kinds of suffering are being experienced by your brotherhood throughout the world. And after you have suffered a little while, the God of all grace, who has called you to his eternal glory in Christ, will himself restore, confirm, strengthen, and establish you.

1 PETER 5:8–10 ESV

God, the devil is a master sidetracker. He would like nothing more than to push me off course through temptation and discouragement. He seeks to *devour*—strong word for a serious threat. But Your Word says to resist, to stand strong in my faith. I will continue on the path You have set before me. I will not waver in obedience to You. Use this time, God, to deepen my faith and character. You will bring me through—better than before. Amen.

THINK ABOUT IT:
Does knowing that God Himself is perfecting you encourage you to resist Satan?

Morning
LIGHT TO SEE

"Your eye is the lamp of your body. When your eye is healthy, your whole body is full of light, but when it is bad, your body is full of darkness. Therefore be careful lest the light in you be darkness. If then your whole body is full of light, having no part dark, it will be wholly bright, as when a lamp with its rays gives you light."

LUKE 11:34–36 ESV

Father, when my physical vision is murky, when I can't clearly see even my hand in front of my face, life will be hard. The same is true of spiritual sight. When I can't perceive Your truth, life will be difficult. I pray for clear spiritual vision, Father, for eyes to see Your truth. With healthy vision, my whole being is full of life-giving light. Amen.

THINK ABOUT IT:

How does faulty spiritual eyesight affect the whole of you—from your actions to your beliefs?

Evening
COUNTED

You have kept count of my tossings; put my tears in your bottle. Are they not in your book? . . . This I know, that God is for me. In God, whose word I praise, in the LORD, whose word I praise, in God I trust.

PSALM 56:8–11 ESV

When I'm tossing and turning at night, Lord, it's easy to feel alone with grief or worries. The world is still—at rest—while my heart is restless. All is quiet except for my tears. But You are there. And not only do You witness my struggle, but You count my tossings; You collect my tears as they fall. It's not just another lost night of sleep. You take note of it. Lord, King David had much to fear when he wrote Psalm 56. Yet he knew one thing with certainty: You were for him. I place my trust, my praise, with You too because You are for me. Amen.

THINK ABOUT IT:

Have you ever considered that your restless nights are not lost on God?

Morning
EAT YOUR FILL

"Why do you spend your money for that which is not bread, and your labor for that which does not satisfy? Listen diligently to me, and eat what is good, and delight yourselves in rich food. Incline your ear, and come to me; hear, that your soul may live."
ISAIAH 55:2–3 ESV

Father, are You frustrated with all the ways I try to fill my soul apart from You, as I run around seeking comfort in buying things, in working to build a nest here on earth? When will I learn—for good—that nothing, absolutely nothing, will fill me like You? While earthly pursuits alone will leave me hungry for more, what You provide satisfies deeply. I turn to Your Word for the rich food—the joy, the peace, the assurance—that gives life. Amen.

THINK ABOUT IT:
Do you go to the world or God first to find satisfaction?

Evening
THE MASTER'S PLAN

"Woe to him who strives with him who formed him, a pot among earthen pots! Does the clay say to him who forms it, 'What are you making?' or 'Your work has no handles'? Woe to him who says to a father, 'What are you begetting?' or to a woman, 'With what are you in labor?'"
ISAIAH 45:9-10 ESV

Father, like a child, at times I don't understand why certain things happen in my life. And I can't always see the purpose in Your plans for me. In my heart, I throw a tantrum and pout when my desires don't align with Your sovereign will. Quiet my soul, Father, long enough for me to hear You speak: "Be still. I am God." You only have my good in mind as You form my life. Please grant me patience as I wait for Your plans to unfold. I trust in Your design. Amen.

THINK ABOUT IT:
Is it difficult to rest in God's work when the result isn't what you expected?

Morning
QUARREL-LESS

Have nothing to do with foolish, ignorant controversies; you know that they breed quarrels. And the Lord's servant must not be quarrelsome but kind to everyone, able to teach, patiently enduring evil, correcting his opponents with gentleness. God may perhaps grant them repentance leading to a knowledge of the truth.

2 TIMOTHY 2:23–25 ESV

Quarrels. Bickering. God, as Your children, You would have us avoid the ugliness of arguments. When we do speak out, we shouldn't mirror the world that seeks to be "right" no matter what. We are to speak with kindness. Gentleness. You are the master of using any situation for Your good. You can use our words to draw others to You. Or if we are rude and uncaring, we can repel others just as quickly. Act as a holy filter in my mind, God, that only beauty would flow from me. Amen.

THINK ABOUT IT:

Is there a greater cost to ugly quarrels—even if what you seek to point out is well meant?

Evening
IF NOT FOR LOVE

If I speak in the tongues of men and of angels, but have not love, I am a noisy gong or a clanging cymbal. And if I have prophetic powers, and understand all mysteries and all knowledge, and if I have all faith, so as to remove mountains, but have not love, I am nothing. If I give away all I have. . .but have not love, I gain nothing.

1 CORINTHIANS 13:1–3 ESV

Father, in Your Book, everything hinges on love. "For God so loved." Your great love put in motion Your plan of salvation, the greatest news the world has ever heard. The centrality of love should reflect in my life. I could do many remarkable deeds, but if they do not begin with love, they amount to nothing. I can do lots out of selfishness, but what really counts is what I do out of love. Fix my life on love, I pray. Amen.

THINK ABOUT IT:

How can love become a starting point for all you do?

Morning
HISTORY OF DOING

I will give thanks to the LORD with my whole heart; I will recount all of your wonderful deeds. I will be glad and exult in you; I will sing praise to your name, O Most High. . . . And those who know your name put their trust in you, for you, O LORD, have not forsaken those who seek you.

PSALM 9:1–2, 10 ESV

God, Your Word is a rich history of Your faithfulness and wonderful deeds. Across generations and through turbulent times, You have remained steadfast. A firm rock, an unwavering focus, a guarantee. You, God, I can count on! With each day, You are writing a rich history in my own life. From Your willingness to forgive—again—to the times You've stood by me, strengthening me in hardship and celebrating in joy, to Your rescuing hand when I've all but given up, You remain. I praise You and I thank You for all You've done. Amen.

THINK ABOUT IT:
What "wonderful deeds" has God done in your life?

Evening
LIKE HAGAR

And as she sat opposite him, she lifted up her voice and wept. And God heard the voice of the boy, and the angel of God called to Hagar from heaven and said to her, "What troubles you, Hagar? Fear not, for God has heard the voice of the boy where he is. Up! Lift up the boy, and hold him fast with your hand, for I will make him into a great nation."

GENESIS 21:16–18 ESV

I can only imagine how Hagar felt, Lord. Used by Sarah to gain a child then cast aside; now wandering in the wilderness and in dread of her son's death. While it appeared that everyone had abandoned her and all was lost, You heard! You protected Hagar and Ishmael. You planned a future. Lord, in my most desperate times, remind me of Hagar. You follow us to the remotest places. You have a plan even when all seems hopeless. Amen.

THINK ABOUT IT:
How does Hagar's story encourage you?

Morning
YOU ARE WHAT YOU BEAR

"For no good tree bears bad fruit, nor again does a bad tree bear good fruit, for each tree is known by its own fruit. For figs are not gathered from thornbushes, nor are grapes picked from a bramble bush. The good person out of the good treasure of his heart produces good, and the evil person out of his evil treasure produces evil."

LUKE 6:43–45 ESV

Lord, this is such a simple illustration but so true. Good trees bear good fruit. Likewise, out of a good heart, good flows. I can't harbor sin and ugliness and expect to yield good in my life. But if I fill myself with good—Your Word, Your love, Your will—good is the result. Help me clear out the brambles, Lord, and replace them with healthy fruit. I want others to recognize You when they see the good in me. May I be known for good! Amen.

THINK ABOUT IT:

What do you consider good fruit in the life of a Christian?

Evening
MY MANNA

Then the LORD said to Moses, "Behold, I am about to rain bread from heaven for you, and the people shall go out and gather a day's portion every day, that I may test them, whether they will walk in my law or not."

EXODUS 16:4 ESV

God, as I read about the Israelites in the wilderness, I sometimes catch myself being critical. You told them how and when to collect manna; You revealed Your plan clearly. Yet some doubted; they disobeyed. How foolish! God, You tell me in Your Word that You will take care of me. You teach me to be content, to trust, to pray: "Give us day by day our daily bread" (Luke 11:3 KJV). Yet at times I doubt You and carve my own way through the wilderness. How foolish! I choose today to rest in Your sovereign plan. Amen.

THINK ABOUT IT:

How are you like the Israelites when faced with the test of trusting in God's provision?

Morning
STEADY AS A ROCK

"Everyone who comes to me and hears my words and does them, I will show you what he is like: he is like a man building a house, who dug deep and laid the foundation on the rock. And when a flood arose, the stream broke against that house and could not shake it, because it had been well built."

LUKE 6:47–48 ESV

Lord, You were a teacher to Your disciples. What You told them was for their good, their best. The same is true for me. Through Your Word, You lead me and teach me, and what I hear, even if I don't understand, is for my good, my best. I can choose to build my life on our commands and have a firm base when stormy times come, or I can live without Your foundation and fall apart. I choose to listen and do Your will. Amen.

THINK ABOUT IT:
How is God's Word like a rock for your life?

Evening
ILL-FITTED

But Moses said to the LORD, "Oh, my Lord, I am not eloquent, either in the past or since you have spoken to your servant. . . ." Then the LORD said to him, "Who has made man's mouth? Who makes him mute, or deaf, or seeing, or blind? Is it not I, the LORD? Now therefore go, and I will be with your mouth and teach you what you shall speak."

EXODUS 4:10–12 ESV

Father, in service, in relationships, in missions, in parenting, in jobs—in the many roles we are called to fill—how often do we feel like Moses? Ill-equipped, ill at ease, ill-suited. . .we don't measure up! When I feel like this, Father, remind me that You made me just as I am. Your plan for my life is custom fit—even my weaknesses. You will be there upholding me in the roles You call me to. Be with me as I go, I pray. Amen.

THINK ABOUT IT:
Is God using limitations to strengthen your faith?

Morning
SPIRIT OF THE SABBATH

And he said to them, "The Sabbath was made for man, not man for the Sabbath. So the Son of Man is lord even of the Sabbath."
MARK 2:27–28 ESV

A day of rest! Lord, with all the responsibilities of living, it's easy to become tired or even exhausted. As to-do lists lengthen, time to rejuvenate seems to shorten day by day until resting is all but forgotten. You have designed me wonderfully, and part of that design is rest. A time to put aside work and trust in Your provision. A time to abandon worldly pursuits and turn my heart heavenward in worship. A time to reset for the week ahead. Lord, Your Sabbath is a beautiful reflection of how You created, resting on the seventh day, and how You continue to care for Your creation. May I never forget Your blessing or twist it into duty but keep it as You intended: a day of rest. Amen.

THINK ABOUT IT:
How can you establish a Sabbath rest this week?

Evening
COMPASSIONATE GOD

And a leper came to him, imploring him, and kneeling said to him, "If you will, you can make me clean." Moved with pity, he stretched out his hand and touched him and said to him, "I will; be clean." And immediately the leprosy left him, and he was made clean.
MARK 1:40–42 ESV

At this time in Jesus' ministry, He was a busy man. He traveled from town to town, preaching to crowds and sharing about Your great love. Everywhere He went, crowds pressed in to see Him. Yet He wasn't too busy or too important to care for the needs of this one man, a leper, an outcast. It's comforting to know You have compassion and that You care about my problems. Like the leper, I ask You now: if You will, please fix my problems and take away my fears. You're the only one who can.

THINK ABOUT IT:
What problem do you need to bring to Jesus today? He cares deeply about all your concerns.

Morning
CAST OUT

And he healed many who were sick with various diseases, and cast out many demons. And he would not permit the demons to speak, because they knew him.

MARK 1:34 ESV

I know Your power still heals the sick and casts out demons. I ask, with faith, please heal the diseases plaguing me, my family, and all those I love. Cast out demons that are causing havoc in my life. I know I have nothing to be afraid of as long as You are on my side. Give me the kind of faith that looks trouble in the face and casts it out in Your name. I know I carry Your power within me, but often I allow that power to lie dormant as I cower in fear. Give me the faith of David as he stood against Goliath. I trust Your power, Lord.

THINK ABOUT IT:

What sickness or problem needs healing or casting out? Speak now, in Jesus' name, believing in God's goodness and power.

Evening
YOUR WILL BE DONE

And going a little farther he fell on his face and prayed, saying, "My Father, if it be possible, let this cup pass from me; nevertheless, not as I will, but as you will."

MATTHEW 26:39 ESV

Jesus was afraid. He didn't want to endure the things He knew were coming. Jesus understands fear and anxiety because He felt those things too. Still, He said, "Your will be done." Father, right now I lay it all on the table. I'm worried and afraid. Like Jesus, I beg You to "let this cup pass from me." I don't want to endure the things I'm afraid will happen. Yet I know You love me, and even through the fire, You will uphold me. You'll give me strength to endure what I must in order for Your perfect will to be accomplished. Like Christ, I pray that Your will is done.

THINK ABOUT IT:

What "cup" do you want to pass from you? Are you willing to pray, "Your will be done"?

Morning
THAT KIND OF FAITH

And Jesus answered them, "Truly, I say to you, if you have faith and do not doubt, you will not only do what has been done to the fig tree, but even if you say to this mountain, 'Be taken up and thrown into the sea,' it will happen. And whatever you ask in prayer, you will receive, if you have faith."

MATTHEW 21:21–22 ESV

Where does my faith end? Do I believe You'll do some things but not others? The disciples were amazed at what Jesus did to the fig tree. Jesus said, "You think that's impressive? You ain't seen nothin' yet!" I want my faith to be so large it has no borders. I want to believe that any problem, any giant can be obliterated with just a word from You. I want my faith to be infinite and unending. Give me that kind of faith, Lord.

THINK ABOUT IT:

What problem seems too big for God? Can you stretch the borders of your faith?

Evening
PARTY TIME

"Again I say to you, if two of you agree on earth about anything they ask, it will be done for them by my Father in heaven. For where two or three are gathered in my name, there am I among them."

MATTHEW 18:19–20 ESV

Dear Father, You must be an extrovert! You like it when we get together and have prayer and praise parties. Forgive me for trying to carry my burdens alone. It takes humility to ask for prayer for myself. I don't want to share my worries and weaknesses with others. But when two or three people ask for the same thing, You show up! Give me a few trustworthy people that I can share my requests with. Help me to join them in praying for their problems as well. I look forward to seeing what happens when You come to the party.

THINK ABOUT IT:

What friends or family members can you share your concerns with? Will you commit to pray for them as well?

Morning
MOUNTAIN MOVER

Then the disciples came to Jesus privately and said, "Why could we not cast it out?" He said to them, "Because of your little faith. For truly, I say to you, if you have faith like a grain of mustard seed, you will say to this mountain, 'Move from here to there,' and it will move, and nothing will be impossible for you."

MATTHEW 17:19–21 ESV

So many things in my life seem like impossible mountains. I look at my problems and see something bigger than I am, something that can't be moved, and I feel defeated. I need to stop focusing on the size of the mountain and focus on the size of my God. Any problem is nothing but a tiny anthill from Your point of view. I may not be able to conquer my difficulties, but You can. I put it all in Your hands. I can't wait to see what You do.

THINK ABOUT IT:

What mountain do you believe God will move for you? Have faith that He can.

Evening
KINGDOM KEYS

"I will give you the keys of the kingdom of heaven, and whatever you bind on earth shall be bound in heaven, and whatever you loose on earth shall be loosed in heaven."

MATTHEW 16:19 ESV

When you give someone the keys to something, you're giving them ownership. If they have the keys, they have power and control over it. When I believe. . .when I have faith. . .You give me the keys to Your kingdom and all that is in it. When I have faith in You, Your power supports me. When I have faith in You, Your authority lifts my status and allows me to have more control over any situation. Worry and fear give me a victim's status, but faith gives me a sense of dominance over my problems because I know Your strength belongs to me.

THINK ABOUT IT:

In what situation have you felt powerless? Reframe that situation in your mind, and picture yourself in authority over that problem with God's full support.

DAY 250

Morning
YOU'VE GIVEN YOUR ANGELS INSTRUCTIONS!

For he will command his angels concerning you to guard you in all your ways.
PSALM 91:11 NIV

Do You have daily meetings with Your angels, Lord? I often wonder about this. Are specific angels assigned to me? If so, I surely keep them very busy. You're probably having to give them instructions around the clock. They probably hear the words "Keep a special eye on this one!" a lot.

I rest easy in the knowledge that You have a plan for my protection, Lord. You've commanded Your angels to guard me, not just during good seasons but during the hard times as well. Your Word assures me that they're watching over me in all my ways. When I make mistakes. When I do well. When I'm stressed. When I'm walking in peace. They're right there, watching over me. Thank You for caring so much, Lord. I take comfort in Your care. Amen.

THINK ABOUT IT:
Are your angels working overtime?

Evening
I WANT WHAT I WANT

Incline my heart to your testimonies, and not to selfish gain!
PSALM 119:36 ESV

Sometimes my stress is caused by not getting my way, Lord. I want what I want, and I want it now. It's hard for me to acknowledge that not getting my way often leads to pity parties or anxiety, but that's the truth.

You never meant for Your kids to be selfish, did You? You long for us to keep our eyes riveted on You, not ourselves. Your heart's desire is for us to love others as we love ourselves. Selfish gain was never part of Your plan for any of us.

Help me with this, I pray. I don't want to get worked up over every little thing that doesn't go my way. Instead, I want to remain true to Your calling—to love You first with a deep and abiding passion, to love others sincerely, and to love myself as You love me. Help me, I pray. Amen.

THINK ABOUT IT:
How can you trade your way for God's way?

Morning
AUTHENTICITY

For our boast is this, the testimony of our conscience, that we behaved in the world with simplicity and godly sincerity, not by earthly wisdom but by the grace of God, and supremely so toward you.

2 CORINTHIANS 1:12 ESV

I've seen phony-baloney people, Lord. Many are over-the-top, an exaggerated version of themselves. I wonder how others can fall for their nonsense.

You long for me to be authentic even if it means I'm not the most popular person out there. "Fitting in" isn't as important as pleasing Your heart, so I'll do my best to be who You created me to be—nothing more and nothing less. Sincerity is far more important to You than anything else. You're not keen on fakes.

May I live with authenticity, use my gifts with a genuine desire to serve others, and worship You with a sincere heart. May there be no pretense in me, I pray. Amen.

THINK ABOUT IT:
Does God want you to fake it until you make it?

Evening
GREAT AND UNSEARCHABLE THINGS

"Call to me and I will answer you and tell you great and unsearchable things you do not know."

JEREMIAH 33:3 NIV

You will show me great and unsearchable things, Lord. Things my finite mind could never begin to comprehend. Things so far beyond me that people will stand in awe. You have wisdom, Lord, that can't be found in books or university classrooms. The kind of knowledge I gain from You comes from on high, not gleaned from humans but imparted straight from the heart of the Creator of all.

You have asked me to call on You. When I do, You answer. But You don't just give a short, quick answer. No, You begin to pour out Your heart, revealing great and unsearchable things that, until that very moment, were completely unknown to me. What a gift! What a blessing! Oh, to hear from You daily! Amen.

THINK ABOUT IT:
Have you ever received unsearchable knowledge straight from the heart of God?

Morning
I'M ON A LEARNING CURVE

Now when Jesus saw the crowds, he went up on a mountainside and sat down. His disciples came to him, and he began to teach them.
MATTHEW 5:1–2 NIV

Some days I feel like a student in a classroom. The learning curve is steep, Lord! Just about the time I think I've got things figured out, I realize there are areas of my life where I need a tutorial. Thank goodness You're the best tutor around! You're gentle, patient, and loving in the way You share your wisdom and knowledge with me.

Today I open my heart, my mind, and my imagination so that I can learn all that You have for me. Even the circumstances that are stressing me out or causing pain can be teaching tools in Your hands, Father. Have Your way in me today, I pray. Amen.

THINK ABOUT IT:
Are you on a learning curve at the moment?

Evening
PROTECTOR AND DEFENDER

What then shall we say to these things? If God is for us, who can be against us?
ROMANS 8:31 ESV

You are for me. Those four words change absolutely everything, Lord. When I'm facing trials. When I come up against a health crisis. When I'm battling manipulation or narcissism. You are for me. You are not against me. You want me to succeed.

My enemies stand no chance, no matter how hard they fight. No matter how tricky their schemes. No matter how sly their approach. You see all, hear all, and intervene in all. What You have ordained cannot be stopped. Thank You, God, for serving as my protector and defender, the one who is always on my side. Amen.

THINK ABOUT IT:
Do you believe that God is bigger than your problems?

Morning
I GIVE UP, LORD!

From inside the fish Jonah prayed to the LORD his God. He said: "In my distress I called to the LORD, and he answered me. From deep in the realm of the dead I called for help, and you listened to my cry."

JONAH 2:1–2 NIV

I'm tired of running, Lord! I give up. You've been chasing me down for a long time. And now You've caught up with me, finding me in a deep place, a trap of my own choosing. Like Jonah, I'm stuck. . .stressed, worried, defeated.

You have me right where You want me. You finally have my undivided attention, Lord! I'm all Yours. What else can I do but listen? What else can I do but ponder Your way instead of my own? I cry out to You today from the belly of the whale. Thank You, God, that even here You hear my cry and respond in love. Amen.

THINK ABOUT IT:

Has God ever placed you in the belly of a proverbial whale?

Evening
MORE TIME WITH YOU, LORD!

Draw near to God, and he will draw near to you. Cleanse your hands, you sinners, and purify your hearts, you double-minded.

JAMES 4:8 ESV

My life tends to be a little crazy, Lord. I feel like I'm always rushing here or there, shuttling the kids to T-ball practice or gymnastics, taking someone to the doctor, dealing with work-related challenges. Chaos abounds most days, and there's no time left over to draw near to You. Or so I claim.

Quiet time with You has been the missing ingredient in my life. Do I wonder why things are stressful? I haven't invited You in. Today I step away from the chaos long enough to say, "Lord, here I am." You have my full attention. I am Yours, not just for a few moments but for all eternity. Nothing is more important than spending time with You. May I never forget it. Amen.

THINK ABOUT IT:

What does it mean to draw near to God?

Morning
BABY STEPS

The Lord makes firm the steps of the one who delights in him; though he may stumble, he will not fall, for the Lord upholds him with his hand.

PSALM 37:23–24 NIV

The chunky little toes grab and stretch, providing balance for the toddler who is depending on them so wholeheartedly. The child's eyes fixate on the toy he wants. He wavers a little as he stands, looking and longing. Then a chubby hand reaches out, fingers spread wide. The dimpled knee bends, the sole of the foot lifts off the floor and comes down again with a thump. And there it is—one step. A small step for this little man, but a giant leap for his parents. Lord, help me rejoice in moments like this. As I watch first steps, please remind me that You are with me every step of my life. Amen.

THINK ABOUT IT:

What "first" moments have you enjoyed lately? How does it feel knowing you've got God's support every first, every second?

Evening
THE EVILS OF FRETTING

Refrain from anger and turn from wrath; do not fret—it leads only to evil.

PSALM 37:8 NIV

Lord, You know that "Fret" could be my middle name. I tend to act as though I'm at peace, and yet underneath I'm doing it—fretting. And I totally get how it leads to evil. Fretting steals my joy and distracts me from my hope. It takes a good situation and throws a veil of uncertainty over it. Many times I fret over my children—about whether I have clothed, fed, or taught them well enough. Fretting is the devil's game to keep me so occupied with worry and anxiety that I get irritated and angry at everyone around me. Help me not to fret anymore, Lord. Help me break the habit. Amen.

THINK ABOUT IT:

What do you fret about? What scripture might you cling to in order to de-fret?

Morning
TAKING UP THE CROSS

"Whoever wants to be my disciple must deny themselves and take up their cross daily and follow me."

LUKE 9:23 NIV

I wonder, Lord, did You know what my cross would be? I wonder if You knew I would one day be struggling with mounting debt and unmet standards. I wonder if You considered how much I would battle against rule-following, rigid bureaucrats, or tight-lipped, tightly wound authoritarians. I wonder if You knew I would chafe against the ties that were binding me and keep wandering away to find my path. I wonder, Lord, if You knew that every day little hands would remind me to take up my cross yet again and, once on my shoulders, how that cross wouldn't seem so heavy after all. Thank You, Lord, for waiting for me to catch up. And thanks for sharing my load. Amen.

THINK ABOUT IT:

What does your daily cross look like? How does God lighten that load?

Evening
MORE HOPE FOR A FOOL

Do you see someone who speaks in haste? There is more hope for a fool than for them.

PROVERBS 29:20 NIV

When will I finally learn to hold my tongue, Lord? The words seem to tumble out of my mouth before I even know they are in my brain. And why is it that the words that come out the fastest always seem to be the ones that are the nastiest? Why can't the nice, pleasant, and kind words come out first? Never mind. I think I know the answer. Lord, please, please, *please* help me to slow my mouth down. Shut me up, Lord. When nasty words are jumping at the gates, help me to remember that I want more hope than there is for a fool. I want to make You proud, Lord. Amen.

THINK ABOUT IT:

When do you have the most trouble holding your tongue? What scripture can you mentally recite to help you curb your tongue in such situations?

Morning
BEACH BABIES

He leads me beside quiet waters,
he refreshes my soul.
PSALM 23:2–3 NIV

Lord, today I am thankful for oceans, and for sand, and for sand castles. I'm thankful for the glow of sunbeams and the reflecting sparkles that dance on the waves. These waters are not so quiet—the waves roar and crash on the rocks. These waters trickle and spit and spray and slosh. But oh! They do refresh my soul, Lord! Thank You for knowing exactly what I need, and thank You for providing a way to rest. I know I can't always come to a beach, but I can always come to You. And sitting in Your presence is as warm as lying in the sun and as comforting as an old familiar story. I love being here and watching my child discover every seashell and pebble—each time with a look and shout of wonder. Oh Lord, wherever we may be, You refresh us all. Thank You! Amen.

THINK ABOUT IT:

Where is one of your happy places to be with your family? Where is one of your happy places to be alone with God?

Evening
HUMBLE AND GENTLE

Be completely humble and
gentle; be patient, bearing
with one another in love.
EPHESIANS 4:2 NIV

I can be humble, Lord. I often have a hard time being proud of myself—though I am always proud of my loved ones. But gentleness, Lord? That one is a little more difficult. I have learned to be tough—all my life I have worked hard and had to prove myself. I have had difficult things happen to me and have been treated harshly. So sometimes when a friend comes to me with hurt feelings or flesh, I am not patient. I tend to want him to just get over it and move on. And I sometimes catch a glimpse of the surprise in his eyes when I am too harsh or speak too quickly. Lord, help me to find the right words to use, to take time, to find the gentleness I know You have placed in me. Amen.

THINK ABOUT IT:

What is most difficult for you—humility, gentleness, or patience? What Bible verse might help you grow in that area?

Morning
EARLY MORNINGS

*"Arise, shine, for your light
has come, and the glory of
the LORD rises upon you."*

ISAIAH 60:1 NIV

Lord of the dawn, I know there is much glory to behold in the pinky-orange glow of the sun as it peeks up over the horizon. But oh Lord! I am not made for mornings. Or perhaps, just not for this morning. My brain is foggy and my body is slow, Lord. Help me wake up! Help me have the energy and enthusiasm I need to get these kids moving. Help me be a good example with a pleasant attitude, not to mention patience and kindness—even when it's 6:00 a.m. Lord, I'm so thankful You are the God of every hour. There is not a time when I can't come to You. You are an all-day, every-day God, and I praise You and thank You for the light. (Even though it is a little too bright at the moment.) Amen.

THINK ABOUT IT:

*What's your favorite time of
day? Where is God for you
in that stretch of time?*

Evening
OUT OF HIDING

*Whoever conceals their sins does not
prosper, but the one who confesses
and renounces them finds mercy.*

PROVERBS 28:13 NIV

My Deliverer, I have sinned. I am weighed down by shame. I am troubled by my weakness to temptation, neglect of my duties, and lack of self-control. I am deeply disturbed by things that seem to take over my thoughts. I want to be clean. Yet so often I also just want to hide away— even from You. Help me to find someone trustworthy to confide in. Help me to find people who will keep me accountable and to have the courage to invite them into my life. And help me to come to You even when my strongest desire is to run far away. I don't want these sins to eat away at me and hurt my family. Please help me. Amen.

THINK ABOUT IT:

*What sins do you need to confess?
How does it feel knowing God
loves you—no matter what?*

Morning
LORD OF MY SCHEDULE

Now listen, you who say, "Today
or tomorrow we will go to this or
that city, spend a year there, carry
on business and make money."
Why, you do not even know what
will happen tomorrow. What is
your life? . . . Instead, you ought
to say, "If it is the Lord's will, we
will live and do this or that."

JAMES 4:13–15 NIV

Wow, God, sometimes I feel like You are talking directly and solely to me. Have You been checking out my calendar? Do You see how every day is filled with one activity after another (and sometimes two or three on top of each other)? Lord, I know that sometimes I get caught up in the frenzy of my life. Help me not become imprisoned by the schedule. Help me to leave space for You, Lord. No— help me instead to put You first! Amen.

THINK ABOUT IT:

Have you left space on your
calendar for God? If not, what
can you do to schedule Him in?

Evening
HOW ABUNDANT

How abundant are the good things
that you have stored up for those who
fear you, that you bestow in the sight
of all, on those who take refuge in you.

PSALM 31:19 NIV

Lord of safety, Lord of my security, Lord of refuge, Lord who saves me—I thank You for the many times You have kept me from real danger. I pray that You keep watch over my loved ones as well. I know You love them more than I ever could, and You can see any harm in their way far before I could. God, I don't really know how to thank You for all that You've already done for my family. I just know that I need to keep telling people about it. I want people to hear our stories and trust in You. And every time I tell our stories, I'm reminded once again of the abundant blessings You have poured out on me and my family. Amen.

THINK ABOUT IT:

What good things has
God bestowed on you?

Morning
NO PROBLEM

*"With your help I can advance
against a troop; with my
God I can scale a wall."*

2 SAMUEL 22:30 NIV

Lord, we have a big transition coming up. And there's so much to organize and sort and pack. . .just so much to do. And guess who's been put in charge of all that? Yep, it's me. I suppose I nominated myself, and that's okay. I can do it. But I need my family members to be helpful. And it wouldn't hurt if they were also gracious and, well, would just give me a break every now and then. I'm so glad I can count on Your help always, Lord. Whenever I need a friend, a listening ear, or a wise reply, I know I can come to You. With Your help, I can do anything. I can even pack and move all our belongings in two weeks or less. No problem. Right, Lord? Amen.

THINK ABOUT IT:
*What's one big problem that
God has helped you with?*

Evening
FORGIVEN MUCH

*"Her many sins have been forgiven—
as her great love has shown.
But whoever has been
forgiven little loves little."*

LUKE 7:47 NIV

God, I can't believe I've messed things up yet again. It's just a silly mistake. A stupid misunderstanding. I blame sleep deprivation. But I've really done it, and it's totally my fault. Lord, help me, please. Give me the best words to use to ask for forgiveness. And please help my friend to understand. Let this moment be a lesson for both of us. A lesson in forgiveness and grace. A lesson in generosity of spirit, Lord. A lesson in humility for me. Lord God, it seems like I've had a lot of these lessons, doesn't it? I guess I have so much to learn! And I guess I should love a lot more! Amen.

THINK ABOUT IT:
*What have you needed to ask
forgiveness for lately? How does
receiving God's forgiveness feel?*

Morning
GOOD AND RIGHT

"Be careful to obey all these words that I command you, that it may go well with you and with your children after you forever, when you do what is good and right in the sight of the Lord your God."

DEUTERONOMY 12:28 ESV

I know that when I worry and fret and become anxious over the future, I'm not focusing on what You want me to. Worry won't help my future a bit, but loving You and following Your commands will help set up my future for Your blessing. Help me shift my focus, Lord. Instead of thinking about how I can fix my own future, I need to simply do what is good and right in Your sight. Thank You for Your promise to care for those who love You.

THINK ABOUT IT:

What things can you do today and every day that are good and right in God's sight?

Evening
TREASURED

"For you are a people holy to the Lord your God, and the Lord has chosen you to be a people for his treasured possession, out of all the peoples who are on the face of the earth."

DEUTERONOMY 14:2 ESV

How is it possible that You've chosen me? How is it that You consider me a treasured possession? According to this verse, You've selected me out of all the people on the face of the earth. If I am Your treasure, I know You'll take care of me. If I'm Your treasure, I don't have to worry about anything because You'll make sure I have everything I need—financially, physically, spiritually, and emotionally. Because I'm Your treasure, I know my anxieties and fears are nothing more than lies intended to steal my peace. Forgive me for doubting Your love for me. I trust You, Father. Thank You for choosing me.

THINK ABOUT IT:

How has God demonstrated that you're His treasured child?

Morning
GOD'S WORD

"And it shall be with him, and he shall read in it all the days of his life, that he may learn to fear the LORD his God by keeping all the words of this law and these statutes, and doing them."
DEUTERONOMY 17:19 ESV

This verse shows me the importance of reading Your Word every single day. You commanded the kings of Israel to do this because Your Word gives wisdom for life. Your Word is a treasure, Lord. I have this treasure right at my fingertips, and yet too often, I don't choose to use it. Draw me to Your Word, Lord. Remind me each day to read it, to soak it in, to make it a part of me. Thank You for Your Word, Father.

THINK ABOUT IT:
Do you make daily Bible reading a habit? If not, how can you arrange your schedule to make God's Word a priority?

Evening
PURITY AND STRENGTH

"When you go forth against your enemies and are in camp, then you shall keep yourself from every evil thing."
DEUTERONOMY 23:9 RSV

Evil weakens us. Sin destroys us. You tell us to avoid evil because You want us to be strong. There is a battle going on for my spirit, and I remain strong in that fight by remaining pure. It's really hard to stay pure in this world, Lord. Evil seeps in from every side, through every crack and crevice. The evil around me causes my fears to flare, my anxieties to amplify. But I know if I want to stand strong against the enemy, I must remain pure. Help me to keep myself from evil and sin, for I know purity equals strength. Move my focus from the evil around me to the source of my strength: You.

THINK ABOUT IT:
How have you focused on evil and negative things? Shift your focus to your heavenly Father, who loves you.

Morning
CIRCUMCISE YOUR HEART

"And the LORD your God will circumcise your heart and the heart of your offspring, so that you will love the LORD your God with all your heart and with all your soul, that you may live."

DEUTERONOMY 30:6 RSV

Circumcision is a painful process. Its purpose is to cut away the excess so germs can't breed and cause infection. When You circumcise my heart, You're removing the excess, the things that can hide evil and impurity. It's a painful process but a necessary one to keep me pure and guard me against the effects of sin. I know that true life, true living, happens when I love You with all my heart and soul, and I love You best when I'm pure and clean from sin. Thank You for this reminder that You allow the painful things in my life to keep me pure, so I can live the best life possible.

THINK ABOUT IT:
How has God used painful events in your life to purify you?

Evening
CHOOSE LIFE

"I call heaven and earth to witness against you this day, that I have set before you life and death, blessing and curse; therefore choose life, that you and your descendants may live."

DEUTERONOMY 30:19 RSV

I know I choose life—beautiful, abundant life—when I choose to love and trust You with all my heart. I don't know why I choose not to trust You sometimes. It's a constant battle of faith versus fear. When I'm tempted to give in to anxiety, remind me that I always have a choice. Though it may be a struggle, I can force those anxious thoughts from my mind and focus on You, on Your goodness, on Your kindness, and on Your love. My default setting is often worry and fear, but I can *choose* faith. Today and every day, I choose to trust You.

THINK ABOUT IT:
In what ways can you choose abundant life instead of worry and fear?

Morning
DO NOT FEAR

"It is the LORD who goes before you; he will be with you, he will not fail you or forsake you; do not fear or be dismayed."

DEUTERONOMY 31:8 RSV

Thank You for this reminder. I fear all the time. I feel dismayed all the time. I don't know why it's so hard for me to remember that You're with me. You're before me, behind me, and on either side. When I feel afraid, remind me of Your presence. In both Genesis and Revelation, You're called the lion of Judah. Help me to picture You as a powerful lion, walking with me wherever I go. With You as my guard, I have nothing to fear. I know You'll never fail me or forsake me. Thank You for being there, Father.

THINK ABOUT IT:

What situation leaves you feeling afraid and dismayed? Trust that God has it under control.

Evening
ENCOMPASS US

Of Benjamin he said, "The beloved of the LORD, he dwells in safety by him; he encompasses him all the day long, and makes his dwelling between his shoulders."

DEUTERONOMY 33:12 RSV

Make me Your beloved. Make each person in my family, each person I love, make us Your beloved. Encompass us all day long, and cause us to dwell in safety. When I'm tempted to worry about my children, my parents, my family members, and my friends, remind me that You are the one who keeps them safe, and Your care is worth a lot more than my worry. I give them to You, Father. I call each of them by name before You and ask that You hold them close in the palm of Your hand. Thank You for Your protection over those You love.

THINK ABOUT IT:

Who are you worried about today? Call them by name in prayer, and trust that God will protect them.

Morning
STRONG AND COURAGEOUS

*"Only be strong and very courageous,
being careful to do according to
all the law that Moses my servant
commanded you. Do not turn
from it to the right hand or to
the left, that you may have good
success wherever you go."*

JOSHUA 1:7 ESV

I need to memorize this verse and quote it every time I feel anxious. You are with me wherever I go. You set Your bodyguards before me, behind me, and on either side. I have nothing to fear. Nothing can intimidate me. Through You and because of You, I am strong and courageous! Help me to play this verse on repeat in my mind and bring it forward whenever I'm tempted to fear. Thank You for these words, Father. Thank You for making me stronger and more courageous than I ever thought possible.

THINK ABOUT IT:

*In what ways can you change
your behavior to reflect strength
and courage instead of fear?*

Evening
MY ONLY HOPE

*With my whole heart I cry; answer me,
O LORD! I will keep your statutes. I call
to you; save me, that I may observe
your testimonies. I rise before dawn
and cry for help; I hope in your words.*

PSALM 119:145–147 ESV

Sometimes it feels like You're not listening. I pray and pray. I cry to You with my whole heart. Please show Yourself, Lord. You are my only hope. You are the only one who can help me. I know You love me, Father. Please rescue me from this situation. You know every need and every detail, and I beg You to intervene. Give me patience as I wait for You to act. I know that even when it feels like You're ignoring me, You're not. You're always working on my behalf. I trust You, and I place all my hope in You.

THINK ABOUT IT:

*Do you truly believe God is working
on your behalf? He is. Trust Him.*

Morning
PREPARE YOUR PROVISIONS

"Pass through the camp, and command the people, 'Prepare your provisions; for within three days you are to pass over this Jordan, to go in to take possession of the land which the LORD your God gives you to possess.'"

JOSHUA 1:11 RSV

"Prepare your provisions." You simply wanted the people to obey, to get ready for the great things You were about to do. They didn't have to do any of it on their own. They just had to be ready. I love this reminder that all You require is my obedience. I don't have to be successful by the world's standards. I don't even need to be particularly capable. You only want my pure-hearted obedience as I wait expectantly, ready for You to act.

THINK ABOUT IT:

How can you "prepare your provisions" today? How can you obey God in a way that shows you're ready for Him to do something that only He can do?

Evening
BLESSED

Blessed is the man who walks not in the counsel of the wicked, nor stands in the way of sinners, nor sits in the seat of scoffers; but his delight is in the law of the LORD, and on his law he meditates day and night.

PSALM 1:1–2 RSV

In Your Word, You direct us to stay away from evil, wicked people and stay close to You. When we do these things, You bless us. Teach me to avoid negative people, people who try to draw me in. Whether it's gossip and slander, negative talk, or something else, give me wisdom as I deal with these people. Show me how to treat them with love and respect but not to make them my close advisors and friends. At the same time, draw me into Your presence each day. Remind me to spend time reading Your Word and talking to You. When I'm close to You, I'm blessed by Your nearness.

THINK ABOUT IT:

What steps can you take to be blessed, according to these verses?

Morning
TEARS

I am weary with my moaning; every night I flood my bed with tears; I drench my couch with my weeping. My eye wastes away because of grief, it grows weak because of all my foes.

PSALM 6:6–7 RSV

You have seen my tears. You've heard my cries. You know every thought, as if I've spoken them out loud. You know my fears, my anxieties. You know every detail of every situation that keeps me awake at night. And even though I know I should trust You more, I don't feel condemned by You. Instead, I feel Your compassion, Your kindness, Your love. I sense You holding me, wiping my tears, and rocking me in Your presence. Thank You for being there for me, Father. Thank You for loving me through my doubts and fears and worries. I'm so grateful that You are my God.

THINK ABOUT IT:

What have you lost sleep and tears over? God knows. He sees. And He longs to comfort you with His presence.

Evening
REFUGE

O LORD my God, in thee do I take refuge; save me from all my pursuers, and deliver me, lest like a lion they rend me, dragging me away, with none to rescue.

PSALM 7:1–2 RSV

You are my refuge. You're my safe place from everything that pursues me, causes me to worry, and steals my sleep. Sometimes it's people who crank up my anxieties. Sometimes it's money, or work issues, or health concerns. I'm afraid they'll overcome me, Lord. But when I take a moment to remember who You are, my heart rate slows and my anxieties calm. Those problems are nothing compared to You! I know You love me more than I can fathom. With that kind of love, why do I ever doubt that You'll take care of me? Save me from the people and circumstances that pursue me, Father. I love and trust You with all my heart.

THINK ABOUT IT:

Who or what do you feel is pursuing you right now? Picture God standing between you and the circumstance.

Morning
THE SHIELD

*My shield is with God, who saves
the upright in heart. God is a
righteous judge, and a God who
feels indignation every day.*
PSALM 7:10–11 ESV

Sometimes I foolishly think You don't know what I'm going through. I worry and fret in my belief that bad things will happen if I don't somehow take control of the situation. But when I give myself a moment to breathe, when I take time to consider things, I remember who You are. You are my shield, Lord. You love and care for me not because of anything I've done but simply because I'm Yours. You are righteous and good, and when bad things happen to Your children, You are indignant. Thank You for this reminder that You know, You see, and You will protect me.

THINK ABOUT IT:
What are you going through right now? God already knows, and He sees everything that happens to you. He stands in front of you like a shield, ready to protect and defend you.

Evening
GIVE THANKS

*I will give thanks to the LORD with
my whole heart; I will tell of all
thy wonderful deeds. I will be glad
and exult in thee, I will sing praise
to thy name, O Most High.*
PSALM 9:1–2 RSV

Thank You for all the amazing things You've done for me. When my thoughts turn to worry and fear, remind me how You've loved me, cared for me, and carried me through even the most difficult of circumstances. Give me opportunities to share the great things You've done in my life. I know when I talk about Your goodness, it helps to focus my thoughts on You and not on my anxieties. Like the verse says, I will tell of Your wonderful deeds. I will be glad in You. I will sing praise to Your name, O Most High.

THINK ABOUT IT:
What do you thank God for today? Set your thoughts on those things.

Morning
FAR AWAY?

*Why, O Lord, do you stand
far away? Why do you hide
yourself in times of trouble?*
PSALM 10:1 ESV

Thank You for allowing me to question You. I know You welcome my honest conversations, my sincere inquiries about what's going on and how You're working. Sometimes, I just need to talk about my fears and frustrations, and it's a comfort to pour out my thoughts to You. When I talk to You in this way, Lord, I always walk away from the conversation feeling better, more at peace. Even though You don't always answer the way I want or on my timeline, I know You've heard my pleas, and You have it all under control. Even when You seem far away, when it feels like You're hiding, I know You're actively working on my behalf. I trust You.

THINK ABOUT IT:
*Does it feel like God is far away?
Tell Him, and ask Him to show Himself.*

Evening
HOW LONG?

*How long must I bear pain in my
soul, and have sorrow in my heart
all the day? How long shall my
enemy be exalted over me?*
PSALM 13:2 RSV

According to some scholars and evidenced by the psalms, David struggled with depression. So many of the psalms are written from a broken, anguished heart. Yet in each of these, David comes back around to praising God. I've found the same to be true. When I sincerely pour out my heart to You, I find comfort and peace in Your presence. When I lift You up in prayer and praise, I get lifted up as well. I have pain in my soul today, Lord, and sorrow in my heart. But I know You are faithful and that Your love is never ending. Thank You for being so good to me, Father.

THINK ABOUT IT:
*What pain and sorrow do you
carry in your heart right now?
How has God shown Himself
faithful to you in the past?*

Morning
GOD IS WITH ME

There they shall be in great terror, for God is with the generation of the righteous.

PSALM 14:5 RSV

Evil is all over the news. It's everywhere. Even when I try to shelter myself from the onslaught of negative media, it seeps in. I can't escape it. But I know that You are with the righteous. You are actively working for those who love You. One day, every evil deed will be called to account, and every person who has rejected Your ways will pay for the things they've done. Thank You for sending Jesus to pay for my sins, and thank You for being with me and protecting me every step I take. Thank You for counting me among the righteous not because of my own deeds but because of what Christ did on the cross.

THINK ABOUT IT:

Are you worried about evil in the world? Trust that God will one day bring justice.

Evening
FULLNESS OF JOY

You make known to me the path of life; in your presence there is fullness of joy; at your right hand are pleasures forevermore.

PSALM 16:11 ESV

You have so many good things in store for me. I can look back on my life and see Your fingerprints all over the place. In light of Your goodness, I don't know why I struggle with fear and anxiety. All I need to do is stay close to You, and Your joy will surround me. It's all about focus, isn't it? I can choose to see the sunset, or I can focus on the telephone wires that get in the way. I can look at fields of flowers, or I can home in on one dead tree. Make known to me the path of life and joy and peace, Lord. Draw my attention to all the beautiful gifts You've placed in my life for me to enjoy.

THINK ABOUT IT:

Where is your focus today? Think of something good to dwell on.

Morning
LIKE WATER

"For as the rain and the snow come down from heaven and do not return there but water the earth, making it bring forth and sprout, giving seed to the sower and bread to the eater, so shall my word be that goes out from my mouth; it shall not return to me empty, but it shall accomplish that which I purpose, and shall succeed in the thing for which I sent it."

ISAIAH 55:10–11 ESV

Father, water is so essential to life. Every living thing—from plants to humans—needs it. It rains down from the sky to support life, and it does. I can see how water falling on parched ground brings renewal; water causes delicate saplings to grow. Your Word is like the water. With it, we quench our thirsty souls and nourish our faith. And just as physical water meets physical needs, Your Word will not fail to meet our spiritual needs. Thank You for sending Your Word. Amen.

THINK ABOUT IT:
What spiritual needs does God's Word fulfill?

Evening
BURDEN BEARERS

If anyone is caught in any transgression, you who are spiritual should restore him in a spirit of gentleness. Keep watch on yourself, lest you too be tempted. Bear one another's burdens, and so fulfill the law of Christ.

GALATIANS 6:1–2 ESV

Lord, we all struggle with walking in Christlike ways at times. We all have weaknesses and fail in the face of temptation. Bearing the burden alone can be overwhelming, and we would fall under its weight. Thank You for those You place in our lives who come alongside to shoulder the burdens together. May I be that person for someone. May I be a source of encouragement, accountability, strength, and prayer. As I reach out in love and faith, guard my heart, Lord. Keep me steady to help support another, I pray. Amen.

THINK ABOUT IT:
How have your sisters in Christ been a blessing when you struggle with sin?

Morning
HEAVEN AWAITS

"Now God's presence is with people, and he will live with them, and they will be his people. God himself will be with them and will be their God. He will wipe away every tear from their eyes, and there will be no more death, sadness, crying, or pain, because all the old ways are gone." The One who was sitting on the throne said, "Look! I am making everything new!"

REVELATION 21:3–5 NCV

God, heaven sounds like. . .heaven! I can only begin to imagine all that it will be. A place with no more tears, no more death, no more pain. This old life that is so wearisome will be gone, replaced with new, perfect life. Even more unimaginable: You will dwell with us. What we have only begun to experience through Your Holy Spirit in our hearts will surround us. What a glorious place it will be! Thank You for the promise of heaven, God. Amen.

THINK ABOUT IT:
What do you look forward to most in heaven?

Evening
WONDERFULLY MADE

For you formed my inward parts; you knitted me together in my mother's womb. I praise you, for I am fearfully and wonderfully made. . . . Your eyes saw my unformed substance; in your book were written, every one of them, the days that were formed for me, when as yet there was none of them.

PSALM 139:13–14, 16 ESV

Father, when I look in the mirror, sometimes I begin to pick apart what You lovingly created. Why not a different nose? Different hair, skin? Why not a thinner this, curvier that? In these moments, Father, remind me of the words of the psalm. You formed every cell of me before I was born. My body is miraculous in all its uniqueness. And more than just creating the physical me, You form my days before I live them. You are master of body and life. I praise You for Your design. Amen.

THINK ABOUT IT:
Do you look at yourself and your life with criticism or praise?

Morning
SHE LAUGHED

So Sarah laughed to herself, saying, "After I am worn out, and my lord is old, shall I have pleasure?" The Lord said to Abraham, "Why did Sarah laugh and say, 'Shall I indeed bear a child, now that I am old?' Is anything too hard for the Lord?"

GENESIS 18:12–14 ESV

God, You are almighty. You reign over heaven and earth. Considering that, Sarah's laughter itself is laughable. How could she laugh at Your promise, Your plan? But we all are Sarahs at times, aren't we? Whether we doubt Your ability or dislike the timing, we lack faith. God, forgive me for my Sarah moments. Open my faith wide so that I view my life with You in mind. Nothing is too hard for You. Through the seemingly impossible ways You work, Your glory shines. Amen.

THINK ABOUT IT:

How does God use Sarah's example and our own "Sarah moments" to teach us about Himself?

Evening
CHILD OF GOD

The disciples came to Jesus, saying, "Who is the greatest in the kingdom of heaven?" And calling to him a child, he put him in the midst of them and said, "Truly, I say to you, unless you turn and become like children, you will never enter the kingdom of heaven. Whoever humbles himself like this child is the greatest in the kingdom of heaven."

MATTHEW 18:1–4 ESV

The greatest in Your kingdom, Lord, will have childlike faith. The disciples were focused on what they could achieve to be the greatest, but You showed them that it is what they believe that makes them great in Your sight. To approach You as a child means trusting You as my heavenly Father. To approach You as a child means resting in Your care. To approach You as a child means looking to You for all my needs. I sit at Your feet today as Your child. Amen.

THINK ABOUT IT:

What are some examples of God taking the least and making it great?

Morning
INNER ADORNMENT

*Do not let your adorning be external—
the braiding of hair and the putting
on of gold jewelry, or the clothing
you wear—but let your adorning
be the hidden person of the heart
with the imperishable beauty of
a gentle and quiet spirit, which
in God's sight is very precious.*

1 PETER 3:3–4 ESV

God, what's on the outside is important to most women. From our hair to our shoes and everything in between, we expend a lot of time, energy, money, and thought on how to adorn our physical selves. While You bless us with beautiful things, real beauty—a beauty that will outlast even the most precious jewels—resides in our hearts. A beautiful spirit is precious to You, God. Each day, may I pour more effort into beautifying my spirit than my body. May I be truly gorgeous in Your sight. Amen.

THINK ABOUT IT:
*Why is a gentle and
quiet spirit beautiful?*

Evening
OF HEAVEN

*"These things I speak in the world,
that they may have my joy fulfilled in
themselves. I have given them your
word, and the world has hated them
because they are not of the world, just
as I am not of the world. I do not ask
that you take them out of the world, but
that you keep them from the evil one."*

JOHN 17:13–15 ESV

A square among polka dots. Lord, as a Christian, it's natural to feel out of place in the world. Once I believed in You, my true home became a future home in heaven. And while I *feel* at odds, the world should *see* me as different. A daughter of the King with a mission to spread Your love—even if it is met with hate. Lord, You knew that Your disciples, You knew that I, would experience this. So You prayed. You prayed for our protection. You prayed for our joy. Thank You for Your prayers. Amen.

THINK ABOUT IT:
What is Christ's prayer for you?

Morning
SMALL BUT MIGHTY

*No one can tame the tongue. It is wild
and evil and full of deadly poison.
We use our tongues to praise our
Lord and Father, but then we curse
people, whom God made like himself.
Praises and curses come from the
same mouth! My brothers and
sisters, this should not happen.*

JAMES 3:8–10 NCV

Sticks and stones can break my bones. . .
and words can wound even deeper. God,
the tongue and the words it forms have
great power. Power for good as I bless
and pray and praise, but also power to
curse and do harm. When ugly words
slip out, the truth of James is so clear.
Who can tame the tongue? Only You. Use
my tongue to speak of Your love, Your
healing, with words that penetrate to the
soul and uplift. May my words always be
in harmony with my faith. Amen.

THINK ABOUT IT:
*Do you need to ask God
for a tongue taming?*

Evening
E-V-E-R-Y

*Rejoice always, pray without
ceasing, give thanks in all
circumstances; for this is the will
of God in Christ Jesus for you.*

1 THESSALONIANS 5:16–18 ESV

When I read these words in 1 Thessalonians, God, they seem so simple,
and yet doing them seems impossible.
Rejoice *always*. Pray *without ceasing*.
Give thanks *in all circumstances*. How can
that be? How can I keep up? Because of
You. Because of Your love and salvation,
every moment is cause for joy. Because
of Your promise to hear me when I cry
out in faith, every need, every answer
is a reason to never give up on prayer.
Because of Your presence, every day I
can give thanks no matter what happens.
I won't be perfect, but place in me a heart
to rejoice, to pray, to offer thanks continually. Amen.

THINK ABOUT IT:
*What ways can joy, prayer,
and gratitude become essential
parts of everyday life?*

Morning
HIGHER THOUGHTS

If then you have been raised with Christ, seek the things that are above, where Christ is, seated at the right hand of God. Set your minds on things that are above, not on things that are on earth. For you have died, and your life is hidden with Christ in God. When Christ who is your life appears, then you also will appear with him in glory.

COLOSSIANS 3:1–4 ESV

When You redeem my life at the moment of salvation, Lord, You reserve a place for me in heaven. My new life is hidden with You above, yet my mind lags behind as my thoughts still center on this life. It's easy to get discouraged when my focus is downward instead of heavenward. It's easy to become distracted when my eyes aren't on You. Lord, set my mind on things above. May I never lose sight of my new life and my future home. Amen.

THINK ABOUT IT:

Do this life's disappointments pale when seen in the light of heaven's hope?

Evening
TOXIC PEOPLE

Too long have I had my dwelling among those who hate peace. I am for peace, but when I speak, they are for war!

PSALM 120:6–7 ESV

Much of my worry, stress, and anxiety comes from within me. But I think part of it comes from being around toxic people. It's hard to break away from the negative people in my life. Some of them are permanent fixtures, and I don't know how to avoid them. Give me wisdom for how to act when I must be around them and how to stay away from them whenever possible. Help me pray for them instead of becoming like them. Whenever a conversation or climate turns hateful or negative, show me ways to turn things around in a way that honors You. I know by avoiding toxic people and situations, I'll alleviate much of the stress in my life.

THINK ABOUT IT:

Can you think of people or situations that increase your anxiety? Talk to God about how to change your reaction.

Morning
BOLD SPIRIT

For this reason I remind you to fan into flame the gift of God, which is in you through the laying on of my hands, for God gave us a spirit not of fear but of power and love.

2 TIMOTHY 1:6–7 ESV

God, You want me to be bold. When I use the gift You have given me and walk in Your will, You equip me not with fear but with power, with love. Far from a shriveling flower cowering in the shade, I can bloom. I can stand tall, knowing that You have supplied all I need to weather even the harshest times. I can bring brightness by living out and sharing Your love. Just as Paul told Timothy to fan into flame his gift, remind me each morning to cultivate my gift. May it flourish in power and love. Amen.

THINK ABOUT IT:
How can you bring a renewed energy to using your spiritual gift?

Evening
A CLEAN SWEEP

Create in me a clean heart, O God, and renew a right spirit within me. Cast me not away from your presence, and take not your Holy Spirit from me. Restore to me the joy of your salvation, and uphold me with a willing spirit.

PSALM 51:10–12 ESV

God, I know how good it feels to spring-clean, to reorganize and refresh my home. Getting rid of ignored cobwebs and dust, letting a fresh breeze flow in, removing clutter, and opening up space. . . Much more important is the "spring-cleaning" You can do in me. Sweep out sin to reveal a clean heart, God. Breathe into my life so I approach today and the days to come with a renewed spirit. Open me to Your joy, I pray. It feels so good to start fresh! Amen.

THINK ABOUT IT:
What areas of your life need a little spring-cleaning?

Morning
THE SHELTER OF HIS WINGS

He will cover you with his feathers, and under his wings you can hide. His truth will be your shield and protection.

PSALM 91:4 NCV

Father, in Your design, You have programmed in us the comfort of a hug. When a child falls and scrapes her knee or awakes at night from a bad dream, a hug can soothe and let her know that she is not alone. A hug means belonging, being wrapped in love. Even the birds of Your creation know the power of gathering precious ones together. As a parent bird enfolds and guides and protects chicks with loving wings, so You, our heavenly Father, enfold Your children, guiding and protecting us with Your love. Cover me today; let me hide in Your care. Amen.

THINK ABOUT IT:

Have there been moments in your life when you felt God's love surround you like wings of refuge?

Evening
MORE THAN LIP SERVICE

Let the words of my mouth and the meditation of my heart be acceptable in your sight, O Lord, my rock and my redeemer.

PSALM 19:14 ESV

In Old Testament times, God, those who worshipped You made sacrifices—physical displays of their devotion. They prayed that the sacrifices would be acceptable. Today, Christians are living sacrifices; it is with our lives that we show worship and devotion. God, I pray along with King David that my "sacrifices" go deep—beyond physical. I want the meditation of my heart, what my heart dwells on, to be pleasing to You. Then from a heart attitude of sacrifice will flow words of beauty, reflections of the God my life is sacrificed for. May my words and heart be acceptable in Your sight. Amen.

THINK ABOUT IT:

Do you believe God cares just as much about your inner self as He does about what others hear or see?

Morning
THE FIRST STEP

If we confess our sins, he is faithful and just to forgive us our sins and to cleanse us from all unrighteousness.

1 JOHN 1:9 ESV

God, thank You for forgiveness. Because of Your awesome love, You chose not to stand aside and let me perish in my sin but provided a way out, a way to You. Without You, God, I have no future, but with You I have life. Because of Your precious Son's death and resurrection, I chose Your saving grace. Now as Your child, when sin confronts me, I must take the first step. I must confess my sin; then in Your faithfulness, You will forgive. Incredible! May I never take Your forgiveness for granted but always reach for Your help after I stumble. You will wipe the dirt from my knees and set me on the path again. Amen.

THINK ABOUT IT:
Do you sometimes skip confession in prayer, assuming that God has forgiven by default?

Evening
WHERE ARE YOU GOING?

Let me hear in the morning of your steadfast love, for in you I trust. Make me know the way I should go, for to you I lift up my soul.

PSALM 143:8 ESV

Father, direction is important in life. North, south, east, west. . .knowing where I'm headed keeps me focused, keeps me in line with Your will. But I'm only human. My compass is faulty. It points to my desires and comfort and ease as true north, even when the best way might be the opposite way. I need Your compass, Father. Each morning as I face a new day, grant me a keen desire to bend my knees and ask for Your direction. You love me steadfastly. I can trust You completely. Point me in the right direction, I pray. Amen.

THINK ABOUT IT:
Have you ever felt as if God's leading is off but later discovered that He had you right on course?

Morning
WISE WORDS

But the wisdom from above is first pure, then peaceable, gentle, open to reason, full of mercy and good fruits, impartial and sincere.

JAMES 3:17 ESV

Father, if women are supposedly born communicators, why do we struggle with the ugly side of communicating? Gossip, quarrels, backbiting. . .we use our words to hurt rather than heal, to uplift ourselves instead of uplifting others. We want to be heard first and listen later; we try to be polished when we should be honest. There's still so much we can learn about communicating! We can become so much *wiser* with our words. Teach us how, Father. Describing wisdom, James used the words *pure, peaceable, gentle, reason, mercy, good, impartial, sincere.* The beautiful side of communicating. May I think on these words before I speak. May I become a wise communicator, I pray. Amen.

THINK ABOUT IT:
How can you incorporate James' words on wisdom into your relationships?

Evening
A HAND TO HOLD

For I, the LORD your God, hold your right hand; it is I who say to you, "Fear not, I am the one who helps you."

ISAIAH 41:13 ESV

God, when I think about holding hands, I envision beautiful things. I see a father reaching out to grasp his child's hand before they cross a busy street. I see two people in love walking side by side. I see hands held to comfort and reassure in times of trial. I see hands held in unity when facing opposition—and raised together in triumph. But more beautiful than all these is the thought of You holding my hand as You guide my steps. As You pour out Your love and encouragement. As You uphold me; as You celebrate with me. You, my God, stand beside me, our hands clasped. Amen.

THINK ABOUT IT:
What has God's presence meant to you in troubling and joyous times?

Morning
GREATER THINGS AHEAD!

For I consider that the sufferings of this present time are not worth comparing with the glory that is to be revealed to us.

ROMANS 8:18 ESV

Sometimes I look at the sufferings going on around me, and I get overwhelmed. So much drama is going on in the world today, Lord. So much sickness. So much division and anger. I wonder how long humanity can go on like this.

When I see things through Your lens, I'm reminded that these current sufferings, whether they are my own or ones affecting my loved ones, can't begin to compare with the glory that is coming. The contrast of chaos to glory is going to be breathtaking. So please guard us during these tumultuous times. Prepare our hearts for greater things ahead. Amen.

THINK ABOUT IT:

When you look through the lens of eternity, is your current situation more tolerable?

Evening
YOU'LL WORK IT OUT

And we know that for those who love God all things work together for good, for those who are called according to his purpose.

ROMANS 8:28 ESV

You haven't called me to excel so that eyes can be drawn to me, Lord. The purpose behind my successes is to draw humankind to You. That's why You are working all things out—not so that I can be glorified for my achievements but so that others will see You for who You are.

You promise to work things out. That's enough for me. Confusion, misunderstandings, frustrations. . .they are not too big for You. In fact, they are springboards to something better ahead. I can't wait to see what You're going to do, Lord—how You're going to turn my messes into messages for a lost world. Amen.

THINK ABOUT IT:

Are you called according to God's purpose?

Morning
YOU'RE STRAIGHTENING MY PATH

Trust in the Lord with all your heart and lean not on your own understanding; in all your ways submit to him, and he will make your paths straight.

PROVERBS 3:5–6 NIV

Oh boy, have I ever had some crooked paths over the years! I feel like I've been lost in the wilderness more times than I can count. From the mountains to the valleys, I've trekked a mile or two. . .and often in the wrong direction.

Today I will be the first to admit that my internal compass isn't always the best. Sometimes I set off on my way only to discover it's the wrong way. Thank You for stopping me in my tracks. Thank You for caring enough to straighten the road before me. I'm so grateful for Your intervention in seasons like these. You are my guardian, my protector, my true compass. How I praise You for Your perfect direction. Amen.

THINK ABOUT IT:

When was the last time you realized God was straightening your path?

Evening
A CLOUD OF WITNESSES

Therefore, since we are surrounded by so great a cloud of witnesses, let us also lay aside every weight, and sin which clings so closely, and let us run with endurance the race that is set before us.

HEBREWS 12:1 ESV

Whenever I feel alone, Lord, I reflect on the biblical giants from years past. Men like Abraham, Isaac, and Jacob. Women like Sarah, Deborah, and Mary. Warriors like Gideon, David, and Jehoshaphat.

I can picture them all in the grandstands watching me run my race. They're waving banners and cheering me on. I can hear them shouting, "You've got this!" I can hear Mary crying out, "Keep the faith! Don't give up!" Their voices ring loud in my ears as I continue to run. Thank You for the stories of the saints of old, Lord. They inspire me to keep going. Amen.

THINK ABOUT IT:

Who do you imagine is cheering in the grandstands, giving you the courage to keep going?

DAY 282

Morning
STEADFAST UNDER TRIAL

Blessed is the man who remains steadfast under trial, for when he has stood the test he will receive the crown of life, which God has promised to those who love him.
JAMES 1:12 ESV

I will stand the test. Maybe I should embroider that on a sampler and hang it on the wall. To be reminded daily would encourage me so much.

You have a lovely prize waiting on the other end of my steadfastness, Lord. I'll spend eternity with You, where the testing will be behind me. The victory came not by my own actions, but by Your sacrifice on the cross, Jesus. And I get to share in the prize—eternal bliss with You.

Thank You for helping me stand during the various tests I go through. I've got this with You leading the way. Amen.

THINK ABOUT IT:
What does it mean to stand the test?

Evening
OUT OF MY DISTRESS

Out of my distress I called on the Lord; the Lord answered me and set me free. The Lord is on my side; I will not fear. What can man do to me?
PSALM 118:5–6 ESV

As a parent, I know what it's like for my child to come to me when he's in distress. I want him to come to me with everything, but I'm especially attuned to his pleas when he's hurting or in turmoil. I wonder if that's how You feel when I cry out to You in my distress, Lord.

Your heart is touched, I know, because I've seen Your swift and loving responses to those cries. You're on my side, so I have nothing to be afraid of. That reality brings me great comfort no matter what I'm facing. And knowing I have someone to turn to, especially when everything and everyone seems to be against me? Priceless.

Thank You, Lord, for hearing my cries. Amen.

THINK ABOUT IT:
When you're in distress, who do you call on?

Morning
TABLE FOOD

Anyone who lives on milk cannot understand the teaching about being right with God. He is a baby.

HEBREWS 5:13 NLV

I've enjoyed my baby food for years now, Lord. I'm comfortable hearing sermons about love, joy, and happiness. Easy messages like "Three Steps to a Better Life" get my vote every time. It's tougher to hear messages about pain, valleys, and sacrifice. Those things require work on my part.

You're calling me to bigger, better things. I can only get there if I'm willing to go deep with You. So today I'll start digging—past the chaos, past the confusion, past the point where I'm comfortable. I'll keep going until I reach that place of revelation where Your truth plants itself deep in my heart. No more milk for me, Lord. I want to fully understand what it means to walk in fullness of peace with You. Amen.

THINK ABOUT IT:

Are you interested in knowing more about the deep things of God?

Evening
CALLED BY KINDNESS

In his kindness God called you to share in his eternal glory by means of Christ Jesus. So after you have suffered a little while, he will restore, support, and strengthen you, and he will place you on a firm foundation.

1 PETER 5:10 NLT

Your kindness, Lord, is what leads me to repentance. I would still be moving in the wrong direction, headed down a dark path, if not for Your gentle and loving ways.

You love me so completely that You would go to great lengths to win my heart. Your kindness draws me to You, and in Your presence I find restoration. I find support. I garner the strength to keep moving ahead.

Best of all, Lord, You've placed my feet on solid rock. Everything in my life is made new because of Your great kindness. How grateful I am! Amen.

THINK ABOUT IT:

How have you personally witnessed the kindness of God in a recent situation?

Morning
LET ANXIETIES GO

And he said to his disciples, "Therefore I tell you, do not be anxious about your life, what you will eat, nor about your body, what you will put on."

LUKE 12:22 ESV

You've told me, "Don't worry about it!" But I still fret, Lord. I wonder how the light bill will get paid this month. Should I juggle the other bills around so I can pay that one? I'm also worked up about a situation at work. My coworkers aren't getting along, and the tension is grating on my nerves, making my job more difficult.

In moments like these, when I'm stressed out, You say, "Don't be anxious about your life—what you eat, put on, and so forth." I need Your help to refrain from worry, though. It's not coming naturally to me. Help me to let go of the anxieties I'm clinging so tightly to today, Father! I need Your help to unwind my fingers from them! Amen.

THINK ABOUT IT:

How do you keep from fretting when you're in a season of lack?

Evening
YOUR SPIRIT IS THERE

In the beginning God created the heavens and the earth. Now the earth was formless and empty, darkness was over the surface of the deep, and the Spirit of God was hovering over the waters.

GENESIS 1:1–2 NIV

Your Spirit hovered over the waters at creation. How miraculous that must have been—how powerful! Your Spirit changes everything!

I read this verse and realize Your Spirit is hovering over me right now, in this very moment, even as I read these words. Your Spirit is here to comfort, to lead, to guide. To give power. To stir me to action.

I have nothing to fear, no matter what I face. Your Spirit is with me. How grateful I am! Amen.

THINK ABOUT IT:

Can you think of a particular time when you deeply sensed God's presence?

Morning
JOY IN PLACE OF SORROW

"So also you have sorrow now, but I will see you again, and your hearts will rejoice, and no one will take your joy from you."
JOHN 16:22 ESV

You're not content for me to live in sorrow, Lord. No way! You have a plan to replace it with joy. The thought of being able to rejoice again seems impossible when sorrows are fresh, but hindsight is 20/20. You've refreshed my spirit so many times in my life, and I know You will do it again.

Joy is birthed out of hope, so today I place my hope in You. I won't let circumstances dictate how I move forward. I'll press onward with Your hand in mine. I'll allow joy to lead the way, even when troubles come. I won't let my struggles zap my joy. It's Your gift to me, after all! I'll hold on tight, for in You I find my strength. Amen.

THINK ABOUT IT:
Has God ever changed your sorrow to joy in an instant?

Evening
EYES WIDE OPEN

Be alert and of sober mind. Your enemy the devil prowls around like a roaring lion looking for someone to devour.
1 PETER 5:8 NIV

You tell me to be alert, Lord. Yet half the time I forget to keep my eyes open, and then I wonder how the enemy sneaks in to catch me off guard. If I'm really staying alert, if I'm not allowing emotions and turmoil to cloud my mind, then I'll see his tactics. Problem is, I'm often worked up about something or frustrated with someone, and the enemy uses my angst as the perfect opportunity to waltz into the room.

I won't let him prowl today, Lord. My eyes are wide open. I'm on to him. When that roaring lion comes around, I'll take him down in Jesus' name. Amen.

THINK ABOUT IT:
What happens when you're not paying attention?

Morning
YOU'RE CLOSE WHEN MY HEART IS BROKEN

The LORD is close to the brokenhearted; he rescues those whose spirits are crushed.

PSALM 34:18 NLT

You're always nearby, Lord, but I feel especially comforted knowing You're there when my heart is broken. Usually when I reach that point, I feel completely isolated, all alone. But You've made a point of telling me that You're there even then.

Best of all, You're there with a plan to rescue me. You long to scoop my crushed spirit into Your tender hands and gently breathe life into it again. So I give You the broken pieces inside of me, Lord. I say, "Come and do what only You can do." Mend. Repair. Heal. Restore. Draw close and do a deep work, I pray. Amen.

THINK ABOUT IT:

Can you think of a time when God healed your broken heart?

Evening
PRAISING IN THE STRESSFUL SEASONS

Rejoice always, pray continually, give thanks in all circumstances; for this is God's will for you in Christ Jesus.

1 THESSALONIANS 5:16–18 NIV

My head hurts, Lord. My stomach is churning. I feel like I'm tied up in knots! The very last thing I feel like doing right now is praising You. But Your Word says I should praise even in these stressful circumstances. When I'm off my game. When everything is against me. Right here. Right now. Without hesitation.

To be honest, I'd rather pull the covers over my head. But I'll try it Your way, Father! I lift Your name right now, Lord, and I say, "Thank You for being such a good and loving Father! Thank You for Your provision. Thank You for answers to my many questions. Thank You for bringing calm in the middle of the storm."

Aah, that's better! One moment of praise changes everything! Amen.

THINK ABOUT IT:

Are you in a stressful season? If so, why not lift your eyes to heaven and begin to praise Him!

DAY 287

Morning
I WON'T LEAN ON MY OWN UNDERSTANDING

Trust in the Lord with all your heart, and do not lean on your own understanding.

PROVERBS 3:5 ESV

I'm one of those people who thinks I have to figure everything out on my own, Lord. I work things out in my head and then rework them to come up with a better plan, one that will surely succeed. Many times I've moved forward, confident with my decision, only to find out it was the wrong one.

You ask me to place my confidence in You, not myself. You want me to lean on Your understanding, not my own. Show me how to do that, I pray. Lead me in Your ways that I might be more effective for You. Amen.

THINK ABOUT IT:
Where does your own understanding lead you?

Evening
MY SPIRIT IS WILLING, LORD

"Watch and pray so that you will not fall into temptation. The spirit is willing, but the flesh is weak."

MATTHEW 26:41 NIV

How many times have I said, "I'll do that tomorrow"? My desire is strong as long as I don't have to step out in faith immediately. But when it comes time to actually take that first step? Too often my flesh is weak. I can't seem to get myself going. The energy just isn't there.

I especially need Your help on those days, Lord! You can energize me with Your Spirit and give me all I need to take that first step! I thank You in advance for strengthening this physical body. Amen.

THINK ABOUT IT:
How do you move forward on days when your spirit is willing but your flesh is weak?

Morning
ESCAPE HATCH

The only temptation that has come to you is that which everyone has. But you can trust God, who will not permit you to be tempted more than you can stand. But when you are tempted, he will also give you a way to escape so that you will be able to stand it.

1 CORINTHIANS 10:13 NCV

You don't want me to get caught in the enemy's traps, Lord. That's why, with every tempting situation that comes along, You provide an escape. You make provision in advance, knowing I'll need it!

I don't always see the way out, so today I'm asking for Your supernatural vision so that I can see what You see. Show me the escape hatch, and then give me the guidance I need to take it! I'm so grateful for a way out of life's temptations. Amen.

THINK ABOUT IT:

Can you think of a particular time when God provided a supernatural escape hatch to get you out of a tempting situation?

Evening
YOU'RE SENDING HELP!

Two are better than one, because they have a good return for their labor: If either of them falls down, one can help the other up. But pity anyone who falls and has no one to help them up.

ECCLESIASTES 4:9–10 NIV

You never meant for us to do life alone, Lord. It was always Your plan that we would lean on each other, learn from each other, and benefit from each other.

Many times, especially during stressful seasons, I pull away from the people in my circle. I don't want to burden them. But through this verse You are reminding me that two really are better than one. My plan for getting out of life's messes needs to involve leaning on the ones You've given me to love. Thank You for this reminder. Amen.

THINK ABOUT IT:

Who do you want by your side during the tough seasons?

DAY 289

Morning
EVERY GOOD WORK

And God is able to bless you abundantly, so that in all things at all times, having all that you need, you will abound in every good work.

2 CORINTHIANS 9:8 NIV

In all things at all times, You want me to abound in good works, Lord! *All things.* Every venture. Every relationship. Every financial decision. Every academic endeavor. You want me to be blessed abundantly. *All* is a lot!

I'm preparing my heart even now for Your blessing. I feel such great joy knowing that You passionately want to provide for me so that I can thrive in every situation. How I praise You for Your loving care! May I be found worthy of it as I work for You, Lord. Amen.

THINK ABOUT IT:

What does it mean to "abound" in every good work?

Evening
YOU'VE GOT THIS

"For I know the plans I have for you," says the LORD. "They are plans for good and not for disaster, to give you a future and a hope."

JEREMIAH 29:11 NLT

You know the plans You have for me, Lord. In fact, You know them well because You are the one who came up with them in the first place.

I'll confess, there are times I wish I could know them too. The "not knowing" is difficult. But I take comfort in the fact that You not only know what's coming but are working out the details even now. In this very moment, You are putting together plans for my tomorrows. How wonderful to know that You are already there, and what a privilege to be able to step into those plans with Your hand in mine! Thank You, heavenly Father. Amen.

THINK ABOUT IT:

Are your current plans His or yours?

Morning
AS ABOVE, SO BELOW

"Our Father in heaven, reveal who you are. Set the world right; do what's best—as above, so below."
MATTHEW 6:10 MSG

I've been blessed in so many ways, Lord, but when I look around, I realize that many people are not as fortunate as I am. People are suffering injustice and oppression; the sins of hatred and division seem to grow stronger with each day. I'm tempted to throw up my hands and say, "There's nothing I can do"—and then retreat back into my own safe little world. Instead, God, give me courage to follow You. Reveal who You are through my words and actions. Use me in whatever way You can to build Your kingdom of love and justice here on earth.

THINK ABOUT IT:

How might God want you to speak out against injustice? Have you asked Him?

Evening
LESS OF YOU AND MORE OF GOD

"You're blessed when you're at the end of your rope. With less of you there is more of God and his rule."
MATTHEW 5:3 MSG

Lord, You know how important it is to me to succeed—but this time, I've run out of ideas. I've run out of energy too. And most of all, I've run out of patience. I can't turn this situation around. No, I've completely and utterly failed. There's nothing else I can do. But as I think that, I hear Your Spirit whisper in my heart, "At last! Now that you're finally ready to step back, I'll have room to get to work." Okay, Lord. I'll stay out of Your way. Show me what You want to do.

THINK ABOUT IT:

Have you ever thought that your need to look good to others might be getting in the way of the Spirit working through you?

Morning
EVEN TO THE POINT OF DEATH

"Do not be afraid of what you are about to suffer. . . . Be faithful, even to the point of death, and I will give you life as your victor's crown."

REVELATION 2:10 NIV

I get so scared, Lord, when I think about the future. So many threats hang over our world—violence, disease, disaster—and I know I can't assume that my loved ones and I will escape them all. These aren't things that just happen to *someone else*; they could very easily happen to me or someone I care about. That terrifies me. But I know, God of love, that no matter what happens, You are with us. You will keep us safe, through violence, disease, disaster, and even death. Our bodies may suffer, but our spirits are safe with You. And so I ask, Lord, that You take my fear from me. Give me the courage to be faithful.

THINK ABOUT IT:

Can you believe that God will keep you and your loved ones truly safe, even if you are asked to suffer in this life? What does the word safe *mean to you?*

Evening
AS A MOTHER COMFORTS HER CHILD

"I will comfort you there in Jerusalem as a mother comforts her child."

ISAIAH 66:13 NLT

No one comforts like a mother does. Her heart is intrinsically tied to her child. She feels their pain. She senses their frustrations. She knows their cries, their needs, and she's right there, ready to step in at a moment's notice.

You are like that tender mother, Lord! You know Your children so well. You know when I sit and when I rise. You know when my heart is broken and when I'm feeling strong. And You are right there, ready to comfort, to touch, and to wipe away every tear. What a tender Father You are. I am Your grateful child. Amen.

THINK ABOUT IT:

How has God comforted you in the past? How is He comforting you even now?

Morning
KEEPING MY COOL

*Do not be quickly provoked
in your spirit, for anger
resides in the lap of fools.*
ECCLESIASTES 7:9 NIV

I've been in some situations where I erupted quickly, like a volcano that offered no warning. I'm sure my swift reaction startled others in the room! I was a little startled myself. Talk about a lava flow.

You ask me *not* to erupt, Lord. Today's verse reminds me that it's not good to be quickly provoked in my spirit. Only fools blow up like that! Oops! Calm my heart in the moment, I pray. The next time I'm tempted to blow my top, stop me in my tracks and bring peace to my soul. Intervene, I pray. Amen.

THINK ABOUT IT:
*What techniques do you use when
you're about to lose your cool?*

Evening
IN HIS SHADOW

*The LORD is your keeper; the LORD is
your shade on your right hand. The
sun shall not strike you by day, nor the
moon by night. The LORD will keep you
from all evil; he will keep your life.*
PSALM 121:5–7 ESV

Shade is caused by something blocking the light. In order for a shadow to be present, something has to come between. I stand in Your shadow, don't I? You stand over me, blocking me from evil and protecting me from harm. I know I live in a fallen, broken world, and sometimes bad things will happen. But I also know You walk each step with me, sheltering me from the very worst of things. . .things I might not even be aware of. Thank You for keeping me in Your shadow. May I never leave the safety of Your presence.

THINK ABOUT IT:
*What do you need God to shade you
from? Talk to Him about it now.*

Morning
ARMED AND READY

You have armed me with strength for the battle; you have subdued my enemies under my feet.

PSALM 18:39 NLT

You saw this battle coming, didn't You, Lord? You knew the enemies I would face. You knew the struggles in my heart. You saw it all long before it happened.

Best of all, You've already made provision for this battle. You have armed me. You have made me strong. All along You've been prepping me for this moment. With Your hand in mine, I will take down the enemy of my soul. I will let him know that the God of creation is on my side! How I praise You for joining me in the battle. Amen.

THINK ABOUT IT:

Do you feel armed and ready right now?

Evening
MUSTARD-SEED FAITH

"You don't have enough faith," Jesus told them. "I tell you the truth, if you had faith even as small as a mustard seed, you could say to this mountain, 'Move from here to there,' and it would move. Nothing would be impossible."

MATTHEW 17:20 NLT

I've seen a mustard seed, Lord! They're teensy tiny, so small I could barely pick one up with my fingertips. So delicate they could fly right out of my hand, and I wouldn't even know it.

How many times have I used the excuse that my faith isn't big enough? That I'm not strong enough? This verse belies those feelings! You say I only need a tiny bit of faith and mountains can be moved. Today I offer You what I have, microscopic as it might seem. Thank You for moving the mountains in my life with my tiny offering of faith. Amen.

THINK ABOUT IT:

How big is a mustard seed?

Morning
I KNOW YOU'RE LISTENING

The Lord is far from the wicked, but he hears the prayer of the righteous.
PROVERBS 15:29 ESV

It's remarkable to think that You can hear my prayers, Lord. I don't even have to speak them out loud, yet You hear them as if I've shouted them in Your ear!

Me, on the other hand? I don't always hear so well. Sometimes You whisper things to my heart, and I miss them altogether. I'm so glad You never miss the prayers of Your people. I'm so grateful for Your consideration of my every need. May I never take Your attention for granted, Lord. I will walk with confidence, knowing You hear me. Amen.

THINK ABOUT IT:

Do you ever feel like your prayers are hitting the ceiling? How do you get past those feelings to the truth?

Evening
I TRUST YOU

Trust in the Lord with all your heart; do not depend on your own understanding. Seek his will in all you do, and he will show you which path to take.
PROVERBS 3:5–6 NLT

You ask me to trust You with my whole heart. Not just pieces of it but every nook and cranny. Every hidden pocket. Every secret chamber.

Trusting You this way is not as easy as it sounds, Lord! How many times have I placed my trust in myself or kept things from You? How many times have I placed my trust in money or my job or other people instead of taking my concerns to the one who loves me most?

Today I choose to put You first. I will trust You above all. You are the faithful one, and You love me passionately. I can trust You, Lord. Fully. That knowledge brings great peace to my soul. Amen.

THINK ABOUT IT:

Who (or what) do you put your trust in when troubles come?

Morning
I WILL BE STILL

He says, "Be still, and know that I am God; I will be exalted among the nations, I will be exalted in the earth."
PSALM 46:10 NIV

You will be exalted among the nations. What a remarkable thought, Lord! Every city in every country on every continent will come to know You. Every human being will one day bow the knee to You. Until that day, You ask me to be still and to trust—to know in my heart that You are Lord of all.

You are Lord of those cities. You are Lord of those countries. You are Lord of those continents. You are Lord of this planet and, indeed, of the whole universe! How could I not trust the one who holds the entire world in His hands? I do, Lord! I trust You from now through eternity. Amen.

THINK ABOUT IT:
Is "stillness" hard for you?

Evening
ANOINTED AND APPOINTED

"Before I formed you in the womb I knew you, before you were born I set you apart; I appointed you as a prophet to the nations."
JEREMIAH 1:5 NIV

How I love this verse, Lord! You not only anointed me before I was born; You've appointed me as well. You have an assignment for me. Many of them, in fact!

This verse clues me in to a special secret: You set Your plans for me in motion before I even existed. Even then I was anointed to do great things for You! And I am appointed at this time in history to reach a certain group of people with the gospel message. Wow!

How can I help but feel confident when I realize You went to such efforts to get me ready? Why would my knees ever knock? You have plans, and they are big ones! Your provision for me is staggering, really!

Let's do this, Lord! Amen.

THINK ABOUT IT:
Do you sense God's anointing and appointing in your life?

Morning
THE BIG PICTURE

Yet God has made everything beautiful for its own time. He has planted eternity in the human heart, but even so, people cannot see the whole scope of God's work from beginning to end.

ECCLESIASTES 3:11 NLT

You make everything beautiful in its time, Lord. If it's not beautiful. . .it's not time. The fulfillment has not yet come. If it's not beautiful, I'll keep waiting until it is. If it's not beautiful, I'll keep trusting that one day it will be.

You see the big picture, far beyond what these earthly eyes can make out. You see the beauty in my mess. All I see is chaos and confusion, but You know what's ahead. You see the whole scope from beginning to end. I can walk with confidence, knowing You see it all. How wonderful to walk out Your plans in faith, knowing the outcome will be beautiful! Amen.

THINK ABOUT IT:

Are you a "big picture" person, or do you have trouble seeing the big picture?

Evening
YOU'RE WORKING IT OUT

We know that God makes all things work together for the good of those who love Him and are chosen to be a part of His plan.

ROMANS 8:28 NLV

Sometimes I feel like all I ever do is work. From the moment I get up in the morning to the time I rest my head on my pillow at night, I'm on the go.

It doesn't seem fair at times, if I'm being honest. Then I'm reminded of how hard You work! You go 24-7 (not that You're limited by time, Lord, but You get the point). You never stop. You're working on my behalf even now! And You are working all things together for my good, which lets me know that my welfare is always on Your mind. My heart overflows with gratitude. Thanks for working so hard, Lord! Amen.

THINK ABOUT IT:

Is it easy or hard for you to remember that God is eventually going to work things out?

Morning
IT'S LIKE THIS, LORD. . .

*If we confess our sins, he is faithful
and just to forgive us our sins and to
cleanse us from all unrighteousness.*

1 JOHN 1:9 ESV

You have asked me to come to You and confess my sins, Lord. I don't always do that. Sometimes I just try to get away with them and hope You don't notice.

Why would I ever doubt Your kindness? You're not going to slap me down when I tell You what I've done. It's not like You don't already know all about it, anyway! But You have asked me to confess, not for Your sake but for my own. I am cleansed and purified as I lay my sins at Your feet. And then I'm free to rise up and walk in confidence, fully forgiven.

Today I come, ready to get a few things off my chest. Here goes, Lord! Amen.

THINK ABOUT IT:

*Is it easier for you to
confess to God or to people?*

Evening
COMING WITH CONFIDENCE

*Let us then with confidence draw
near to the throne of grace, that
we may receive mercy and find
grace to help in time of need.*

HEBREWS 4:16 ESV

There have been times, Lord, when the little ones in my world have come to me with heads bowed low, eyes shifted to the ground. They were so filled with shame over what they had done that they couldn't even look me in the eye.

I know that feeling well! How many times have I come to You with my gaze shifted downward? Far too many to count, such is the shame I've borne. You've asked me to come with confidence no matter what burdens I carry, no matter what sins I've committed. When I come confidently, You offer mercy and grace. What a good God You are!

Today, Lord. . .I come. Amen.

THINK ABOUT IT:
Are you intimidated by God's presence?

Morning
YOU MAKE ME WORTHY

*To this end we always pray for
you, that our God may make you
worthy of his calling and may
fulfill every resolve for good and
every work of faith by his power.*

2 THESSALONIANS 1:11 ESV

I have struggled with feelings of unworthiness my whole life, Lord. Perhaps these feelings came about as a result of how I was spoken to as a child. Or maybe I have just carried so much guilt and shame that I couldn't imagine how You could see me as anything other than intrinsically flawed.

My heart fills with joy as I realize that I am made worthy through the blood of Your Son, Jesus, on the cross. Because of His free gift of grace, worthiness is mine for the taking. I can enter Your chambers boldly, confidently, not because of my goodness but because of His. How grateful I am for salvation in Him, Lord! I've been made worthy in Your sight. Amen.

THINK ABOUT IT:
Do you feel worthy?

Evening
YOU LIVE IN ME

*I have been crucified with Christ and
I no longer live, but Christ lives in
me. The life I now live in the body,
I live by faith in the Son of God, who
loved me and gave himself for me.*

GALATIANS 2:20 NIV

This is such a fascinating verse, Lord! You tell me that I have been crucified with Christ. What a concept! The old me is dead and gone. (Bye-bye, old me!) The sins of yesterday? Wiped away to exist no more.

Because of what Jesus did on the cross, I have a brand-new life. It's a life of faith. It's a life of gratitude. It's a life of hopeful possibilities. The death I have experienced was a necessary part of my journey with You, Lord, a transition from one world to another. I can hardly wait to thank You in person! Amen.

THINK ABOUT IT:
*What does it mean to
lay down your life?*

Morning
I CALL, YOU ANSWER!

"He will call on me, and I will answer him; I will be with him in trouble, I will deliver him and honor him."
PSALM 91:15 NIV

People don't always respond when I call them, Lord. Sometimes the phone will ring, but nobody picks up. It's the same with my pets. When they're being naughty, I call out to them, but they hide under the bed to avoid my stern gaze.

You, though? You *always* answer. You want me to call. In fact, You're sitting by the phone right now, waiting! There's no incessant ringing when I dial Your number! You pick up immediately. You listen patiently, and then, sometimes to my surprise, You respond. You give me answers for all I'm facing. It's a two-way conversation laced with love.

How I love our chats. I'll be calling again soon, Lord! Amen.

THINK ABOUT IT:

Do you consider your prayer time to be a two-way street?

Evening
THE BEST IS YET TO COME

For I consider that the sufferings of this present time are not worth comparing with the glory that is to be revealed to us.
ROMANS 8:18 ESV

I've had some pretty amazing adventures in this life, Lord. You've taken me places I never dreamed I would go, both in the natural and in the spiritual. Have I mentioned how grateful I am?

When I look ahead, I can see that You have even bigger things in store! I'm so curious. . .if the best is yet to come, then what's out there for me? I guess I'll just have to take it one day at a time and see for myself.

As I walk it out, I lay down any need to know the details. I push my worries aside. All stresses disappear with the wind as I place my trust in You. What fun this will be, Lord! I'm ready if You are! Amen.

THINK ABOUT IT:

What does it mean to live with a sense of anticipation?

Morning
DELIVER ME

You delivered me from strife with the people; you made me the head of the nations; people whom I had not known served me.

PSALM 18:43 ESV

It's easy to focus on the end result of this prayer without thinking about the beginning. You delivered David, but in order to be delivered, he had to go through some pretty rough things. If he hadn't, he wouldn't have needed saving. Father, I know the difficult things I go through are often necessary to shape me and change me into the person You want me to be. But I'm tired of all the strife, Lord. I'm anxious and scared and weary, and I need You to rescue me. Please deliver me like You delivered David. Let my end result be a place of peace, and let it come soon.

THINK ABOUT IT:

What is causing you strife today? Ask God to deliver you from it.

Evening
GOD'S WORD

The law of the LORD is perfect, reviving the soul; the testimony of the LORD is sure, making wise the simple; the precepts of the LORD are right, rejoicing the heart; the commandment of the LORD is pure, enlightening the eyes.

PSALM 19:7–8 ESV

I know Your Word is the most valuable learning tool available to me. It's the most precious thing I can fill my mind with. No news or television show, popular music, or bestselling novel can compare. I know from experience that when I fill my mind with Your thoughts and Your words, my anxiety decreases. Draw me to Your Word, Lord. Remind me to spend time with You each day. Protect my time and my schedule so nothing can crowd You out, Lord. You are my priority.

THINK ABOUT IT:

Are you in the habit of spending time each day reading God's Word? If not, what can you do to make that a priority?

Morning
IN GOD I TRUST

Some trust in chariots and some in horses, but we trust in the name of the Lord our God. They collapse and fall, but we rise and stand upright.
PSALM 20:7–8 ESV

In David's time, people trusted in a mighty army with the best chariots and horses to keep them safe. The better the military forces, the lower the anxiety. Today, I might be tempted to trust in our military as well. I also might trust in my bank account, my job, my family, my friends, or any number of things. But I know any of these people or things may fail me at any moment. You are the only constant. You are the only one in my life who will never fail. I trust in You alone for everything I need.

THINK ABOUT IT:

Other than God, what are you tempted to trust in for your safety and well-being? How is God better than those things?

Evening
HE RESTORES

The Lord is my shepherd; I shall not want. He makes me lie down in green pastures. He leads me beside still waters. He restores my soul. He leads me in paths of righteousness for his name's sake.
PSALM 23:1–3 ESV

Dear Father, You restore. This indicates hardship, because why would You restore something that doesn't need restoration? I know You will restore my dry, thirsty soul. Later in this chapter, it says, "Surely goodness and mercy shall follow me all the days of my life" (Psalm 23:6 ESV). When I'm tempted to worry, remind me of these promises, Lord. You will restore what's been lost. You will send goodness and mercy to pursue me. Thank You for the confidence I can have in Your love for me and in Your restorative power over my life.

THINK ABOUT IT:

What do you need God to restore for you? Talk to Him about it now.

Morning
GOD'S ADDRESS

*Yet you are holy, enthroned
on the praises of Israel.*
PSALM 22:3 ESV

Sometimes I feel so far from You. I look for You, but it seems like You're hiding. Thank You for this verse, which reveals Your personal address. You live in the praises of Your people! When You feel far away, all I need to do is praise You, and there You'll be. When I feel worried and stressed, anxious and afraid, Your praise will bring You near. Father, I praise You right now, in this moment. You are amazing, awesome, wonderful, beautiful. You are more than I can ever think or imagine, and I'm so humbled and grateful to be allowed into Your presence. Thank You for making me Your child and for always being within my reach.

THINK ABOUT IT:

When was the last time you dedicated a specific amount of time to simply praise God? Do that today.

Evening
WAIT ON GOD

*Indeed, none who wait for you shall be
put to shame; they shall be ashamed
who are wantonly treacherous.*
PSALM 25:3 ESV

When I'm patient and wait on Your timing, it always pays off. But when I carelessly act on my own, that's when disaster strikes. Help me to calm down and wait on You. I know I need to stop trying to control my circumstances. I need to stop trying to force things to happen in my own way, my own time. Your plan is so much better than anything I can bring about on my own. Teach me to be calm and simply rest in Your love, Father, as I wait for You to act according to Your will. I love You and trust You, and I will wait on Your timing.

THINK ABOUT IT:

Are you trying to control a circumstance instead of waiting on God? Step back, take a deep breath, and trust His timing.

Morning
HOLY REVERENCE

Who is the man who fears the Lord? Him will he instruct in the way that he should choose.
PSALM 25:12 ESV

Dear Father, I fear You. . .not because You are unkind but because You are powerful. This kind of fear is really reverence. I revere You, Father, and I want to please You. Your Word says that when we fear You with a holy reverence, You will show us which way to go. You'll direct our paths and assist us in our decisions. Instead of worrying about things, I know I just need to honor You with my life and listen to Your Holy Spirit's guidance. Help me, Father, to follow Your instruction instead of trying to figure things out on my own. I trust Your timing.

THINK ABOUT IT:
Do you need God's help in your decisions? Spend some time in sincere, reverent prayer, and listen for His guidance.

Evening
I WAIT

Oh, guard my soul, and deliver me! Let me not be put to shame, for I take refuge in you. May integrity and uprightness preserve me, for I wait for you.
PSALM 25:20–21 ESV

There is that word again: *wait.* I am waiting for You, Father. It seems I've waited for such a long time. Please deliver me from the circumstances that worry my heart, plague my mind, and steal my sleep. You are my refuge, my safe place. Let me feel Your presence, Lord, and let me see You working. I know You are the only one who can change the trajectory of my life. You have the power to change relationships, finances, even people's hearts. I'm waiting, Lord, knowing You will work in Your time. Please let it be soon.

THINK ABOUT IT:
In what circumstance are you waiting for God to act? Remember, even when we can't see progress, He is working.

Morning
SO MANY STORIES

Proclaiming thanksgiving aloud,
and telling all your wondrous deeds.
PSALM 26:7 ESV

There are reasons You tell us to talk about all the great things You've done. When we share with others how You've brought us through difficult things in the past, those who hear are drawn to You. It also sets our minds on Your mighty works instead of on our fears. Finally, praising You causes You to lean close, drawing near to Your children. Make me bold to tell others about all the amazing things You've done and continue to do in my life. There are so many stories to tell; the most wondrous is the story of my salvation. I can think of so many other things You've done for me, Father. I don't know why I ever worry about anything. You have proven Yourself to be good and kind, gracious and merciful, time and again.

THINK ABOUT IT:

What are some of your favorite
stories about God's goodness in
your life? Thank God for them now.

Evening
ACTIVE FAITH

I believe that I shall look upon the
goodness of the LORD in the land
of the living! Wait for the LORD;
be strong, and let your heart
take courage; wait for the LORD!
PSALM 27:13–14 ESV

You want me to wait. While I wait, You want me to have sturdy faith. The writer of this psalm believed, without doubt, that he would see good things in this life, while he was still alive. Job reflected the same kind of faith in the midst of the worst trials imaginable. I want that kind of faith, Father. I know faith is an action more than a feeling. It's a decision to push aside all worry and doubt and fear in favor of a belief in Your goodness. Sometimes, shoving that worry aside feels like a physical task. It's heavy and stubborn. But with all my strength, I will practice faith. I will believe in Your kindness with expectation, and I'll wait, knowing good things will come.

THINK ABOUT IT:

How can you practice faith today?

Morning
PRAISE AND FEAR

Blessed be the LORD! For he has heard the voice of my pleas for mercy. The LORD is my strength and my shield; in him my heart trusts, and I am helped; my heart exults, and with my song I give thanks to him.
PSALM 28:6–7 ESV

Dear Father, I love these psalms that are so filled with positive thinking. Worry and fear cannot coexist with praise and thanksgiving. I want to add my voice to the psalmist's and bless You! Thank You for always hearing my prayers. Thank You for jumping at my cries for help and coming to my rescue. You truly are my strength, getting me through the most difficult times. You are my shield, surrounding and protecting me physically, spiritually, and emotionally. I trust You, I praise You, and I thank You for every good thing. I love You with my whole heart.

THINK ABOUT IT:

For what do you praise God today? When fear sets in, praise will push it out.

Evening
KING OF MY LIFE

The LORD sits enthroned over the flood; the LORD sits enthroned as king forever.
PSALM 29:10 ESV

You truly are King over everything. You rule over every place, every time, every circumstance. When good things happen, You get the credit. When bad things happen, You see, and You work to bring about justice. This verse says You're enthroned over the flood, which means You are enthroned over things that can seem threatening and scary. Just as You used the flood in the Old Testament to bring about Your perfect plan, I know You use the frightening, uncomfortable circumstances in my life to make me stronger, more resilient, and more like You. Thank You for being the King of my life and for reigning over every detail.

THINK ABOUT IT:

Over what circumstance do you need to acknowledge God as King? Picture Him on His throne, reigning over every aspect.

Morning
SING PRAISES

Sing praises to the LORD, O you his saints, and give thanks to his holy name. For his anger is but for a moment, and his favor is for a lifetime. Weeping may tarry for the night, but joy comes with the morning.

PSALM 30:4–5 ESV

Thank You for this reminder that although not everything in my life is perfect or happy, those difficult times are only temporary. Though some circumstances bring a flood of tears, I will eventually find relief. I know You love me. I'm Your child, and You don't want me to hurt forever. Though things may seem desperate and impossible right now, I know nothing is impossible with You. You are the God of hope, and You will surely send joy in the morning. Even in the middle of the storm, I'll praise You and thank You. And I'll wait expectantly, knowing You have good things in store.

THINK ABOUT IT:

What is the most difficult circumstance in your life right now? Hang in there. Joy is on its way.

Evening
NO STANDARD-ISSUE PEACE

"Peace I leave with you; my peace I give to you. Not as the world gives do I give to you. Let not your hearts be troubled, neither let them be afraid."

JOHN 14:27 ESV

Lord, I've heard it said: "Pray for peace." I pray for peace—that there be an ease in conflict and that hurting souls find relief. But I also pray for *Your* peace in my life. Your peace goes deep. Your peace is a sense of calm that let You sleep even during a raging storm at sea. Your peace offered security in Your Father's will— even when following led to anguish and a cross. Your peace means hope in hopeless situations, comfort during pain, a future when all seems lost. This kind of peace comes only from You, Lord. I need a dose today; please settle me with Your deep peace. Amen.

THINK ABOUT IT:

How is Christ's peace different from the world's?

Morning
SHOW. . .

Was not also Rahab the prostitute justified by works when she received the messengers and sent them out by another way? For as the body apart from the spirit is dead, so also faith apart from works is dead.

JAMES 2:25–26 ESV

Father, from the outside and at first glance, Rahab doesn't seem like a faith-filled woman. Her occupation is less than holy, and she lies to help the messengers, but deep inside, her faith is true. Putting herself in great risk, she takes a stand for You. She remains a reflection of faith lived out, a reflection of each godly woman. Father, sin is a part of all of us; and while You abhor sin, You extend grace to sinners. I pray that my faith shines brighter than my sin so those who see my life will know that I'm alive in You. Amen.

THINK ABOUT IT:

What ways can you show that your faith is a living faith?

Evening
. . .AND TELL

Jesus said to her, "I who speak to you am he." . . . So the woman left her water jar and went away into town and said to the people, "Come, see a man who told me all that I ever did. Can this be the Christ?"

JOHN 4:26, 28–29 ESV

Lord, I confess the Samaritan woman's response humbles and challenges me. Because of her reputation, she was an outcast among outcasts to the Jewish people. Yet once You reached out to her and she embraced You, she was bold to tell her story, to tell Your story. She did not tuck what she'd received deep inside but abandoned her water jug and went straightaway to share with others. Too often I shrink from telling how You continually transform my life. Forgive me, Lord. Embolden me! Let nothing—my past or what's to come—keep me silent. Amen.

THINK ABOUT IT:

How are you like the Samaritan woman? How can you become more like her?

Morning
REMEMBER WHEN

And he said to the people of Israel, "When your children ask their fathers in times to come, 'What do these stones mean?' then you shall let your children know, 'Israel passed over this Jordan on dry ground.' For the LORD your God dried up the waters of the Jordan for you until you passed over."

JOSHUA 4:21–23 ESV

God, the Bible is a rich record of what You've done in the lives of believers. Remembering Your mighty works keeps us praising You and following You, even in grim moments. Besides reading the biblical accounts, God, remind us that we, as families and as a community, have our own rich history to pass down to the children in our lives. Please show us ways to mark the times You have come through for us. There are so many! Use our memories to fill the next generation with Your truth so that they never forget. Amen.

THINK ABOUT IT:
What events or periods of your life will you preserve?

Evening
HUMBLE ME

[Christ Jesus], though he was in the form of God, did not count equality with God a thing to be grasped, but emptied himself, by taking the form of a servant, being born in the likeness of men. And being found in human form, he humbled himself by becoming obedient to the point of death, even death on a cross.

PHILIPPIANS 2:6–8 ESV

Lord, You embody humility—something that seems foreign in our culture. Everywhere I see people who prize being better than, who look after themselves before others. I'm guilty of the same mindset more than I'd like to admit, Lord. It's not easy to put *self* aside. In part, that's what makes You remarkable, Your love incomprehensible. You are one with God, yet You "emptied" Yourself, humbled Yourself, in order for me to thrive. Remind me of Your great humility as I approach my days emptied of self and ready to serve. Amen.

THINK ABOUT IT:
Why is being truly humble so hard?

Morning
CLEAR THE AIR

"So when you offer your gift to God at the altar, and you remember that your brother or sister has something against you, leave your gift there at the altar. Go and make peace with that person, and then come and offer your gift."

MATTHEW 5:23–24 NCV

Grudges, tiffs, squabbles. . .whatever we call them and however justified they are, Father, they get in the way of true worship. You sacrificed everything to reconcile us to You, to heal a severed relationship. Why should we not do everything in our power to right what is wrong before praising You? Prod my heart, Father. Don't let me ignore conflict out of pride or a false sense of entitlement. You know what's best for me when I'm blinded by emotion. "Go. . .make peace," Jesus said. May I do just that. Amen.

THINK ABOUT IT:
Do you need to make peace with someone today?

Evening
HOME AWAY FROM HOME

"In my Father's house are many rooms. If it were not so, would I have told you that I go to prepare a place for you? And if I go and prepare a place for you, I will come again and will take you to myself, that where I am you may be also."

JOHN 14:2–3 ESV

Home. Lord, that word can mean so many good things. A place of belonging, a safe haven. . .it's where the heart is. But this world can rip "home" from us. Dysfunctional families, foreclosures, natural disasters, rising rent—sadly, our home on earth isn't always so good. While we can't count on the blessing of a sound earthly home, we can count on Your promise of a glorious home to come. There we will have a place beyond anything we imagine. There we will be home. Amen.

THINK ABOUT IT:
What do you look forward to most in your heavenly homecoming?

Morning
TO LOVE DEEPLY

Above all, love each other deeply, because love covers over a multitude of sins.

1 PETER 4:8 NIV

I'll confess that I don't always love others as I should, Lord. Perhaps some of the stresses in my life have come about because I'm going through the motions instead of genuinely, deeply caring about the situations of those around me. Maybe I don't really care as much as I should or I feel taken advantage of when they involve me.

Would You help me with my attitude? Give me Your heart for those You have placed in my life, a love that covers a multitude of sins. Give me compassion. Give me patience. Give me the right words to say when it's time to minister to them. Most of all, make me a reflection of You to the people in my world. I want to represent You well, Lord. Amen.

THINK ABOUT IT:

Can you think of a time when God's love covered a multitude of your own sins?

Evening
YOUR WAYS ARE HIGHER

"For my thoughts are not your thoughts, neither are your ways my ways, declares the LORD."

ISAIAH 55:8 ESV

Sometimes I meet people who seem so far above me in their thinking. College professors. People with brilliant minds. I listen to them talk, and I'm overwhelmed trying to figure them out!

Your thoughts are even higher than theirs, Lord! All of the earthly knowledge can't come close to what You know. So when I wonder why things in my life aren't going according to my plan, I'll trust that You—the one with the highest thoughts and ways of all—are working out something far bigger, far greater than my finite mind could dream up.

I'm excited to see what You have for me as I journey forward, Lord. Thank You for working out big plans for me. Amen.

THINK ABOUT IT:

What would it be like to think like God?

Morning
ABOUNDING IN HOPE

*I lift up my eyes to the mountains—
where does my help come from?
My help comes from the LORD, the
Maker of heaven and earth.*
PSALM 121:1–2 NIV

I look up, Lord. Up to You. Up to hope. Up to the future. Up to great things ahead.

When life is tough—and I'll admit, it often is—my tendency is to look down. To give up. But no more! I'm shifting my gaze to the heavens because that's where my help, my hope, comes from. You are in charge of the universe and in charge of my life—every teensy-tiny bit of it—and I can trust You with it all.

So I'll look up and keep my focus on You, not on the circumstances swirling around me. They're nothing but a distraction, Lord. You are the immovable Rock. Thank You for holding steady. Amen.

THINK ABOUT IT:
Are you overflowing with hope today?

Evening
YOU WILL GIVE ME REST

*"Come to me, all you who are weary
and burdened, and I will give you rest."*
MATTHEW 11:28 NIV

I'm seeing this verse in a new light today, Lord. I see now that rest is a gift from You. It's something You "give" me, not something that just happens. When I consider it through that lens, my entire approach to rest changes. I don't have to wonder why rest doesn't come easily to me. I see the reason in the first part of the verse. It's because I'm not coming to You when I'm weary and burdened.

No wonder I get burned out. No wonder I always reach the breaking point. You're right there, ready to hand me the antidote, but I have to humble myself and come to You. Today, Lord, I choose to do just that. Oh, how I long for Your supernatural rest! Amen.

THINK ABOUT IT:
Does resting come naturally to you?

Morning
PRESSING ON

*Not that I have already obtained
this or am already perfect, but I
press on to make it my own, because
Christ Jesus has made me his own.*

PHILIPPIANS 3:12 ESV

I'm thinking of a time I tried to run on the beach, Lord. That loose sand was beautiful, but it sure made running difficult. I felt bogged down. Held back. Unable to move at my usual pace.

Sometimes I feel like that with the circumstances I face. They're just too much for me. I get bogged down in them. I can't put my finger on what's wrong, but it just feels like I'm not free to run, to soar, in the usual way.

Then You step in and offer a word of encouragement. I'm off and running again, ready to press on until I reach the goal. Thank You for giving me the courage to keep going, even when I don't feel like it. Amen.

THINK ABOUT IT:

*When do you struggle the
most with pressing on?*

Evening
NEARER, NEARER

*Come near to God and he
will come near to you.*

JAMES 4:8 NIV

When I am feeling down on myself and a little bit depressed, sometimes I wander away from You, Lord. I don't know why—maybe it's because I know You will remind me of all the goodness in my life, and maybe I'm not ready to hear about that. Or maybe it's because I'm afraid You will be ashamed of my behavior. But, Lord, I know You love me. Just as surely as I would hold out my arms to my own child for a big bear hug, I know You are holding out Your arms to me. Help me to remember to come to You with any problem, big or small. Help me to remember that little eyes are watching me. . .to see where I go for help when trouble comes. Amen.

THINK ABOUT IT:

*Who do you turn to when you are
feeling low? Where is God on that list?*

Morning
AS A MOTHER

"As a mother comforts her child, so will I comfort you."
ISAIAH 66:13 NIV

A cool palm on a hot forehead. A sweet whisper in the ear of a mind full of hurt feelings. A soft breath blowing on a boo-boo. A generous handful of change when only a quarter was asked for. A word of praise at just the right moment. A beam of pride when a goal is reached. A warm, plush hug when sorrow is heavy. A quiet tear that expresses understanding. A guiding principle when instruction is needed. Lord, You know the ways to comfort us, as well as our own mothers do. You know us even better, and Your comfort is always available. Thank You for that promise. And thank You for moms. Amen.

THINK ABOUT IT:

Think about one way your mom used to comfort you. What did that feel like? How does it feel knowing God will comfort you both now and forever?

Evening
NO COMPARISON

With whom, then, will you compare God? To what image will you liken him?
ISAIAH 40:18 NIV

So many screens, Lord. My life is filled with screens. TV screens, phone screens, tablet screens, and computer screens. And they all seem to be screaming for my attention. *Look at me! Be distracted! Waste your time!* Lord, I want my eyes to be on You. I want my mind to be filled with Your Word. I want my heart to be fully devoted to You. Help me, Lord. Help me block out all the distractions that are nothing, *absolutely nothing*, compared to the life You have planned for me. There is no image, no item, no video, no article that can benefit me as much as spending more time with You.

THINK ABOUT IT:

What is distracting you lately? What small routine can you incorporate into your life to increase your God focus?

Morning
BEAUTY

Your beauty should not come from outward adornment, such as elaborate hairstyles and the wearing of gold jewelry or fine clothes. Rather, it should be that of your inner self, the unfading beauty of a gentle and quiet spirit, which is of great worth in God's sight.

1 PETER 3:3–4 NIV

God, I look in the mirror, and I wish I could see myself like You see me. I see the shadows under my eyes, the frowny forehead, and the five pimples that have shown up to the party. I don't see beauty. But then I think about how I kissed my beautiful daughter's face this morning. And I remember smelling the top of my handsome son's head. All that beauty has come from me and is being nurtured by me. And I think if all of that is somehow growing because of me, even a little bit, then somewhere that beauty is inside me too. Thank You, Lord, for helping me feel beautiful. Amen.

THINK ABOUT IT:

What is beautiful in your life? What steps can you take to increase your own inner beauty, the beauty God really values?

Evening
SLUMBER

He will not let your foot slip—he who watches over you will not slumber.

PSALM 121:3 NIV

Lord, have mercy. I. Need. Sleep. Night after night, I have been jolted out of bed by a child's cry, a creaky step, or nature's call. I think those last five pounds I gained must all be in my eyelids. I drink cup after cup of coffee, and it doesn't even make a dent in the fatigue. I am so thankful, Lord, that *You* don't require sleep. I'm so grateful that I can rest in the peace that comes from knowing You are always looking out for me. But, Lord, I most certainly do need sleep. Could You please give me just five more minutes of it? Or maybe five more days? Hey—it's really quiet here right now. No one's around. And the dishes can wait. Thanks, Lord! I'll just be going . . .amen.

THINK ABOUT IT:

What changes can you make to help you get the sleep you need? How does it feel knowing God will watch over you whenever you do catch some z's?

Morning
A PRAYER FOR LEADERS

Encourage one another and build each other up, just as in fact you are doing. Now we ask you, brothers and sisters, to acknowledge those who work hard among you, who care for you in the Lord and who admonish you.

1 THESSALONIANS 5:11–12 NIV

Holy God, today I want to remember those who are leading in our church. Sometimes it must be hard to care for our brothers and sisters in Christ. There are so many different personalities, troubles, backgrounds, and baggage. People in the church have human emotions and needs, just like everyone else. And it must be so stressful to hear so many stories and not always be able to fix the problems. On top of that, the church leaders are the target for so much criticism, both from within the church and beyond. Lord, help me be a voice of encouragement and a comfort to those who are leading. Amen.

THINK ABOUT IT:

What might God be prompting you to do to encourage and lift up your community's pastors and leaders today?

Evening
SMALL VICTORIES

"Do not despise these small beginnings, for the LORD rejoices to see the work begin."

ZECHARIAH 4:10 NLT

Lord of the universe, I didn't make any worlds today or move any mountains (unless you count a mountain of wet towels and dirty socks). I didn't save any souls or even make much of a sacrifice (unless you count letting my daughter in the shower first). But here's what I did do. I managed to get out of bed on time, even though *someone* woke me up three times in the night because "dinosaurs are in my underwear drawer." I delivered breakfast to the table and packed lunches. I shoved kids out the door and onto the bus. And at the grocery, I performed the miracle of multiplication and somehow stretched fifty bucks into twice that (with the blessing of coupons). I know it may not seem like much, Lord. But I'm rejoicing anyway. And I'm thankful for every little thing. Amen.

THINK ABOUT IT:

What small victories have you experienced today? Do you feel God rejoicing with you?

Morning
PONDERING

*Mary treasured up all these things
and pondered them in her heart.*

LUKE 2:19 NIV

Sweet baby Jesus, what did You hear when Your young mother first held You in her arms? What song did she sing to calm Your cries? And what did You feel as she wrapped the cloth around You? Did You feel warm and safe in her arms? Jesus, I know Your mother loved You. Oh, how she loved You! She risked so much just to let You be born into this world. She took on so much responsibility. She trusted in Your Father, even when she didn't fully understand. Sweet baby Jesus, thank You for coming to us. I am forever grateful. I will forever treasure You. Amen.

THINK ABOUT IT:

*What must it have felt like
to hold the infant Jesus?*

Evening
HELP IS ON THE WAY

*"I will talk to the Father, and he'll
provide you another Friend so that you
will always have someone with you."*

JOHN 14:16 MSG

God, You know how much I want to be a helper. Someone I know is in trouble, and I want more than anything to drop all my plans, reach out my two hands, and lift up my friend. But I can't. My plans are not my own. My day is wrapped up in my children's needs and wants. And they are things that just can't be postponed. Not now. So, Lord, my prayer is that You send someone to help my friend. Someone to fill my shoes and take my place. Someone to give her everything she needs. And, Lord, if there's anything else I can do, please show me. Amen.

THINK ABOUT IT:

*What things can you do to help
someone when you can't be physically
present? How does God help you
without Him being physically present?*

Morning
BE GRACIOUS TO ME

Be gracious to me, O Lord, for I am in distress; my eye is wasted from grief; my soul and my body also. For my life is spent with sorrow, and my years with sighing; my strength fails because of my iniquity, and my bones waste away.

PSALM 31:9–10 ESV

Just as David cried out to You, so do I. Deliver me, Lord. Deliver my children, my spouse, my loved ones, my friends. Heal us of pride, stubbornness, laziness, selfishness, fear, anxiety, and anything else that stands in the way of Your perfect plan for our lives. These traits are our adversaries, stronger than any human opponent, and we need Your help. Turn our hearts to You, and help us trust You. Mature us and draw us daily into Your presence. Hear my cries for myself, my family, my friends, Lord. Be gracious and deliver us.

THINK ABOUT IT:
What keeps you awake at night? Talk to God about it today. Tell Him what's on your heart, and ask Him for deliverance.

Evening
STOP THE SILENCE

For when I kept silent, my bones wasted away through my groaning all day long. For day and night your hand was heavy upon me; my strength was dried up as by the heat of summer.

PSALM 32:3–4 ESV

I don't know why I'm prone to hold things in. When I keep my sin, my fear, my anxiety inside, it destroys me. It's like an infection that slowly spreads through my body; it zaps my strength and steals my sleep. Today I want to confess, Lord. Everything that's in me that doesn't please You, expose it, Lord. Bring it to the surface. I'm sorry for all my sins. I'm sorry for my anger, my bitterness, my lack of forgiveness to others. I'm sorry for my lack of faith. I don't want to keep silent anymore, Father. It feels good to get it all out in the open and leave it with You.

THINK ABOUT IT:
What do you need to confess today? Tell Him.

Morning
WAIT

Our soul waits for the Lord;
he is our help and our shield.
For our heart is glad in him,
because we trust in his holy name.

PSALM 33:20–21 ESV

Why do You tell us so many times in scripture to wait? You must know how prone we are to impatience. Am I trying to move ahead of You in some situation? If so, hold me back, Lord. Calm my spirit and help me to just rest in the confidence that You are working on my behalf even when I don't see or feel it. Trust is hard for me, Lord, and I'm sorry for that. I have no reason to doubt Your faithfulness, Your goodness, or Your love. Today, when I try to step in front of You and force things to happen the way I want them to, whisper a reminder to trust You, to rest in Your love for me, and to wait.

THINK ABOUT IT:

In what situation are
you waiting on God?

Evening
HOPE IN YOU

Let your steadfast love, O Lord,
be upon us, even as we hope in you.

PSALM 33:22 ESV

Dear Father, I love the word *hope*. It is the belief that something good will happen. It's the opposite of fear, which is the belief that bad things are coming. Your Word tells me again and again that You are the God of hope and that fear is from Satan. When I let myself be ruled by anxiety, I'm really saying that I believe Satan is more powerful than You are. I don't mean to do that. Satan is really good at his game, and he knows how to feed my fears. Give me strength to resist his lies and to stand strong in hope. I love You, I trust You, and I know You are good.

THINK ABOUT IT:

In what situation are you struggling
for hope? Trust in God's goodness
today, knowing He loves you and
He's working on your behalf.

Morning
KEYS TO LIFE

What man is there who desires life and loves many days, that he may see good? Keep your tongue from evil and your lips from speaking deceit. Turn away from evil and do good; seek peace and pursue it.

PSALM 34:12–14 ESV

So many of my fears and anxieties stem from wanting to live a good, long, prosperous life. But what good is a long life if it's filled with worry? You've given me all the keys to have a good, successful life. In 2 Timothy 1:7, Your Word tells me that fear is not from You. Instead, You give power and love and a sound mind. Here, You've told me to keep my mouth closed to negative things, turn away from evil and do good, and seek peace and chase after it. Thank You for such a specific list, Father. Help me as I take action to live a life that pleases You.

THINK ABOUT IT:

What things on this list of life-giving actions will you pursue today?

Evening
DELIGHT IN HIM

Let those who delight in my righteousness shout for joy and be glad and say evermore, "Great is the LORD, who delights in the welfare of his servant!"

PSALM 35:27 ESV

Your righteousness is truly a delight. When I worry about things, I know I'm not focusing on Your goodness but on Satan's lies. When I worry, I'm succumbing to the belief that You're not good, You're not righteous, and that I'm doomed. That's not how I want to live my life. Forgive me for the negative thought patterns I've allowed to rule me, and heal me of them, Father. Whenever those bad thoughts show up, help me shove them aside and focus on Your goodness, Your righteousness, and Your faithfulness. I know You delight in doing good things for me, and I trust in Your love.

THINK ABOUT IT:

Do you delight in God's righteousness? Spend time today thinking about all the good things He's done for you and others.

Morning
A DIFFERENT LENS

For we walk by faith, not by sight.
2 CORINTHIANS 5:7 ESV

I'm figuring it out, Lord—there are two ways to view life: with my physical eyes and with my spiritual eyes. Moving forward according to what I can see with my physical eyes is tempting. That's the way modern culture thinks I should move. But life with You is a faith journey. It's a thrilling, trail-blazing adventure filled with opportunity after opportunity to impact the world if I will just do things Your way.

So I'll use a different lens to move forward from here, Lord. I'll do my best to walk by faith, not by sight. Thanks for leading and guiding when I can't see what's coming. Amen.

THINK ABOUT IT:
*Which lens are you looking through—
your circumstances or your faith?*

Evening
I'LL TAKE EVERY THOUGHT CAPTIVE

We demolish arguments and every pretension that sets itself up against the knowledge of God, and we take captive every thought to make it obedient to Christ.
2 CORINTHIANS 10:5 NIV

I've been in situations where I felt trapped, Lord. In those moments, I felt like a prisoner in a cage, unable to break free.

You're asking me to take my thoughts captive in much the same way. To see them bound up, tied down, unable to move to the right or the left. Unable to rule me in any way. You don't want my emotions to outweigh my faith. You're calling me to a higher way of living.

So I'll take my thoughts captive. Only then will the stresses I'm facing quiet down. Only then will I rise above my circumstances and walk with hope, peace, and joy. Help me, Lord, I pray. Amen.

THINK ABOUT IT:
*Do you struggle with discouraging
or negative thoughts?*

Morning
THE DESIRES OF
MY HEART

May he give you the desire of your heart and make all your plans succeed.

PSALM 20:4 NIV

You want to meet my needs, Lord. I'm so grateful. But there have been times I was scared to ask You for what I wanted because I felt I didn't deserve it. Or maybe I felt I didn't really need it.

This verse is startling to me! I read it, and I'm overwhelmed that You actually *want* me to be more detailed with You when I pray. You don't just long to meet my needs; You want to give me the desires of my heart. How deeply You must love me! Thank You for caring so much about the longings of my heart. You bring me such joy, Father! Amen.

THINK ABOUT IT:

What are the desires of your heart at this very moment? Are you going to make them known to the Lord?

Evening
MY STRENGTH FOREVER

My flesh and my heart may fail, but God is the strength of my heart and my portion forever.

PSALM 73:26 NIV

Just enough and just in time. That's the kind of God You are. You give me what I need exactly when I need it, not a moment before and never too late!

Sometimes I feel like You're not going to come through for me, but You always do. I'll be honest, there are times when I'm waiting with bated breath—hoping, praying, believing. . .but often harboring a smidgen of doubt that things will turn out.

Then You show up! You infuse me with strength in the waiting. You give me my "portion" of hope, and I'm able to keep hanging on, even when it makes no sense to hang on. You're my strength and portion forever, Lord. I won't give up. Amen.

THINK ABOUT IT:

What changes would you need to make to walk in God's supernatural, eternal strength?

Morning
TRANSCENDENT PEACE

And the peace of God, which transcends all understanding, will guard your hearts and your minds in Christ Jesus.

PHILIPPIANS 4:7 NIV

It's inexplicable, Lord! Your peace transcends everything. It's an ethereal cloud hovering over me and enveloping me just when I'm about to panic. Your supernatural peace settles deep in my heart, and my attitude begins to shift. Stress fades. Calm settles over me.

I don't understand Your ways sometimes, Father, but that's part of the beauty of walking with You. I don't have to get it. I just have to trust, in spite of what I don't understand. And I have to walk in the assurance that You'll guard both my heart (which is shaky at best) and my mind (which tends to flitter all over the place). I do trust You, Lord. Thank You for the peace to keep on believing. Amen.

THINK ABOUT IT:
What does "transcendent" peace look like to you?

Evening
ONE DAY I'LL SEE MORE CLEARLY

Now that which we see is as if we were looking in a broken mirror. But then we will see everything. Now I know only a part. But then I will know everything in a perfect way. That is how God knows me right now.

1 CORINTHIANS 13:12 NLV

The scene in front of me is blurry sometimes, Lord—like I'm wearing someone else's glasses with a prescription that's far different from my own. I can't make out what's right in front of me. The story makes no sense. I can't see where You're taking me or how I'm going to get from point A to point B.

Still, You call me to trust in You. This broken image will one day be made clear. Right now You're showing me just enough to increase my faith and give me the wherewithal to keep putting one foot in front of the other. It's not easy. I get scared. But I won't stop. Guide me step by step, I pray. Amen.

THINK ABOUT IT:
Are you looking forward to the day when all will be made clear?

Morning
POWER, LOVE, AND SELF-DISCIPLINE

For the Spirit God gave us does not make us timid, but gives us power, love and self-discipline.
2 TIMOTHY 1:7 NIV

Lord, You've given me everything I need to make it through any tough circumstance. Your Word promises power, love, and self-discipline. A person can go a long way on those three things.

You offer fortitude. I need this supernatural inside-out power to get through the tasks in front of me. I need courage to stop these knees from knocking. I need tenacity to keep going, even when I don't feel like it. And I need self-discipline to stay committed to the tasks in front of me.

You promise it all! And in the process, You'll also give me boldness so that I'm not afraid as I step forward into the great unknown. Thank You, Lord! Amen.

THINK ABOUT IT:
Do you truly believe that God didn't make you timid?

Evening
WHATEVER I ASK FOR

"Therefore I tell you, whatever you ask for in prayer, believe that you have received it, and it will be yours."
MARK 11:24 NIV

Wow, what a promise, Lord! You've said in Your Word that if my faith is strong enough, I can receive whatever I ask for. I have some big things on my list and wonder how far I should take this! Should I believe for the impossible? That child who has wandered from You? That financial situation that seems too big to fix? That coworker who grates on my nerves?

I should bring all of that to You? (Oh, that's right—it was Your idea, not mine!) I'll up my faith, Lord. I'll begin to think bigger, to trust deeper, and to ask with more intention. Only when I increase my faith will I see miracles happen. I'm ready, Lord! Amen.

THINK ABOUT IT:
"Whatever" can mean different things to different people. What does it mean to you?

DAY 324

Morning
OUR SAFE PLACE

Trust in Him at all times, O people.
Pour out your heart before Him.
God is a safe place for us.
PSALM 62:8 NLV

So many times I've wished for a friend to tell my troubles to. Someone who would listen and not butt in. Someone who would genuinely care but not overwhelm me with their ideas and plans to fix my problem. Then I'm reminded that You've been there all along.

You're the best place to run, Lord. You provide safety, compassion, comfort, and gentle wisdom. I can count on You to give the best advice, even in situations where I'm completely overwhelmed. So I'll tell You my troubles. (Thanks for listening!) And I know You'll have solutions to every problem I face, so I'll lean in close to hear what You're whispering in my ear. Amen.

THINK ABOUT IT:

Where do you usually run for safety?

Evening
YOU DELIGHT IN MY WELL-BEING

May those who delight in my vindication shout for joy and gladness; may they always say, "The LORD be exalted, who delights in the well-being of his servant."
PSALM 35:27 NIV

You care about every intricate part of me, Lord—from my trembling hands to my knocking knees. You care when I'm having a good day, and You're fully tuned in when I'm having a bad one. You delight in my well-being, so You're working overtime to make sure I've got what it takes to see this thing through. Even when my enemies are chasing me down, I have nothing to fear. You're right there, ready to come out swinging on my behalf.

Good days or bad, rough situations or smooth, I put my trust in You. My allies will shout victoriously when You come through for me. I can hardly wait for that day! Amen.

THINK ABOUT IT:

Why do you suppose God delights in our well-being?

Morning
I'LL KEEP GOING

Let us not grow weary of doing good, for in due season we will reap, if we do not give up.

GALATIANS 6:9 ESV

I want to give up. Seriously. I'm just not feeling it today, Lord. My "want-to" has flown out the window. It would be easier to do nothing than to put one foot in front of the other.

Then I think about all You went through for me. Your Son put one foot in front of the other on His walk to Calvary, didn't He? You put one (proverbial) foot in front of the other when You raised Him from the grave. How then can I balk at doing good things for You? I'll keep going, even on the days when I'm not feeling it. Why? Because You did, Lord, and I'm a reflection of You! Amen.

THINK ABOUT IT:

How do you keep going when you don't feel like it?

Evening
I PUT MY HOPE IN YOU

Why, my soul, are you downcast? Why so disturbed within me? Put your hope in God, for I will yet praise him, my Savior and my God.

PSALM 42:11 NIV

I love this verse so much, Lord! It reminds me of the many times I've talked to myself: "Self, what's wrong with you? Why do you keep messing up? Soul, why are you so downcast? What are you so worked up about? Have you really forgotten that the God of the universe is on your side and is working on your behalf?"

This verse reminds me to place my trust in You, Lord, which is where it belongs. I put my hope in You and praise You even now because You're a trustworthy God. You've never let me down, and You won't start now! Amen.

THINK ABOUT IT:

When you're down in the dumps, what do you do to turn things around?

Morning
OVERFLOWING

You are making a table of food ready for me in front of those who hate me. You have poured oil on my head. I have everything I need.

PSALM 23:5 NLV

I love how You work, Lord! You don't just protect and guard me from my enemies; You make a show out of how much You love me. . .in front of them! You prepare a table before me in the presence of those who are out to get me. You want them to know You're on my side. And You spread out a feast—the finest foods, the most expensive wines. You lavish oil on my head, giving me peace, even when my enemies are staring me down from across the room.

I won't worry with You on my side, Lord. I have everything I need and more. How grateful I am for Your overflowing provision! Amen.

THINK ABOUT IT:

Why would God prepare a table before you in the presence of your enemies?

Evening
BY THE POWER OF YOUR SPIRIT

May the God of hope fill you with all joy and peace as you trust in him, so that you may overflow with hope by the power of the Holy Spirit.

ROMANS 15:13 NIV

I'll admit it, Lord: I'm not always over-flowing with hope. More often than not, a leak has sprung in the bottom of my proverbial boat, and I feel like I'm sinking instead of overflowing.

Today I ask for what feels impossible—hope, joy, and peace—as I place my trust in You. I know Your Word says this is possible, and I definitely need a change of thinking about my situation, so I'm going to give it a try! I want to overflow with hope by the power of Your Spirit, Lord. Do what only You can do. Turn my situation—and my heart—around, I pray. Amen.

THINK ABOUT IT:

Where does your hope come from?

Morning
GREAT UNDERSTANDING

Whoever is patient has great understanding, but one who is quick-tempered displays folly.

PROVERBS 14:29 NIV

Sometimes my temper gets the best of me, Lord. I flare up and then wonder why my heart is racing and my hands are trembling. I can get hyped up in a hurry, for sure!

Today I'm asking You to calm the tumultuous seas. Do what only You can do. Turn this sometimes-erratic overre-actor into a calm, patient person You can be proud of. I want to represent You well in this life, Lord. You're not flipping out, so I don't need to either.

Replace my quick temper with a steady commitment to You—Your way, Your plan. Rid me of folly, and make me a good example to others, I pray. Amen.

THINK ABOUT IT:

Would people say that you're quick-tempered?

Evening
I WON'T GIVE UP

Do not let yourselves get tired of doing good. If we do not give up, we will get what is coming to us at the right time.

GALATIANS 6:9 NLV

I want to throw in the towel. I really do, Lord. I'm done. Finished. Kaput. I've had it. I'm not taking another step forward. Only You won't let me quit, will You? You have this thing about plowing forward even when I don't feel like it. You tell me that I can finish what I've started if I fight the temptation to give up.

It's not going to be easy, but I'll give this endeavor another shot. Obviously, I can't do it on my own, so I'm placing my trust in You, Lord. I'll trust Your timing and Your strength, in Jesus' mighty name. Amen.

THINK ABOUT IT:

How do you feel knowing good things are coming at just the right time if you don't give up?

Morning
ASK, SEEK, KNOCK

"Ask, and it will be given to you;
seek, and you will find; knock,
and it will be opened to you."
MATTHEW, 7:7 ESV

Lord, You've told me to ask. . .so I'm asking. There are so many needs in my life right now. I want to bring them straight to You because I know You're the only one with any answers. You told me to seek, so I'm seeking—Your will, Your way, Your plan, not my own. You've told me to knock, and here I stand, knocking at Your door. Swing it wide, I pray. Usher me in so that not one moment is wasted doing things the world's way. (I've tried the world's way, Lord, and it only led to stress and chaos.)

Your plan is simple: come to You. So today I choose to bring You every concern, every wish, every problem, and every dream. I lay them at Your feet, Father, and ask You to do with them as You will. Amen.

THINK ABOUT IT:

How are asking, seeking,
and knocking different
from each other?

Evening
REFRESHED

He refreshes my soul. He
guides me along the right
paths for his name's sake.
PSALM 23:3 NIV

I love that "just washed" feeling after taking a shower. It feels wonderful to be cleansed, refreshed, readied for the day ahead.

In many ways, this is the same feeling I have after spending time with You, Lord. I enter into a time of renewal. My weary soul is bathed in Your love. I come away ready to face whatever life throws my way. Thank You for refreshing me. Thank You for giving me the wherewithal to keep moving along life's paths. Amen.

THINK ABOUT IT:

Where is God guiding you during
this current season you're in?

DAY 329

Morning
YOU'RE MORE THAN ABLE

Now to him who is able to do immeasurably more than all we ask or imagine, according to his power that is at work within us, to him be glory in the church and in Christ Jesus throughout all generations, for ever and ever! Amen.

EPHESIANS 3:20–21 NIV

There's no ruler to gauge how deep Your love is for me, Lord. There's no measuring tape to calculate the distance from the cross to the empty tomb. But I know this about You: You would go any distance to reach me. You always do more than I expect. You give more than I think You will. You're an "above and beyond" Creator, working on my behalf at all times out of Your great love for me.

I praise You, Father, for this overwhelming, immeasurable love. It's so much more than I could ever ask or think. How grateful I am. Amen.

THINK ABOUT IT:
What does "immeasurably" mean to you?

Evening
WOUNDS HEALED

"I will give you back your health and heal your wounds," says the LORD. "For you are called an outcast— 'Jerusalem for whom no one cares.'"

JEREMIAH 30:17 NLT

Some of the wounds in my life have run deep, Lord. They haven't been the kind people could see with their eyes, but they were there all the same. They kept me doubled over in pain, and healing never seemed to come.

Then You stepped in! In an instant, You did what I couldn't do in years of trying. You brought healing and wholeness. You restored me, replenishing my hope, my joy, and my peace. I was an outcast no more. I was made whole, thanks to Your great love. Oh, what joy to live a healed life. Amen.

THINK ABOUT IT:
What healing has God brought to your life?

DAY 330

Morning
OVERWHELMING GOODNESS

*Your steadfast love, O Lord, extends
to the heavens, your faithfulness
to the clouds. Your righteousness
is like the mountains of God; your
judgments are like the great deep;
man and beast you save, O Lord.*

PSALM 36:5–6 ESV

I love the poetic beauty of these verses. But more than just beautiful language, these words are true. Your goodness is beyond measure. Sometimes worry and fear drop over me like a thick fog. Anxiety blocks my vision so I can't see You clearly. Remove the fog, Lord. Silence the lies. When they show up, let me hear these words louder, more clearly in my mind: Your love is higher than the heavens, and Your faithfulness reaches to the clouds. Your righteousness is taller than the highest mountains, and Your wisdom is deeper than the ocean. You save Your children because You love us. Thank You for Your overwhelming, everlasting goodness.

THINK ABOUT IT:

*How has God proven His love
to you in the past? Remember,
His love never changes.*

Evening
DELIGHT

*The steps of a man are established
by the Lord, when he delights
in his way; though he fall, he
shall not be cast headlong, for
the Lord upholds his hand.*

PSALM 37:23–24 ESV

Thank You for this promise. Instead of worrying about things, I can rest easy in the knowledge that You will prepare the way for me as long as I delight in You. My mind cannot focus on anxiety and praise at the same time. When my fears creep in and threaten to take hold of my thoughts, remind me to delight in You. Remind me to set my eyes on all the good things You have done, on Your faithfulness and strength and love. Help me find joy in You instead of finding fear in Satan's lies. I commit to spending time with You each day, reading Your Word, talking to You, and thinking about You. Hold my hand today, Lord, and keep me from stumbling into fear.

THINK ABOUT IT:

*What aspect of God's goodness
will you delight in today?*

Morning
FAITH IN TRAINING

*For the LORD loves justice; he will
not forsake his saints. They are
preserved forever, but the children
of the wicked shall be cut off. The
righteous shall inherit the land
and dwell upon it forever.*
PSALM 37:28–29 ESV

Dear Father, I believe this in my head. Why is it so hard to believe it in my heart? You love me, and You will never ever forsake those who love You. One way I show my love to You is simple faith. Hebrews 11:6 says that without faith, it's impossible to please You. Yet when I succumb to worry and fear, I'm not exhibiting faith. My faith may be weak at times, Lord, but I want to exercise to make it stronger. Today, when I'm tempted to worry about things, remind me that I'm in training, building faith muscle. Help me to heft aside my fears and grip on to faith in Your goodness, Your mercy, and Your love.

THINK ABOUT IT:
How will you exercise faith today?

Evening
CRYING OUT

*Do not forsake me, O LORD! O my
God, be not far from me! Make haste
to help me, O Lord, my salvation!*
PSALM 38:21–22 ESV

It's comforting to know that David struggled with fear and anxiety too. His desperation is clear in these verses. He's not resting peacefully, trusting You. Instead, he's crying out to You, and his worry is clear. I love it that You don't get angry at me for worrying. Instead, You want me to bring it to You. When anxiety crowds in, remind me to take it to You again and again and exchange it for Your peace. Help me do this as many times as it takes to rid myself of the weight. Like David, I know You'll never forsake me, but sometimes it's hard not to be afraid. In my fear, I cry out to You, knowing You're the only one who can save me and trusting that You will.

THINK ABOUT IT:
*Have you cried out to
God today? Do it now.*

Morning
MEASURE MY DAYS

*O LORD, make me know my end and
what is the measure of my days;
let me know how fleeting I am! . . .
Surely a man goes about as a
shadow! Surely for nothing they are
in turmoil; man heaps up wealth and
does not know who will gather!*

PSALM 39:4, 6 ESV

Why do I worry about wealth, success,
or status? What does it matter, anyway?
I am but a wisp in the wind. May my wisp
of time please You. May my short vapor
of a life bring a brief moment of delight
to Your heart. That's all I exist for, Abba
Father. Forgive me for focusing on the
things that don't matter and won't make
a difference in light of eternity. Pleasing
You is all that matters. Help me set my
mind on loving You, loving others, and
doing the good things You have planned
for me to do.

THINK ABOUT IT:

*What can you focus on today
that will last for eternity?*

Evening
IN THE FLOOD

*Deep calls to deep at the roar of your
waterfalls; all your breakers and
your waves have gone over me. By
day the LORD commands his steadfast
love, and at night his song is with
me, a prayer to the God of my life.*

PSALM 42:7–8 ESV

Surely the author of this psalm understood anxiety and depression. I can so
relate to the feeling of drowning described
here. Yet the psalmist didn't remain
focused on the breakers and waves wash-
ing over him. Instead, he turned to You,
singing to You, searching for and feeling
Your steadfast love. When worry floods
my soul, help me follow this example. I
will think of Your steady, unfailing love
for me. I will sing to You and pray to You.
Instead of focusing on my problems, I will
focus on You alone.

THINK ABOUT IT:

*What is your favorite
praise song? Sing it now.*

Morning
WHEN GOD HIDES

Why do you hide your face? Why do you forget our affliction and oppression? For our soul is bowed down to the dust; our belly clings to the ground. Rise up; come to our help! Redeem us for the sake of your steadfast love!

PSALM 44:24–26 ESV

As I read this author's words, I identify with the desperation he felt. He doesn't understand why things are so hard. Sometimes it feels like You've forgotten about me, Lord. I feel so low, like things can't get any worse. Please help me! Show me Your face. Let me feel Your presence, Father. I know You love me. I just need a visible reminder of that love. I'm desperate and shaken and anxious. I'm begging You. . .show Yourself to me now.

THINK ABOUT IT:

Have you ever felt like God is hiding? Call out to Him now, and watch for Him to make an appearance.

Evening
PROBLEMS LIKE MOUNTAINS

God is our refuge and strength, a very present help in trouble. Therefore we will not fear though the earth gives way, though the mountains be moved into the heart of the sea, though its waters roar and foam, though the mountains tremble at its swelling.

PSALM 46:1–3 ESV

You are my refuge. When I'm afraid, You're my hiding place. You're also my strength. When I feel weak, like I just can't take another step, You give me the energy and the courage to move forward. Because of this, I will not fear. Though everything in my life may go wrong, though my problems seem like immovable mountains, though I feel like I'll be crushed any moment by an avalanche of my circumstances, I will trust You. I know with certainty that You are stronger than my fears, more powerful than my problems.

THINK ABOUT IT:

What problems feel like they'll crush you? God is bigger. Trust Him.

Morning
YOU ARE GREATER

*You, dear children, are from God
and have overcome them, because
the one who is in you is greater
than the one who is in the world.*

1 JOHN 4:4 NIV

Sometimes I feel so small and inadequate, Lord. I get overwhelmed too easily. In those moments, my perspective is skewed. I look at tiny hills and call them mountains. They loom in front of me like Mount Everest.

But You, Lord? You're bigger than all of them! No matter how large a problem, You're greater still. And You've given me the power to overcome even the biggest foe!

Change my perspective, I pray. Instead of focusing on all the reasons I can't, I want to zero in on the fact that You can. . .and You will. I have nothing to fear as long as my perspective is right, Lord! Amen.

THINK ABOUT IT:

Who is "the one who is in the world"?

Evening
COMMITTED AND ESTABLISHED

*Commit to the LORD whatever you do,
and he will establish your plans.*

PROVERBS 16:3 NIV

Lord, this verse reminds me of the many times in school when I was asked to sign a commitment form. When I put my name on the dotted line, I was making a promise—that I would follow my words with actions. I would commit and would follow through no matter how I felt or how many distractions came my way.

That's what You long from me too. You want my whole heart, every piece of it. When I say yes to You, I'm saying yes for the long haul, not just when I feel like it. I'll remain committed, dedicated, fully on board, no matter what distractions come my way. And I'll enjoy the fruit of my labors when all is said and done as You establish Your plans in my life. Amen.

THINK ABOUT IT:

*What active steps can you take to
commit yourself to the Lord today?*

Morning
BY THE POWER
OF YOUR SPIRIT

Our hope comes from God.
May He fill you with joy and peace
because of your trust in Him.
May your hope grow stronger by
the power of the Holy Spirit.

ROMANS 15:13 NLV

The power of Your Spirit is what gives me energy. The power of Your Spirit breathes new life into these bones. Through Your Spirit, I can do things I never dreamed I could do. I can overcome obstacles. I can conquer foes. I can go above and beyond anything I dared to imagine.

My hope comes only from You, not from me. I don't have to depend on my own power, thank goodness! I would be in a lot of trouble, wouldn't I? No, I will rely solely on You, Father. Shower me with Your power today, I pray. Amen.

THINK ABOUT IT:

Where does your hope come from?

Evening
PRAYER WILL
TAKE US THERE

Therefore confess your sins to
each other and pray for each
other so that you may be healed.
The prayer of a righteous person
is powerful and effective.

JAMES 5:16 NIV

Prayer is the vehicle to get me from point A to point B, isn't it, Lord? In some ways, it's kind of like a car or plane. I wouldn't "wish" myself from one city to another (or one country to another). I would get in a vehicle or board a jet.

I can't just wish and hope that my life will get better. I have to actually reach out to You, talk to You, get into that "vehicle," and be moved from my current situation to wherever You are leading me next.

So today, Lord? I open the door to spend time with You. I can hardly wait to see where You're taking me next. Let's go! Amen.

THINK ABOUT IT:

How powerful are your prayers?

Morning
ORDERED

For God is not a God of confusion but of peace. . . . All things should be done decently and in order.

1 Corinthians 14:33, 40 esv

God, Paul's orderly model for the church in Corinth can serve equally as a model for day-to-day living. Without Your character flowing through all the church did, there would have been little benefit to the gospel. Your nature being mirrored in the Corinthians was vital then, and it remains vital for me now. I know all too well how confusion feels. It muddles my thinking and blurs my purpose. I'm not as fruitful in chaos, God. Still the turmoil, please. Let everything fall into its proper place. Help me order my days so that I can be at my best. . .so I can reflect You best. Amen.

THINK ABOUT IT:

Where can you bring more of God's harmony into your life?

Evening
PLEASE GOD

Do you think I am trying to make people accept me? No, God is the One I am trying to please. Am I trying to please people? If I still wanted to please people, I would not be a servant of Christ.

Galatians 1:10 ncv

God, Your will often goes against the grain of society. What You ask me to do may seem absurd to nonbelievers. Yet You are so much wiser than the world. You clearly see everything that is to come, and You have my best-case path in mind as You lead me. I owe my allegiance to You and look to You for approval. But God, I still struggle with pleasing people. I want to fit in. In those moments when I feel myself bending toward the world, pull me back to You. Remind me of all I know to be true. You are Lord, and I will please You. Amen.

THINK ABOUT IT:

How do your everyday choices shift when you become a God pleaser?

Morning
PRAYER 101

Now Jesus was praying in a certain place, and when he finished, one of his disciples said to him, "Lord, teach us to pray."

LUKE 11:1 ESV

Lord, of the many things the disciples could have asked You to teach them, they asked You how to pray. How does a person talk with God? Your response is beautiful in simplicity, and it remains a model for my prayers today. So as I kneel before God, my Father, I'll offer up my praise. I'll surrender to His will. I'll ask for needs met; I'll ask for spiritual debts forgiven. I'll commit to treating others as He treats me. I'll plead for a life free from the pull of sin. Lord, thank You for Your words that guide me through prayer. Amen.

THINK ABOUT IT:

Read Christ's prayer in Matthew 6 and Luke 11. What does it teach you about praying?

Evening
WHATEVER YOU DO

So, whether you eat or drink, or whatever you do, do all to the glory of God. Give no offense to Jews or to Greeks or to the church of God, just as I try to please everyone in everything I do, not seeking my own advantage, but that of many, that they may be saved.

1 CORINTHIANS 10:31–33 ESV

Lord, it feels as if I've grown up in a culture that's all about personal liberty— "what suits me" instead of "what benefits you." Humans can be very self-centered— myself included. But You would flip this mindset on its head. From the moment You were born, Your agenda was others-centered. I'll admit, it's not easy, Lord. I need You for me to succeed. Keep me centered outward. Help me see the little things that seem *so* important for what they are—mere specks in the light of Your great salvation. Amen.

THINK ABOUT IT:

How often do you consider others— and God—in the personal choices you make?

Morning
SORROW NOT

But I would not have you to be ignorant, brethren, concerning them which are asleep, that ye sorrow not, even as others which have no hope. For if we believe that Jesus died and rose again, even so them also which sleep in Jesus will God bring with him.

1 THESSALONIANS 4:13–14 KJV

Father, words seem empty to describe what the death of a loved one means. Someone once close to us is now gone. But while we mourn for our loss, pour into us the truth of the words of these verses: we have hope in You! Tears may fall, but they will mingle with the promise of eternal life. Our ache, though deep, is only temporary, because in heaven our loved one will once again be near forever. No more tears, just joy everlasting. We await that day, Father, with hope, not sadness. Amen.

THINK ABOUT IT:
What does it look like to grieve with hope?

Evening
PESKY, PURPOSEFUL THORN

A thorn was given me in the flesh, a messenger of Satan to harass me, to keep me from becoming conceited. Three times I pleaded with the Lord about this, that it should leave me. But he said to me, "My grace is sufficient for you, for my power is made perfect in weakness."

2 CORINTHIANS 12:7–9 ESV

Lord, I think I can empathize with Paul. There is something in my life that makes life difficult. I cry out to You to remove it over and over, but You have a greater goal in mind. There is purpose in this circumstance. Help me see the *why*. What am I to learn? Please never let me forget that while You allow the hardship to remain, You don't abandon me to tough it out on my own. Your grace is always present. Your grace is always enough. Let Your glory shine through me, Lord. Amen.

THINK ABOUT IT:
What might be the purpose of a difficult situation in your life right now?

DAY 339

Morning
24-KARAT FAITH

These troubles come to prove that your faith is pure. This purity of faith is worth more than gold, which can be proved to be pure by fire but will ruin. But the purity of your faith will bring you praise and glory and honor when Jesus Christ is shown to you.

1 PETER 1:7 NCV

Father, I am in the middle of troubles, and it's hard to think clearly. It's hard to trust that I will benefit from something that seems to rip me apart. But I've been through rough waters before. Looking back, I can see where I have grown, where my faith has deepened. I know I will come through these difficult times too with faith more precious and lasting than gold. I know that my full reward is yet to come. For now, may I thrive in assurance of faith, even in the middle of troubles. Amen.

THINK ABOUT IT:

How have trials made you more certain than ever of your faith?

Evening
NEVER FORSAKEN

And about the ninth hour Jesus cried out with a loud voice, saying, "Eli, Eli, lema sabachthani?" that is, "My God, my God, why have you forsaken me?"

MATTHEW 27:46 ESV

Lord, too often I think of the cross as just physical. You took my place and suffered brutality as I should have suffered for my sin. But more than the nail-pierced hands and agonizing death, You experienced God forsaking You. You endured unimaginable sorrow—out of boundless love. Because of You, I will never know the cost of sin, I will never feel God turn His back on me. . .saying thank You will never be enough, Lord. So in humility I offer my life to You. When I am tempted to turn my back and follow my will instead of Yours, remind me of the cost I'll never pay. Obedience is such a small price in comparison! Amen.

THINK ABOUT IT:

What motivates you to remain faithful to God?

Morning
ACCEPT ONE ANOTHER

Accept one another, then,
just as Christ accepted you,
in order to bring praise to God.
ROMANS 15:7 NIV

Lord, I watch children sometimes, not to see whether they have been listening to me but because I need to learn from them. They so easily approach those who are different from them. They play with anyone—no one is a stranger. They find out people's names and learn what they like to do. They give hugs at the drop of a hat. They get excited over the smallest of victories. They rejoice together. And if someone is sad, they try to find out what's wrong and fix it right away. Lord, I want to be like a child. I want to be like You. Please help me accept others as Jesus did. I praise You, Father. Amen.

THINK ABOUT IT:
What lessons has God
been teaching you through
children lately?

Evening
UNMOVABLE

God is in the midst of her;
she shall not be moved; God will
help her when morning dawns.
PSALM 46:5 ESV

I know this verse isn't talking about an actual woman. It's talking about Your holy city. Still, as I read it, I like to think it's talking about me. It could be. After all, You are in the midst of me. You live inside my heart, and You shall not be moved. Since my strength comes from You, I'm just as solid and steadfast as You in me. I know You'll help me when evening falls and when morning dawns and every moment in between. Every time I feel overcome with worry and anxiety, fear and depression, remind me of this verse, and remind me of its truth in my life.

THINK ABOUT IT:
Do you feel immovable?
Spend some time thinking about
God's power living inside of you.

Morning
BE STILL

*"Be still, and know that I am God.
I will be exalted among the nations,
I will be exalted in the earth!"*
PSALM 46:10 ESV

So much of my worry is paired with rest-lessness, a need to act, to do something when there's nothing that can be done. But acting on my own, without Your prompting, shows a lack of trust in Your sovereignty. Instead of trying to control things in a nervous frenzy of activity, You've called me to simply be still. To be quiet. To rest in the knowledge that You don't need me or anyone else. You are all-powerful, and You have everything under control. Forgive me for my agitation and impatience. Each time I'm tempted to fill up my days with nervous energy, shush my spirit. Quiet my soul. Remind me to lay my head on Your great shoulder and simply, calmly rest in You.

THINK ABOUT IT:
*Have you taken time to be still
and rest in God's presence today?*

Evening
CATTLE ON A
THOUSAND HILLS

*"For every beast of the forest is
mine, the cattle on a thousand hills.
I know all the birds of the hills, and
all that moves in the field is mine."*
PSALM 50:10–11 ESV

Your power and resources are limitless. Too often, I view You by my own limitations, and I forget how formidable You are. I know You have more than enough of everything I need, whether it's money, food, relationships, good health, or something else. You are the generous provider, and You will take care of everything in my life. I know it's silly that I worry about things I'm certain You will supply, but my mind quickly forgets. Help me to become more disciplined, to train my brain toward trust instead of worry. I know You will take care of me, Father.

THINK ABOUT IT:
*What do you need God to
provide for you? Talk to Him
about it. He won't let you down.*

Morning
SAYING THANKS

*"The one who offers thanksgiving
as his sacrifice glorifies me; to one
who orders his way rightly I will
show the salvation of God!"*

PSALM 50:23 ESV

When I'm overcome with worry and fear, thanksgiving really is a sacrifice. But I know thanksgiving is also the cure to my anxiety. When times get hard, I need to thank You! I need to praise You for the countless good things You've done in my life and in the lives of others. I need my thoughts to live in that place of gratitude instead of fear. Right now, in this moment, I want to express my thanks. You have never let me down. Time and again, You've poured out Your loving-kindness on me. You are good and gracious and generous beyond comprehension, and I love You.

THINK ABOUT IT:
*What do you thank God for
today? Make a list. Nothing is
too small or insignificant.*

Evening
THROUGH THE STORMS

*Be merciful to me, O God,
be merciful to me, for in you my
soul takes refuge; in the shadow of
your wings I will take refuge, till the
storms of destruction pass by.*

PSALM 57:1 ESV

I know that nothing bad comes from You. You are only love, and You are only good. But sometimes I wonder if You allow some bad things into my life because of my tendency to wander from You. When things are good, I often become complacent in spending time with You. But when circumstances bring worry and strife, I run to You. I know You created me to have fellowship with You, and when I don't spend time with You, You miss me. Forgive me for neglecting You, Father. Have mercy on me as I hide in Your arms. Please calm the storms, and help me stay close to You even when things are good.

THINK ABOUT IT:
*What storms are you going through?
Ask God for mercy in the storms.*

Morning
SING LOUD!

But I will sing of your strength; I will sing aloud of your steadfast love in the morning. For you have been to me a fortress and a refuge in the day of my distress. O my Strength, I will sing praises to you, for you, O God, are my fortress, the God who shows me steadfast love.

PSALM 59:16–17 ESV

Life brings difficult things. There's no way around it. When sin entered the world, along came hardship and trials. But as I look back on my life, it's the trials that have brought me closer to You. You've used those things to make me stronger, more compassionate, more gracious. Like David, I will sing loudly of Your steadfast love. I'll sing in the morning, at night, and in the middle of the day. No matter what I've gone through, You've been there. Thank You for loving me through it all, Father.

THINK ABOUT IT:
What is your song of praise today? Sing it loudly, even if it's inside your head.

Evening
I CAN'T SAVE MYSELF

Oh, grant us help against the foe, for vain is the salvation of man! With God we shall do valiantly; it is he who will tread down our foes.

PSALM 60:11–12 ESV

"For vain is the salvation of man." I can't save myself, Lord, no matter how hard I try. I need Your help. I know with You, mountains get moved. Problems get solved. Diseases are healed, and finances are replenished. Whatever comes against me, whether it's a person or a circumstance, will not win as long as You are on my side. I'm helpless without You, Father, but with You all things are possible. Please take over my circumstances. I'm desperate for You to save me. You're the only one who can.

THINK ABOUT IT:
In what circumstances have you tried to save yourself without God's help? How did that work out? Ask God to intervene, and then trust Him to act.

Morning
NOT GREATLY SHAKEN

*For God alone my soul waits in silence;
from him comes my salvation. He
alone is my rock and my salvation, my
fortress; I shall not be greatly shaken.*

PSALM 62:1–2 ESV

Once again, here's a reminder to wait.
Worry and waiting can't coexist, because
when I worry, I'm fidgety and I want to
do something. When I wait in faith, I'm
calm and I trust You. I love the last phrase
of this passage: "I shall not be greatly
shaken." I don't like being shaken, Father.
I want everything to be peaceful all the
time. But without tension, any story is
a dull one. You want me to live a grand
adventure, which requires shaking things
up now and then. You didn't say I won't
be shaken at all. Rather, You said I won't
be greatly shaken. Sometimes life may
rattle me, but You won't allow any permanent damage. Thank You for Your perfect
care over my life.

THINK ABOUT IT:

*What has shaken you recently?
Trust that it won't destroy you.*

Evening
QUIET MY SOUL

*O LORD, my heart is not lifted up;
my eyes are not raised too high; I do
not occupy myself with things too
great and too marvelous for me. But I
have calmed and quieted my soul, like
a weaned child with its mother; like a
weaned child is my soul within me.*

PSALM 131:1–2 ESV

David wrote this psalm. He was not worrying or occupying his thoughts with things
that weren't his concern. Instead, he was
calm, waiting, knowing that, in the proper
time, You would act. A child who isn't
weaned cries the moment hunger hits.
But the weaned child has learned to trust
and waits calmly, knowing food will come.
Thank You for David's wisdom in this
scripture. Teach me to wait peacefully,
calmly, knowing that in the proper time,
You will act in love.

THINK ABOUT IT:

*Do you concern yourself with
things that aren't yours to manage?
Take some deep breaths, calm
yourself, and wait on God to act.*

DAY 345

Morning
CLING

*For you have been my help,
and in the shadow of your wings I
will sing for joy. My soul clings to
you; your right hand upholds me.*
PSALM 63:7–8 ESV

I cling to You. Like a frightened child clings to its parent, I cling to You. It's dark in my world right now, and I'm afraid, but I'll hold on to You with all my strength. I will sing praises to You, Father, in the midst of the storm. Though the tornado may drown out my song, I know You can still hear it. And even when I grow weary, when my grip starts to loosen, I know You have me. You have always had me, and You've never let me down. I love You. I praise You. And I know You are good.

THINK ABOUT IT:

*Are you clinging tightly to God,
or is your grip loose right now?
It's okay. Either way, He's got you.*

Evening
HEMMED IN

*Let the righteous one rejoice in
the LORD and take refuge in him!
Let all the upright in heart exult!*
PSALM 64:10 ESV

I know I am righteous not because of anything I've done but because of what Christ did for me. Because of that gift of salvation, I'm in right standing with You, and that's what *righteous* means. Because I am in right standing with You, I don't have to worry about anything. You have my back. You also have my front and my sides. You hem me in, protecting me from all directions. Even when I don't feel Your presence, even when it seems like You're not there at all, I know You're working on my behalf. I will rejoice in the knowledge that You will never lose sight of me, and You're always protecting me.

THINK ABOUT IT:

*Have you ever pictured God standing
in front of you, behind you, and on
either side, fighting off enemies? Close
your eyes and picture that now.*

DAY 346

Morning
NEAR GOD

But for me it is good to be near God;
I have made the Lord GOD my refuge,
that I may tell of all your works.
PSALM 73:28 ESV

You are truly my refuge. Some things in my life are crazy and scary, but I know You are with me. You have blessed me in more ways than I can count. I know even when it seems like wicked people and circumstances are prospering, You are always in control. When I worry, I get distracted and wander from Your presence. I don't want to do that, Lord. I want to stay close to You. I want my heart and mind to remain so focused on You that I don't even notice the storms around me. I love You. Like the psalmist, I want to tell everyone about how amazing You are.

THINK ABOUT IT:
At what time in your life did you feel closest to God?

Evening
SO THEY WILL KNOW

That they may know that you
alone, whose name is the Lord,
are the Most High over all the earth.
PSALM 83:18 ESV

You know everything that's going on in my life right now. You know all the circumstances, all the details. And You know exactly what they're doing to me. All the fear, the worry, the anxiety. . . You know it all. I'm begging You, Father. Please act. Please make Yourself known in this situation, in my life. Deliver me and my loved ones from these circumstances in a way that brings You glory so people will know You are God. Just as You delivered Daniel from the lions' jaws, just as You delivered Shadrach, Meshach, and Abednego from the fire, please deliver me. I know You are able. Please show off so everyone will know You are the Most High.

THINK ABOUT IT:
Do you believe God is able to deliver you from the things you're worried about? Do you believe He will?

Morning
STRENGTH TO STRENGTH

Blessed are those whose strength is in you, in whose heart are the highways to Zion. As they go through the Valley of Baca they make it a place of springs; the early rain also covers it with pools. They go from strength to strength; each one appears before God in Zion.

PSALM 84:5–7 ESV

Right now, I don't feel strong. In myself, I feel weak. But the blessings aren't found in my own strength. Instead, this passage says, "Blessed are those whose strength is in you." The "Valley of Baca" mentioned here is translated the "Valley of Weeping." That's where I am, Father. But when we're in the middle of that valley of weeping, You turn those tears into flowing, soothing springs. You cause Your children to go from strength to strength, or to never grow weary. Give me Your strength, Father. I need You now.

THINK ABOUT IT:

In what areas do you feel weak right now? Trust God alone for your strength.

Evening
EVERY DAY

I am shut in so that I cannot escape; my eye grows dim through sorrow. Every day I call upon you, O LORD; I spread out my hands to you.

PSALM 88:8–9 ESV

I can't escape from my fears, from the thoughts that plague my mind day and night. Like the psalmist, my eyes grow dim from sorrow. I feel desperate and hopeless, like nothing will ever get better. But I know those feelings aren't based on truth, Father, for You are the God of hope. With You, there is always the assurance of good things to come. So here I am, Lord. Every day, I call on You. Every day, I reach for You. And every day, I will find hope in You alone.

THINK ABOUT IT:

What fears plague you right now? Tell God about them every day. Rest in the knowledge that He knows, He loves you, and He is working on your behalf.

Morning
BECAUSE I'M YOURS

"Because he holds fast to me in love, I will deliver him; I will protect him, because he knows my name. When he calls to me, I will answer him; I will be with him in trouble; I will rescue him and honor him. With long life I will satisfy him and show him my salvation."

PSALM 91:14–16 ESV

What a comforting scripture this is. You don't love me because of anything I've done. You love me because I belong to You. I hold fast to You like a child to its parent. I call out to You like a frightened toddler, afraid of the dark, and You come right away. You won't ever leave me alone in my troubles. Instead, You're right here, rescuing me, setting me in a high, safe place, and pouring out Your love to me. Thank You for loving me like this.

THINK ABOUT IT:

Are you holding fast to God in love? Each time you call His name aloud or in your thoughts, He is there.

Evening
FLOURISH

The righteous flourish like the palm tree and grow like a cedar in Lebanon. They are planted in the house of the LORD; they flourish in the courts of our God. They still bear fruit in old age; they are ever full of sap and green, to declare that the LORD is upright; he is my rock, and there is no unrighteousness in him.

PSALM 92:12–15 ESV

Today, I want to claim this promise for my life. Because I belong to You, I fall under the category of "righteous." This verse states that the righteous will flourish. This means to be in a vigorous state or to thrive. Please take the circumstances that are causing me to worry and turn them around so I'll thrive and so all my loved ones will thrive. I know You don't always act instantly. I'll be patient, knowing and trusting that You're working all things together for my good. Thank You for Your promises, Father.

THINK ABOUT IT:

What do you picture when you think of yourself flourishing?

Morning
SPRINGS IN THE DESERT

*He turns a desert into pools of water,
a parched land into springs of water.
And there he lets the hungry dwell,
and they establish a city to live in;
they sow fields and plant vineyards
and get a fruitful yield. By his blessing
they multiply greatly, and he does
not let their livestock diminish.*

PSALM 107:35–38 ESV

Right now I feel like I'm in a desert. I feel parched and hungry and needy. But You, Lord, are loving and kind and generous, and I know You will turn this desert of mine into a clear, spring-fed pond. You'll fill my hunger and calm my fears. In spite of what I feel right now, I know You have good things in store for me. Have mercy on me, Father. I'm hurting and scared. Please reach down and bless me right here, right now. My hope is in You alone.

THINK ABOUT IT:

What part of your life feels parched and desert-like right now? Picture it saturated with God's blessings.

Evening
EVERY MOMENT

*From the rising of the sun to its setting,
the name of the LORD is to be praised!*

PSALM 113:3 ESV

Praising You takes the focus off myself and my problems and places it where it belongs. Praise is a lifestyle choice, and too often I make the wrong choice. Instead of praise, I choose worry and fear and anxiety and doubt. It's not a conscious choice, but I know when I choose to praise You and thank You for all the good things You've done, my fear dissipates. When I wake up in the morning, remind me to praise You. When I can't sleep at night, remind me of all the things I should be thankful for. Every moment of every day, I want to focus my thoughts on Your goodness, Your grace, and Your love.

THINK ABOUT IT:

What do you normally think about when you first wake up? Place a reminder by your bed to spend some time, first thing in the morning, praising God.

Morning
THIS LITTLE LIGHT

*If you feed those who are hungry
and take care of the needs of those
who are troubled, then your light
will shine in the darkness, and you
will be bright like sunshine at noon.*

ISAIAH 58:10 NCV

God, I want to shine! This world is so dark; there are so many needs. From my own backyard to places I've never been far across the world, people are hungry for relief and hungry for Your love. My soul aches at the pain, but sometimes I feel helpless to help. But I'm not, God—not with You to lead me. Expose my discouragement for what it is: one of the devil's lies. Show me ways I can brighten dark corners with the blessings You've poured out to me. Be with me as I shine, God. Amen.

THINK ABOUT IT:

*How can you shine—even a
glimmer—into others' lives this
week? This month? This year?*

Evening
BREAD OF LIFE

*Jesus then said to them, "Truly, truly,
I say to you, it was not Moses who
gave you the bread from heaven,
but my Father gives you the true
bread from heaven. For the bread
of God is he who comes down from
heaven and gives life to the world."*

JOHN 6:32–33 ESV

Thank You, Lord, for true bread. When speaking about the nourishment You provide, You first reminded the disciples of the miracle manna. For forty years, manna sustained physical life as the Israelites traveled in the wilderness. But with Your arrival on earth dawned an even greater power—God's power to sustain eternal life. Ordinary bread, even supernatural manna, only meets temporary needs, but You, Lord, fill souls to the brim. Never will I be truly hungry with You, the "bread of life" (John 6:35). Amen.

THINK ABOUT IT:

*Do you say grace before meals?
How can you begin to thank
God daily for the spiritual
nourishment He bestows?*

Morning
FOR GOOD, FOR GOD

"Be especially careful when you are trying to be good so that you don't make a performance out of it. It might be good theater, but the God who made you won't be applauding."
MATTHEW 6:1 MSG

Father, applause is sweet to our ears. We long to hear an *attagirl* in response to what we do. While encouragement has its place, my motivation for doing good begins and ends with You, Father. My offerings are still beautiful in Your sight if only You see them. My victory over temptation is still a cause for celebration if only the angels in heaven cheer me on. My acts of kindness, my whispered prayers, and my witness are just as powerful without applause. Keep me focused on You, my audience of one, when I act in goodness. Your applause is the sweetest of all. Amen.

THINK ABOUT IT:
Whose eyes are you most conscious of when you do good things?

Evening
FLESH AND GOD

"And I will give you a new heart, and a new spirit I will put within you. And I will remove the heart of stone from your flesh and give you a heart of flesh."
EZEKIEL 36:26 ESV

God, I am amazed by the intricacy of Your creation, like the flesh that covers and protects me. Flesh can change. And just like cuts that mend, scars that fade, and muscles that strengthen, with a spiritual heart of flesh, You can heal me, renew me, grow me. You enter my life, and my heart changes. Once resistant, I now yield. Once unbendable, I'm now open to Your will. Once tough, I now respond to Your gentle prompting. Day by day, God, please continue to work within so that the very heart of me reflects You. Amen.

THINK ABOUT IT:
Why is a fleshy heart so important in the life of a Christian?

Morning
NOT-SO-BEST FOOT FORWARD

Many of the believers began to confess openly and tell all the evil things they had done. . . . So in a powerful way the word of the Lord kept spreading and growing.

ACTS 19:18, 20 NCV

Lord, sometimes it seems as if I'm surrounded by facades. You know what I mean—everyone trying to present their best self. Jaw-dropping multitasker, breezy artiste, business genius, wonder woman. . .whatever we show others, it's rarely our bad side. But You do Your greatest work in messy, imperfect lives. Why do we try to hide the not-quite-put-together side of us? Our flaws, our mistakes, our fears, our sins. . .You can use them to shout of Your grace. Grant me courage to share my *real* self—good side and bad—so that others hear of You through me. Amen.

THINK ABOUT IT:

When you think back on testimonies you've heard, which ones were the most powerful?

Evening
THE POWER OF A PRAYER

And when they had prayed, the place in which they were gathered together was shaken, and they were all filled with the Holy Spirit and continued to speak the word of God with boldness.

ACTS 4:31 ESV

Father, lately life has been so busy, and I've drifted from prayer. I send up a quick "Hi, goodbye" and then wonder why I don't feel You working in me. I kneel before You today asking for forgiveness. You deserve my best, not my leftovers. And amazingly, humblingly—You, almighty God, long for me, little me, to commune with You. Remind me of the privilege of prayer. Remind me of the *power* of prayer. Your disciples prayed and walls shook. Your children pray and Your Holy Spirit moves in us. Father, may prayer be a vital force in me, my lifeblood. Amen.

THINK ABOUT IT:

When have you seen prayer yield powerful results?

DAY 353

Morning
IF TREES COULD TALK

"But ask the animals, and they will teach you, or ask the birds of the air, and they will tell you. Speak to the earth, and it will teach you, or let the fish of the sea tell you. . . . The life of every creature and the breath of all people are in God's hand."

JOB 12:7–8, 10 NCV

God, the first place I go to learn about You is Your holy Word. There You have laid out a glorious résumé of who You are. But You've also written Yourself into nature. Lift my eyes to see Your creation, God. Beasts and birds and earth and sea helped Job grasp You in troubling times. By pausing to reflect on what's around me, I too can glimpse You. Your power to renew after ruin, Your splendor, Your provision, Your design for life. . .You are everywhere, in everything. Praise to You, God of all. Amen.

THINK ABOUT IT:
How can you spend some time experiencing God through nature?

Evening
NO IN BETWEEN

"I know your works: you are neither cold nor hot. Would that you were either cold or hot! So, because you are lukewarm, and neither hot nor cold, I will spit you out of my mouth."

REVELATION 3:15–16 ESV

Lord, I don't like drinking stale, lukewarm water. It's neither comforting like something hot nor refreshing like something cold. These verses in Revelation say that You don't like lukewarm Christianity. It's somewhere between turning a cold shoulder and being on fire for God—and its superficiality sickens You. I want to be a Christian through and through, not declaring You as Lord and then living in the lukewarm. I want to be a hot Christian! Fill me, fuel me so that my every deed reveals a fervor for You. Amen.

THINK ABOUT IT:
If you are lukewarm in faith, what actions—like immersing yourself in the Bible and prayer—can heat up your Christianity?

Morning
RECIPROCAL

[Hannah] was deeply distressed and prayed to the Lord and wept bitterly. And she vowed a vow and said, "O Lord of hosts, if you will indeed look on the affliction of your servant and remember me and not forget your servant, but will give to your servant a son, then I will give him to the Lord all the days of his life."

1 Samuel 1:10–11 esv

Lord, when I pray for something that I want deep down, it usually doesn't cross my mind to offer it right back up to You. But that's exactly what Hannah did. She desperately wanted a son. She wept and prayed for Your favor—and then she promised to return to You what You gave. Such a beautiful picture of faith beginning and ending with You. To receive and let go with open hands. . .to pray in gratitude and for Your glory. Lord, may what I want for *me* be ever focused on You. Amen.

THINK ABOUT IT:

Do you consider God in your prayer requests?

Evening
TAKE A STAND

Then the king of Egypt said to the Hebrew midwives, one of whom was named Shiphrah and the other Puah, "When you serve as midwife to the Hebrew women and see them on the birthstool, if it is a son, you shall kill him. . . ." But the midwives feared God and did not do as the king of Egypt commanded them.

Exodus 1:15–17 esv

God, Shiphrah and Puah were two gutsy women. Do I have the courage to do the crazy thing—the thing that puts me at risk to honor You? While I may never face such an extreme choice as these midwives, my life is made up of countless chances to choose You over the world. Be with me as You surely were with Shiphrah and Puah. Grant me the courage—in the everyday choices and even once-in-a-lifetime ones—not to cower or water down my faith, but instead remain true to You. Amen.

THINK ABOUT IT:

Why do we often fear humankind more than God?

Morning
ONE, A LONELY NUMBER

Two are better than one, because they have a good reward for their toil. For if they fall, one will lift up his fellow. But woe to him who is alone when he falls and has not another to lift him up!

ECCLESIASTES 4:9–10 ESV

God, You designed us for companionship. Adam worked the garden, but You knew he needed someone by his side to share the toil. Enter Eve. Your design has not changed with passing time. We still need others walking with us, working alongside us. Out of pride or fear of being a burden, how often do I fail to ask for help, to seek someone to share the load? I'm not perfect; I know that very well! Please place companions in my life to offer a hand up when I'm down—and place me in the path of others so I can do the same. Amen.

THINK ABOUT IT:

How have you seen the truth of these verses lived out in your life?

Evening
LIVE IN UNITY

Behold, how good and pleasant it is when brothers dwell in unity! It is like the precious oil on the head, running down on the beard, on the beard of Aaron, running down on the collar of his robes!

PSALM 133:1–2 ESV

When oil was poured out on Your anointed one, it was a sign of Your approval. When the oil was abundant, it symbolized Your pleasure in that anointing. In the same way, You are pleased when Your children get along well together. It makes You happy when we show love and kindness to each other. Father, there are some really difficult people in my life. Help me to live in unity with them as much as possible. Show me how to keep the peace without compromising my convictions. Most of all, make me a beacon of Your light, drawing them to You.

THINK ABOUT IT:

With whom do you have trouble getting along? Ask God to show you the best way to live in peace with everyone.

Morning
STILL FRESH AND GREEN

They will still bear fruit in old age,
they will stay fresh and green.
PSALM 92:14 NIV

Thank You, God, for my parents' lives. Please give me the wisdom and sense of timing to talk to them about what they want for their future care. Enable me to follow their plan, Lord. Help me to be flexible and have the ability to go with the flow as my parents age. I pray that I will not get angry when things don't go as I want, when my parents' unexpected needs arise. Help me to discover the humor in unusual situations; may my parents and I not lose the ability to laugh together. Most of all, Lord, I want my parents to know they are loved. May Your love flow through me to them and through them to me. Bear fruit in all our lives, I pray. Keep us growing and green, no matter how old we get or how life changes.

THINK ABOUT IT:

What fruit might your parents be
bearing even now, in their old age?

Evening
LUST FOR MONEY

Lust for money brings trouble and
nothing but trouble. Going down
that path, some lose their footing
in the faith completely and live
to regret it bitterly ever after.
1 TIMOTHY 6:10 MSG

You know, Lord, that I live in a society that is constantly encouraging me to be greedy for money and the things money can buy. I don't want to excuse my greed, though. Help me to be more aware. Remind me to consciously reject society's values and choose Yours. But I am also aware of being greedy for other "currencies" too. I get greedy for control; I get greedy for people to notice me and appreciate me. Sometimes that greed gets mixed up with my greed for money too, because there's a part of me that believes that if I have more money, I'll have more control over my life, and people will admire me more. I'm sorry, Jesus. Keep my eye fixed on You, I pray, and may I grow less focused on money.

THINK ABOUT IT:

What are the things you are greedy for?

Morning
LIKE JOHN

Now John wore a garment of camel's hair and a leather belt around his waist, and his food was locusts and wild honey. Then Jerusalem and all Judea and all the region about the Jordan were going out to him, and they were baptized by him in the river Jordan, confessing their sins.
MATTHEW 3:4–6 ESV

John didn't worry about wealth, what he wore, or even what he ate. He didn't care what others thought of him. His only concern was what You thought. He wore rags and ate bugs, but he had a tremendous impact on Your kingdom. I'll bet he's wearing some fancy robes now and eating a king's feast! Even though he was considered poor, You cared so tenderly for his needs. Honey is considered a delicacy, after all. Thank You for caring tenderly for my needs as well. Help me follow John's example as I live for You alone.

THINK ABOUT IT:

Have you worried about earthly things instead of focusing on God's plan for your life?

Evening
HARMFUL PATHS

Violent people mislead their companions, leading them down a harmful path.
PROVERBS 16:29 NLT

I have come to realize, Lord, that this friendship is not healthy. In fact, it is poisoning my mind and heart. It has led to me taking paths away from You. And yet, God, I know You love imperfect people extravagantly—and I confess that I am far from perfect. May I not be blind to my own role in this toxic relationship. Help me see the truth about myself. Be my shield and defender, I pray, and show me how, when, and where to set boundaries in this relationship. Bless my friend. May we both be healed so that You can shine through us. Set our feet back on the right path, Lord, the path that leads to You.

THINK ABOUT IT:

Do you have the courage and honesty to ask God to show you where your own responsibility lies in a friendship that has turned toxic?

Morning
A JOYFUL DEATH

"You will come to the grave in full vigor, like sheaves gathered in season."
JOB 5:26 NIV

God, thank You that death can be a time of joy as well as sorrow. As I face the death of this loved one, I give You thanks for shared meals, laughter, long talks, and all the other memories. This person will be forever sewn into the fabric of my being, and I am grateful. May I remember all that I have learned from this relationship, and may I have opportunities to pass that wisdom on to others. As my loved one straddles this world and the next, may we both sense that this is not the end. A great adventure awaits this person I love so much, another chapter in the book of eternity. I release this loved one into Your presence, Lord, knowing I can trust You with this precious life.

THINK ABOUT IT:

What legacy has your loved one left you? What memories will you treasure and take with you?

Evening
FAMILY PAIN

"Do not nurse hatred in your heart for any of your relatives. Confront people directly so you will not be held guilty for their sin."
LEVITICUS 19:17 NLT

God, You know how painful it is when a family member breaks our trust. I ask for Your guardianship of my heart and mind. I know that anyone intending to harm me or treat me abusively is never someone with whom You want me to spend time. At the same time, though, I believe You long to heal our family. Remove the hate and hurt we feel. Show us how to get the help we need to heal. Empower me to seek help and counsel from You, as well as from those who are trained to help with situations like this. May we once more be able to talk openly with one another.

THINK ABOUT IT:

Family issues can be some of the most confusing to solve. Who might God want to use to give you help and insight?

Morning
NOTHING TOO HARD FOR GOD

Behold, I am the LORD,
the God of all flesh: is there
any thing too hard for me?
JEREMIAH 32:27 KJV

I am helpless, God; there's nothing I can do to change this situation. I've tried everything, and nothing has worked. Now I'm giving up. I'm going to stop trying to figure this out on my own, and I'm giving it to You. I know that's what I should have done in the first place, but thank You that it's never too late to ask for Your help. You are the God of all that lives; Your Spirit sustains all creation, so I know You can handle my problems. Nothing is too hard for You. Teach me, Lord, to rely on Your strength and insight instead of my own. Do on my behalf what I am helpless to do for myself.

THINK ABOUT IT:

Are you willing to accept your
helplessness—and wait to
see what God will do?

Evening
REFUGE FROM DEPRESSION

But rejoice, all who take refuge in
You, sing for joy forever! And may
You shelter them, that those who
love Your name may rejoice in You.
PSALM 5:11 NASB

My depression is keeping me from rejoicing, Lord. Please lead me to the right source for help. Thank You for understanding what I am going through, and thank You that Your Word tells me that even Your Son went through hard times emotionally. I pray You will use this difficult time to draw me closer to You. Thank You that I am not defined by this weakness. Help me to focus on what is true and not focus on how I feel. I take refuge in You. Shelter me, I pray, and restore Your joy to my heart.

THINK ABOUT IT:

Depression clouds our understanding
and perceptions. How might
you shift your focus so that
you can see Jesus more clearly?
What action might you take?

Morning
IN EVERYTHING

*In every thing give thanks:
for this is the will of God in
Christ Jesus concerning you.*
1 Thessalonians 5:18 kjv

If I'm honest, Lord, I've always kind of hated this verse. How do You expect me to give thanks in everything? And how can this be Your will for me now, when You know how badly I hurt all the time? I'm sorry, but I just can't thank You for the pain. Now, though, as I read this verse again, I notice something: it doesn't say to give thanks *for* everything but only *in* everything. So, Jesus, in the midst of my pain, show me the things I still have to be thankful for. Remind me of the blessings that are still mine. Teach me to focus on those things rather than the pain. Replace my constant complaints with gratitude for all You continue to give me. Show me ways I can still be of use to You and others. Do Your will through me.

THINK ABOUT IT:

What does it mean to be thankful in the midst of pain—not for the pain but for the other things God has given you? How might this change in focus change your life?

Evening
VENTING

*Fools vent their anger, but the
wise quietly hold it back.*
Proverbs 29:11 nlt

Lord, this relationship with my friend is no longer functioning in a healthy way. When we're together, all we do is vent our anger. We grouch and kvetch about everything, including our husbands, our children, our other friends, the national government, our church, and local politics. We're both equally to blame for we feed off each other's anger so that it grows ever bigger and more bitter each time we're together. While we're talking, it seems like I'm having a good time—but I always come away feeling bummed out with the world. God, I ask for Your help with this relationship that has grown sick. May I be willing to take the first step toward change. Show me what to say to my friend so that we can join forces and work together against this negativity we've allowed to consume us.

THINK ABOUT IT:

We all need to vent our anger and frustration sometimes, and it's good to have a trusted friend who understands. Can you distinguish between the healthy conversations that allow you to leave your anger behind—and the ones that feed your anger and make it grow?

DAY 361

Morning
GOD IS WORKING!

*God is working in you, giving
you the desire and the power
to do what pleases him.*

PHILIPPIANS 2:13 NLT

Lord, I've struggled with this same hidden sin for so long that it seems impossible I'll ever be able to overcome it. I'm so grateful, though, that I don't have to be free from sin for You to love me. You love me just as I am. I don't have to earn Your love by being good. At the same time, I know that You want what's best for me—and this sin I've been hiding isn't what's best. It eats away at me from the inside. It keeps me from being all that You created me to be. Jesus, I want to please You. Give me the strength I need to change. I can't do this on my own; but with Your help, I know I can do anything, even overcome the hold this sin has on me. Thank You that You are working within me even now.

THINK ABOUT IT:

*Instead of trying to overcome your
sin with sheer self-discipline, have
you tried simply giving it to God in
prayer every day and every night?*

Evening
CUTTING CORNERS

*GOD hates cheating in the
marketplace; he loves it when
business is aboveboard.*

PROVERBS 11:1 MSG

It's so easy sometimes, Lord, to cut little corners. I don't mean to cheat anyone (not even the IRS), so I tell myself I'm just trying to get a good deal. . .or I'm getting the most for my money. . .or what I'm doing doesn't really count as cheating because everyone else does the same thing (or at least *almost* everyone else does). And then I read Bible verses like this one, and I hear Your Spirit gently chiding my heart, reminding me that honesty is important to You. It doesn't matter what "everyone else" is doing, and You care far more about what's right than You do about making a profit. Readjust my priorities, Lord, so that I value what You value. Forgive me for my dishonesty, and give me the strength to change my ways.

THINK ABOUT IT:

*When you find yourself being willing
to be dishonest in small ways, where
are you placing your priorities?
What needs to change?*

Morning
GOOD MEDICINE

A cheerful heart is good medicine, but a broken spirit saps a person's strength.
PROVERBS 17:22 NLT

It's hard to have a cheerful heart, Lord, when I'm feeling so sick, but I know that my negative frame of mind won't help me heal. Give me joy even in small things: the pleasure of a good book, the comfort of my bed, the warmth of a cup of tea. Help me to stop fretting about all the things that aren't getting done while I'm sick, and instead, may I relax into the peace of Your presence. Meet me here, Lord, as I lie here sick, and shift my attention away from my discomfort. You are the great Healer, and I need the medicine of Your Spirit. Heal me—heart, spirit, and body—and renew my strength.

THINK ABOUT IT:

What can you do while you are sick that will help to cheer you up? Take time to be kind to yourself!

Evening
QUICK TO HEAR, SLOW TO SPEAK

Be quick to hear, slow to speak, and slow to anger.
JAMES 1:19 NASB

Lord, I know we're meant to be the body of Christ—but lately, whenever our church gets together, all we seem to do is argue. We disagree about the smallest things, and yet it seems so important to each of us to have our own way. I've tried to justify my own behavior by telling myself that I just want things done the right way, but I have to confess that I'm so sure of my own position I haven't really been listening to other points of view. Next time I'm together with church members, remind me, Lord, to listen before I speak. Teach me to hear what others have to say before I react. May I stop trying to get my own way and instead cooperate with Your body.

THINK ABOUT IT:

Are you willing to listen to other points of view? Can you open both your ears and your heart?

Morning
FRETTING

Refrain from anger and turn from wrath; do not fret—it leads only to evil.
PSALM 37:8 NIV

I'm realizing, Lord, that anger and fretting aren't the same thing. Healthy anger is a reaction to a wrong; it impels me to take action to put things right. But when I let my anger stew day after day deep inside my heart, it turns into fretting. It's destructive. It doesn't push me forward toward something better; instead, it's like quicksand, keeping me mired in the memory of past injuries. Any action that rises out of this kind of anger is likely to be hurtful, both to myself and others. So, Lord, I ask You to give me the strength to release my anger into Your hands. Help me not to cling to it, letting it fester inside me. Show me if I need to act but let me turn away from violence and hatred.

THINK ABOUT IT:

The word fret *comes from an Old English word that meant "devour, feed upon, consume." How might anger be devouring your soul?*

Evening
WORK BURDENS

Cast your burden upon the Lord and He will sustain you.
PSALM 55:22 NASB

My job is wearing me down, Lord. I've reached the place where I dread going into work every day. The tension in my workplace is overwhelming. By the end of each day, I'm exhausted. I'm relieved to go home, but then I can't stop thinking about work for the rest of the day. My thoughts keep me awake at night, and then I'm that much more discouraged the next day when it's time to head off to work again. I don't know what the answer is, God. I can't quit, and I don't see any other way out of this situation. But I know You never want me to be miserable; You always want to give me joy and peace. So, Lord, I give You the heavy load that my job has become. Please help me carry it. Give me renewed strength and energy. Sharpen my mind so that I can find new ideas to get me through this. Sustain me, I pray.

THINK ABOUT IT:

Is there a way you can step back from your job even for an hour or two in the evening or on the weekend? You might be able to gain a new perspective that will help you see the situation more clearly.

Morning
FRIENDSHIPS RESTORED

Don't think of them as enemies,
but warn them as you would
a brother or sister.
2 THESSALONIANS 3:15 NLT

Jesus, these people hurt me in the past, and now I'm always expecting them to do so again. Whether they know it or not, my distrust is always between us. I can't think of them the way I used to. Our friendship has been damaged. I feel as though I'm the innocent party in this situation—but Jesus, is there some action I should take to restore our friendship? You know I'm far from perfect myself, and there have been times I've let people down too. With Your help, maybe I can reach past my distrust and talk to these people openly about my feelings. Show me, Lord, what to say. If at all possible, restore the friendship between us, I pray.

THINK ABOUT IT:

When someone hurts us, it's easy to put up walls to protect ourselves from further hurt. What do you think God is asking you to do in situations like this?

Evening
A CURE FOR
THE GIMMES

And do not forget to do good and
to share with others, for with
such sacrifices God is pleased.
HEBREWS 13:16 NIV

Lord, sometimes my family is pretty demanding about what they want. They have even stomped their little feet and hollered at me when I said no. It's so embarrassing when they do that in public. Then I remember that when I don't get the answers to my prayers just when I want them, I act a bit like that. Maybe not with a tantrum, but in my heart things get a little dicey. I'm sorry for that, Lord, when I succumb to this prevailing self-indulgent, give-it-to-me-now mentality. Maybe a cure for the "gimmes" is to take Hebrews 13:16 to heart, which would help to switch my perspective from me, myself, and I to *others*. Please teach my family—please teach *me*—to do good and share with those in need. Amen.

THINK ABOUT IT:

What could you do as a family to help someone in need? How can you keep Hebrews 13:16 fresh in your family's mind?

Morning
WHEN I'M TEMPTED

Finally, brothers and sisters, whatever is true, whatever is noble, whatever is right, whatever is pure, whatever is lovely, whatever is admirable—if anything is excellent or praiseworthy—think about such things.

PHILIPPIANS 4:8 NIV

Lord, the next time I scratch my head concerning how to pick and choose over the world's various forms of entertainment, please remind me of the above verse so that I can help guide our family with good sense. I am painfully aware that much of what society considers family-friendly fun is far from it. Artists tend to think that if they created it—whatever medium it is—then it's worthy of an audience. I know from experience that this ideology isn't true. Lord, when I'm tempted to be careless about entertainment for me and my family, prompt me to search for whatever is true, right, pure, lovely, and admirable above all other things. Amen.

THINK ABOUT IT:

In the past, what form of entertainment has had a negative or positive impact on your family? How can you keep your mind set on God's goodness?

Evening
FORGIVEN

He does not deal with us according to our sins, nor repay us according to our iniquities. For as high as the heavens are above the earth, so great is his steadfast love toward those who fear him; as far as the east is from the west, so far does he remove our transgressions from us.

PSALM 103:10–12 ESV

Lord, how I needed the beauty of these words today! How I needed to remember their rich meaning. You don't love a little, forgive a little; You love and forgive vastly—as high as heaven above earth and as far as east from west. So often I receive Your forgiveness, but the sin taunts me, remaining just in sight, and I wonder that You could ever love me. Expose this for the lie it is. You remove my sin beyond sight; You love beyond understanding. All I can say is thank You! Amen.

THINK ABOUT IT:

Do you limit God's forgiveness? How can you embrace the truth of the psalm—that His forgiveness is complete?

SCRIPTURE INDEX

OLD TESTAMENT

Genesis
1:1–2	Day 3, 284
1:11	Day 29
1:21	Day 4
1:27	Day 4
2:3	Day 29, 183
2:7	Day 5
2:10	Day 30
2:18	Day 6
3:1	Day 30
3:13	Day 7
3:21	Day 7
4:16	Day 31
4:26	Day 31
5:22–24	Day 8
6:9	Day 11
9:12–13	Day 32
9:13	Day 225
12:1–2	Day 8
13:3–4	Day 45
15:1	Day 45
16:2	Day 48
18:2–3	Day 49
18:12	Day 48
18:12–14	Day 272
18:13–14	Day 49
19:23–24, 26	Day 69
21:1–2	Day 166
21:16–18	Day 243
21:22	Day 58
24:15–16	Day 59
24:30–31	Day 61
24:67	Day 61
26:22	Day 63
26:25	Day 24
27:19	Day 70
28:15	Day 71
41:50–52	Day 73
45:8	Day 73
49:33–50:1	Day 90
50:19–21	Day 90

Exodus
1:15–17	Day 354
3:8	Day 91
4:10–11	Day 91
4:10–12	Day 176, 245
12:35–36	Day 92
13:3	Day 93
13:17–18	Day 93
14:13–14	Day 33
14:14	Day 94
14:21	Day 160
15:20–21	Day 67
16:4	Day 244
18:17–18	Day 94
19:5	Day 126
29:45–46	Day 126
32:11–12	Day 147
32:11, 14	Day 83
33:3	Day 147
39:42–43	Day 148
40:36–37	Day 148

Leviticus
6:12–13	Day 149
9:6	Day 149
11:44–45	Day 190
19:17	Day 358

Numbers
6:24–26	Day 227

Deuteronomy
1:26–27	Day 190
2:7	Day 191
3:22	Day 175, 191
4:9	Day 192

5:9–10 . . . . Day 192	**Esther**
5:29 . . . . Day 193	4:13–14 . . . . Day 69
7:6–7 . . . . Day 193	
8:12–14 . . . . Day 84	**Job**
12:28 . . . . Day 260	1:20–21 . . . . Day 197
14:2 . . . . Day 260	5:26 . . . . Day 358
17:19 . . . . Day 261	12:7–8, 10 . . . . Day 353
23:9 . . . . Day 261	12:7–10 . . . . Day 227
30:6 . . . . Day 262	13:15 . . . . Day 109
30:19 . . . . Day 262	19:25–26 . . . . Day 197
31:6 . . . . Day 98	
31:8 . . . . Day 263	**Psalms**
33:12 . . . . Day 263	1:1–2 . . . . Day 265
	4:8 . . . . Day 66
Joshua	5:11 . . . . Day 359
1:7 . . . . Day 264	6:2–3 . . . . Day 184
1:9 . . . . Day 20, 62, 112	6:6–7 . . . . Day 266
1:11 . . . . Day 265	7:1–2 . . . . Day 266
4:21–23 . . . . Day 308	7:10–11 . . . . Day 267
6:20 . . . . Day 200	8:3–4 . . . . Day 118
	9:1–2 . . . . Day 267
Ruth	9:1–2, 10 . . . . Day 243
1:16 . . . . Day 217	9:9 . . . . Day 161
	9:9–10 . . . . Day 58
1 Samuel	10:1 . . . . Day 268
1:10–11 . . . . Day 354	13:1 . . . . Day 64
2:1 . . . . Day 32	13:2 . . . . Day 268
3:10 . . . . Day 212	14:5 . . . . Day 269
17:45 . . . . Day 97	16:8 . . . . Day 64
17:47 . . . . Day 164	16:11 . . . . Day 116, 269
18:3 . . . . Day 224	18:39 . . . . Day 293
30:6 . . . . Day 14	18:43 . . . . Day 300
	19:7–8 . . . . Day 300
2 Samuel	19:14 . . . . Day 77, 277
22:30 . . . . Day 259	20:4 . . . . Day 321
	20:7–8 . . . . Day 301
1 Kings	22:3 . . . . Day 302
17:14 . . . . Day 226	23:1–2 . . . . Day 96
	23:1–3 . . . . Day 301
Nehemiah	23:2–3 . . . . Day 256
2:18 . . . . Day 136	
8:10 . . . . Day 152	

23:3 . . . . .Day 328	41:9 . . . . Day 172
23:4 . . . . Day 99, 129	42:7–8 . . . . .Day 332
23:5 . . . . .Day 326	42:11 . . . . .Day 325
25:3 . . . . .Day 302	44:24–26 .Day 333
25:12. . . . . .Day 303	45:10 . . . . Day 162
25:20–21 . . . . .Day 303	46:1 . . . . Day 162
26:7 . . . . .Day 304	46:1–3 . . . . .Day 333
27:1. . . . . Day 129	46:5 . . . . .Day 340
27:4 . . . . .Day 88	46:10 . . . . Day 5, 101, 295, 341
27:13–14 . . . . .Day 304	50:10–11 . . . . Day 341
28:6–7 . . . . .Day 305	50:23 . . . . .Day 342
28:7 . . . . Day 75, 187	51:10. . . . . Day 221
29:3 . . . . Day 222	51:10–12 . . . . .Day 276
29:10 . . . . .Day 305	55:17. . . . . .Introduction
29:11 . . . . Day 39	55:22 . . . . Day 3, 112, 363
30:4–5 . . . . .Day 306	56:8–11 .Day 240
30:5, 11–12 . . . . Day 215	57:1. . . . . .Day 342
31:9–10. Day 317	59:16–17 .Day 343
31:19. . . . . .Day 258	60:11–12 . . . . .Day 343
32:3–4 . . . . Day 317	62:1–2. . . . . .Day 344
32:7 . . . . .Day 86	62:8 . . . . Day 324
32:8 . . . . Day 10	63:7–8 . . . . .Day 345
33:20–21 . . . . Day 318	64:10 . . . . .Day 345
33:22 . . . . Day 318	68:4–6. . . . . Day 143
34:4 . . . . Day 165	72:14. . . . . Day 15
34:12–14. Day 319	73:26 . . . . Day 321
34:17–18. . . . . .Day 54	73:28 . . . . .Day 346
34:17–20 . . . . Day 179	83:18 . . . . .Day 346
34:18 . . . . .Day 286	84:5–7 . . . . .Day 347
34:19 . . . . Day 177	84:10–12. Day 82
35:27 . . . . Day 319, 324	88:8–9. . . . . .Day 347
36:5–6 . . . . .Day 330	91:1. . . . . Day 165
37:1. . . . . Day 108	91:4 . . . . Day 277
37:4 . . . . Day 53	91:11 . . . . .Day 250
37:8 . . . . .Day 111, 254, 363	91:14–16 .Day 348
37:23–24 . . . . Day 254, 330	91:15. . . . . .Day 299
37:28–29 . . . . Day 331	92:12–15 . . . . .Day 348
38:9 . . . . Day 125	92:14 . . . . .Day 356
38:21–22 . . . . Day 331	94:19 . . . . .Day 135, 208
39:4, 6. . . . . .Day 332	96:11–13 . . . . .Day 141

97:5–6	Day 221	15:1	Day 16
102:25–27	Day 219	15:4	Day 57
103:10–12	Day 365	15:29	Day 294
107:20	Day 174	16:3	Day 334
107:35–38	Day 349	16:9	Day 158
113:2–6	Day 215	16:29	Day 357
113:3	Day 349	17:17	Day 17
116:1–2	Day 187	17:22	Day 35, 362
116:7	Day 145	23:18	Day 228
118:5–6	Day 282	24:10	Day 135
118:5–7	Day 226	24:13–14	Day 23
119:36	Day 250	24:16	Day 28
119:145–147	Day 264	28:13	Day 257
120:6–7	Day 275	29:11	Day 360
121:1–2	Day 311	29:20	Day 255
121:3	Day 314	29:25	Day 44, 196
121:5–7	Day 292	30:8–9	Day 120
131:1–2	Day 344	31:28–29	Day 21, 115
133:1–2	Day 355	31:29–31	Day 21
139:1–6	Day 131		
139:9–10	Day 140	**Ecclesiastes**	
139:13–14	Day 145	1:18	Day 206
139:13–14, 16	Day 271	3:1, 9–11	Day 238
139:23–24	Day 155	3:11	Day 296
141:3	Day 46	4:9–10	Day 288, 355
143:8	Day 278	7:9	Day 292
145:13	Day 9	7:10	Day 63, 185
147:5	Day 185	11:5	Day 114
147:3	Day 95	11:10	Day 167, 199
		12:13–14	Day 201

Proverbs

3:5	Day 232, 287	**Isaiah**	
3:5–6	Day 97, 281, 294	2:12	Day 11
3:24	Day 173	5:20	Day 78
4:26	Day 186	9:6	Day 24
9:9	Day 10	26:3	Day 111, 113, 173
10:11	Day 15	30:18	Day 70
11:1	Day 361	35:3–4	Day 189, 203
12:25	Day 131, 207	40:6–8	Day 142
14:29	Day 327	40:11	Day 65

40:18 . . . . Day 313
40:28 . . . . .Day 78
40:28–29 . . . . Day 130
40:29 . . . . .Day 38
40:31 . . . . Day 52, 105
41:10 . . . . Day 43, 102, 169, 209
41:13 . . . . Day 279
43:2 . . . . Day 27
43:16–19 . . . . .Day 114
43:18–19 . . . . Day 168
45:9–10 . . . . Day 241
49:15–16 .Day 68
53:3 . . . . .Day 36
53:6 . . . . .Day 89
54:13 . . . . .Day 86
55:2–3 . . . . Day 241
55:8 . . . . Day 310
55:10–11 . . . . Day 270
58:10 . . . . .Day 350
60:1 . . . . Day 257
61:7 . . . . .Day 202
66:13 . . . . Day 291, 313

Jeremiah

1:5 . . . . .Day 295
10:12 . . . . .Day 88
17:7 . . . . Day 194
17:7–8 . . . . .Day 44
22:3 . . . . .Day 230
29:11 .Day 156, 289
29:12 . . . . Day 132
30:17 . . . . .Day 329
31:3 . . . . Day 182
32:26 . . . . Day 108
32:27 . . . . .Day 359
33:3 . . . . Day 251

Lamentations

2:19 . . . . .Day 171

Ezekiel

36:26 . . . . Day 351

Daniel

3:16–18 .Day 20, 34
6:22 . . . . Day 223

Joel

2:25–26 . . . . .Day 92

Jonah

1:3 . . . . Day 74
2:1–2 . . . . Day 253

Micah

6:8 . . . . Day 120
7:18–19 . . . . Day 139

Habakkuk

3:17–18 . . . . Day 138
3:19 . . . . Day 232

Zephaniah

3:17 . . . . .Day 117, 203

Zechariah

4:10 . . . . Day 315

NEW TESTAMENT

Matthew

3:4–6 . . . . .Day 357
4:2–4 . . . . Day 132
5:1–2 . . . . Day 252
5:3 . . . . .Day 290
5:3–8 . . . . .Day 151
5:6 . . . . Day 13
5:7 . . . . Day 12
5:8 . . . . Day 14

5:9 . . . . Day 2, 234
5:10 . . . . Day 234
5:11 . . . . Day 233
5:23–24 . . . . Day 79, 177, 309
5:41–42 . . . . Day 81
5:44 . . . . Day 134
6:1. . . . . Day 351
6:2–4 . . . . Day 41
6:7–8 . . . . Day 39, 151
6:9 . . . . Day 224
6:10 . . . . .Day 290
6:11 . . . . Day 13
6:12. . . . . Day 12
6:14–15. . . . . Day 166
6:25 . . . . Day 125
6:27 . . . . .Day 42, 72
6:33 . . . . Day 172, 225
6:33–34. .Day 95
6:34. . . . . Day 146, 186
7:7 . . . . .Day 328
9:20–22 .Day 211
9:37–38 . . . . Day 139
11:28. . . . . .Day 128, 311
11:28–29. . . . . Day 1
11:28–30. Day 71
13:22. . . . . Day 198
13:44 . . . . .Day 42
14:20 . . . . .Day 205
14:28–31. Day 26
14:29–30 .Day 40
15:25–28 . . . . Day 235
15:32. . . . . Day 218
16:8–11 . . . . Day 237
16:19. . . . . .Day 249
16:21–23 . . . . Day 219
17:19–21 .Day 249
17:20 . . . . Day 83, 293
18:1–4. . . . . Day 272
18:19–20. .Day 248
18:21–22 . . . . Day 19

21:21–22 .Day 248
22:37–38 . . . . Day 116, 181
26:39 . . . . Day 247
26:41 . . . . .Day 180, 287
27:46 . . . . .Day 339

Mark
1:34 . . . . Day 247
1:35. . . . . Day 1
1:40–42 . . . . .Day 246
2:24, 27–28 . . . . Day 229
2:27–28 . . . . .Day 246
4:38–40. . . . . Day 237
4:39 . . . . Day 229
8:29 . . . . Day 55
8:34–37 . . . . .Day 236
9:23 . . . . .Day 53, 62
10:14. . . . . .Day 220
11:24 . . . . Day 323
11:25 . . . . .Day 171
13:11 . . . . Day 199

Luke
1:35, 37–38 . . . . Day 150
1:37. . . . . .Day 96, 189
1:38 . . . . .Day 34
2:19. . . . . Day 316
2:48–49. . . . . Day 82
4:1–2. . . . . .Day 99
5:18–19. . . . . Day 202
6:12. . . . . Day 180
6:27–28 . . . . Day 164
6:43–45. .Day 244
6:47–48. .Day 245
6:48. . . . . Day 136
7:47 . . . . .Day 259
9:1–2. . . . . Day 223
9:23 . . . . Day 255
9:62 . . . . Day 76

10:41–42	Day 25
11:1	Day 337
11:34–36	Day 240
12:22	Day 284
12:22–23	Day 206
12:28	Day 127
12:35–37	Day 142
14:28	Day 121
15:4–5, 7	Day 150
18:20	Day 85
19:38–40	Day 119
22:31–32	Day 55

John

4:26, 28–29	Day 307
6:32–33	Day 350
9:15	Day 201
10:3–4, 11	Day 235
11:43–44	Day 133
14:1	Day 74, 208
14:2–3	Day 309
14:6	Day 87
14:16	Day 316
14:18	Day 184
14:26	Day 200
14:27	Day 27, 174, 207, 306
15:1–2	Day 37, 123
15:8–9	Day 56
16:21–22	Day 156
16:22	Day 285
16:33	Day 105, 133
17:13–15	Day 273
20:29	Day 123, 160
21:6	Day 167

Acts

1:8	Day 163
4:31	Day 352
5:29	Day 18
9:36	Day 80
19:18, 20	Day 352
20:35	Day 36
26:16–18	Day 56

Romans

8:1–2	Day 107
8:18	Day 50, 100, 280, 299
8:24–25	Day 154
8:26	Day 66
8:28	Day 280, 296
8:31	Day 103, 252
8:31–32	Day 195
8:38–39	Day 22, 35, 130
10:14–15	Day 144
12:1–2	Day 152
12:12	Day 104
12:15–16	Day 6
12:16	Day 163
12:19	Day 47
15:5–6	Day 158
15:7	Day 340
15:13	Day 76, 326, 335

1 Corinthians

1:27–29	Day 159
2:9–10	Day 23
3:2	Day 183
10:13	Day 40, 288
10:31–33	Day 337
12:17–18	Day 38
13:1–3	Day 242
13:4–5	Day 204
13:4–7	Day 157
13:7	Day 109
13:12	Day 322
14:33, 40	Day 336
15:54–57	Day 214

2 Corinthians

1:3–4 . . . . Day 238
1:8–11 . . . . Day 213
1:12 . . . . Day 251
4:8–9 . . . . Day 233
4:16–18 . . . . Day 153
4:17 . . . . Day 119
5:7 . . . . Day 320
9:6–7 . . . . Day 210
9:8 . . . . Day 205, 289
10:5 . . . . Day 320
12:7–9 . . . . Day 107, 338

Galatians

1:10 . . . . Day 336
2:20 . . . . Day 298
5:1, 7–8 . . . . Day 213
5:22–23 . . . . Day 161
6:1–2 . . . . Day 270
6:4–5 . . . . Day 154
6:9 . . . . Day 85, 325, 327
6:14 . . . . Day 122

Ephesians

3:20–21 . . . . Day 329
4:2 . . . . Day 256
4:2–3 . . . . Day 175
4:22–24 . . . . Day 239
4:26 . . . . Day 188
4:26–27 . . . . Day 168
4:31 . . . . Day 230
4:32 . . . . Day 52
5:15–16 . . . . Day 51
5:15–17 . . . . Day 84
5:19 . . . . Day 87
5:21 . . . . Day 16
6:12 . . . . Day 117
6:14–17 . . . . Day 80

Philippians

1:6 . . . . Day 113, 170
2:6–8 . . . . Day 308
2:13 . . . . Day 361
2:14–16 . . . . Day 212
3:12 . . . . Day 312
3:13–14 . . . . Day 155
3:20–21 . . . . Day 57
4:5–6 . . . . Day 25
4:6 . . . . Day 182
4:6–7 . . . . Day 33, 103, 228
4:7 . . . . Day 322
4:8 . . . . Day 2, 153, 365
4:11–13 . . . . Day 211
4:13 . . . . Day 54, 75
4:19 . . . . Day 59, 98

Colossians

1:15–17 . . . . Day 217
2:6–7 . . . . Day 81
3:1–2 . . . . Day 196
3:1–4 . . . . Day 275
3:9 . . . . Day 127
3:12 . . . . Day 46
3:13 . . . . Day 19
3:15 . . . . Day 110
3:23 . . . . Day 118

1 Thessalonians

2:7–8 . . . . Day 220
4:13–14 . . . . Day 338
5:11 . . . . Day 51, 101
5:11–12 . . . . Day 315
5:16–18 . . . . Day 274, 286
5:17 . . . . Day 79
5:18 . . . . Day 360

2 Thessalonians

1:11 . . . . Day 298
3:15 . . . . Day 364

1 Timothy

4:7–8	Day 122
6:6–8	Day 144
6:7	Day 178
6:10	Day 356
6:11–12	Day 138

2 Timothy

1:6–7	Day 276
1:7	Day 194, 323
2:23–25	Day 242
3:1–5	Day 17, 181
3:16–17	Day 214

Hebrews

2:1–3	Day 218
4:15–16	Day 159
4:16	Day 297
5:13	Day 283
6:17–19	Day 210
10:17–18	Day 47
10:24	Day 104
11:1	Day 9, 26, 43
11:30	Day 124
12:1	Day 68, 281
12:7	Day 18
12:11–13	Day 216
13:3	Day 188
13:5	Day 146
13:8	Day 124
13:14	Day 179
13:16	Day 364

James

1:2–4	Day 106
1:5–6	Day 121
1:6	Day 115, 204
1:12	Day 128, 282
1:17	Day 77
1:19	Day 362

1:22, 25	Day 137
2:25–26	Day 307
3:8–10	Day 274
3:17	Day 37, 65, 231, 279
4:1–3	Day 178
4:3	Day 134
4:4–6	Day 137
4:8	Day 253, 312
4:13–15	Day 258
5:16	Day 335

1 Peter

1:3–5	Day 102
1:6	Day 100
1:7	Day 339
2:1–3	Day 216
2:17	Day 222
3:3–4	Day 273, 314
3:14	Day 195
4:8	Day 310
4:8, 10–11	Day 22
5:6–7	Day 72, 157, 209
5:7	Day 41, 60, 106
5:8	Day 285
5:8–10	Day 239
5:10	Day 283

2 Peter

1:3	Day 50, 169
3:8–9	Day 140

1 John

1:8–9	Day 170
1:9	Day 278, 297
2:15–17	Day 143
3:17–18	Day 141
4:4	Day 334
4:18	Day 60, 110, 231
5:4–5	Day 28

Jude

22 . . . . Day 176
24–25 . . . . Day 67

Revelation

2:10 . . . . Day 291
3:15–16 . . . . Day 353
3:20 . . . . Day 89
21:3–4 . . . . Day 198
21:3–5 . . . . Day 271